GLENN GOULD

ISBN 9781681120652
Library of Congress Control Number 2016914177
© Dargaud 2016
© 2016 NBM for the English translation
Translated by Montana Kane
Lettered by Ortho
Printed in China
1st printing December 2016

This book is also available wherever e-books are sold

SANDRINE REVEL

GLENN GOULD

A LIFE OFF TEMPO

nbm GRAPHIC NOVELS

Nantier · Beall · Minoustchine
NEW YORK

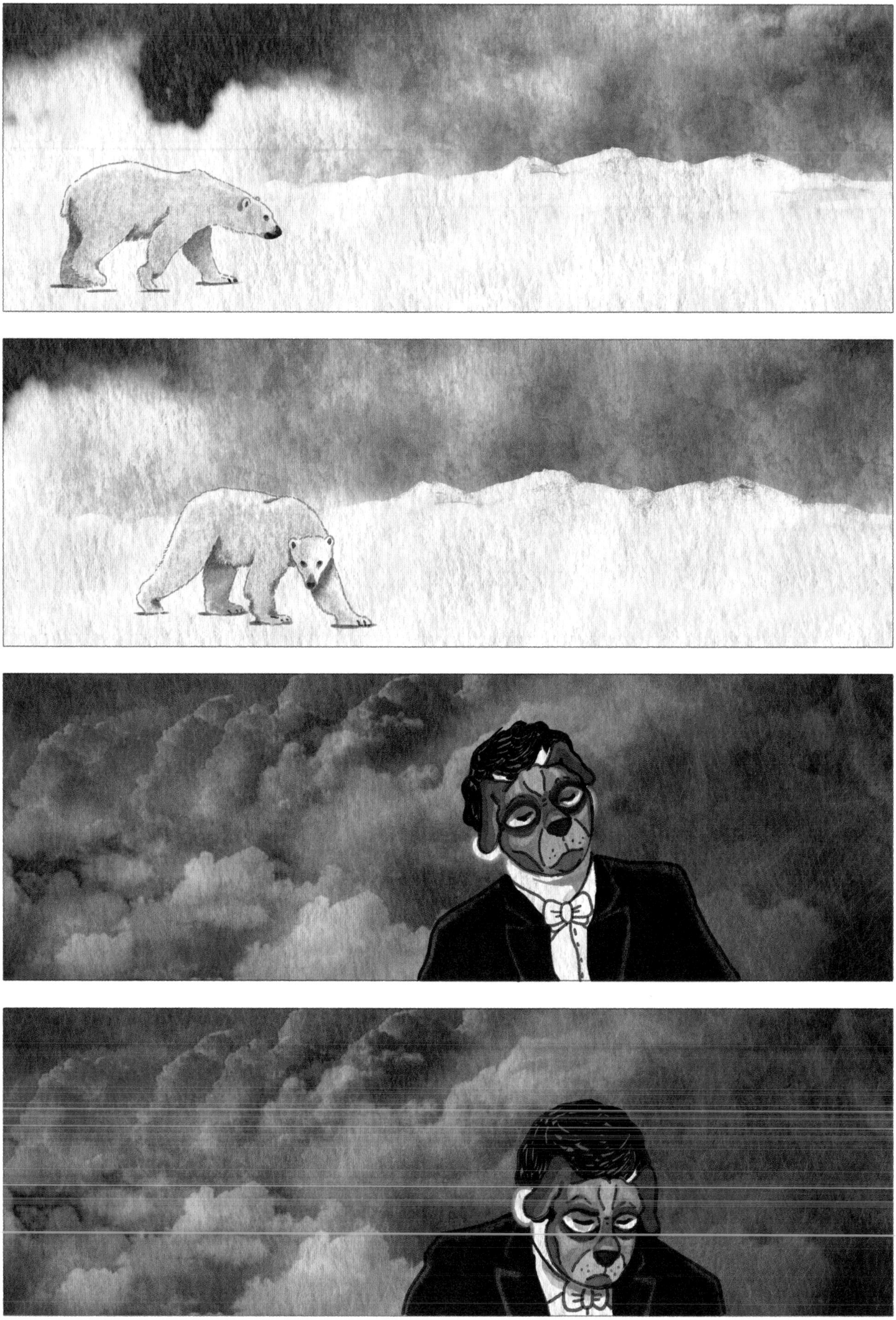

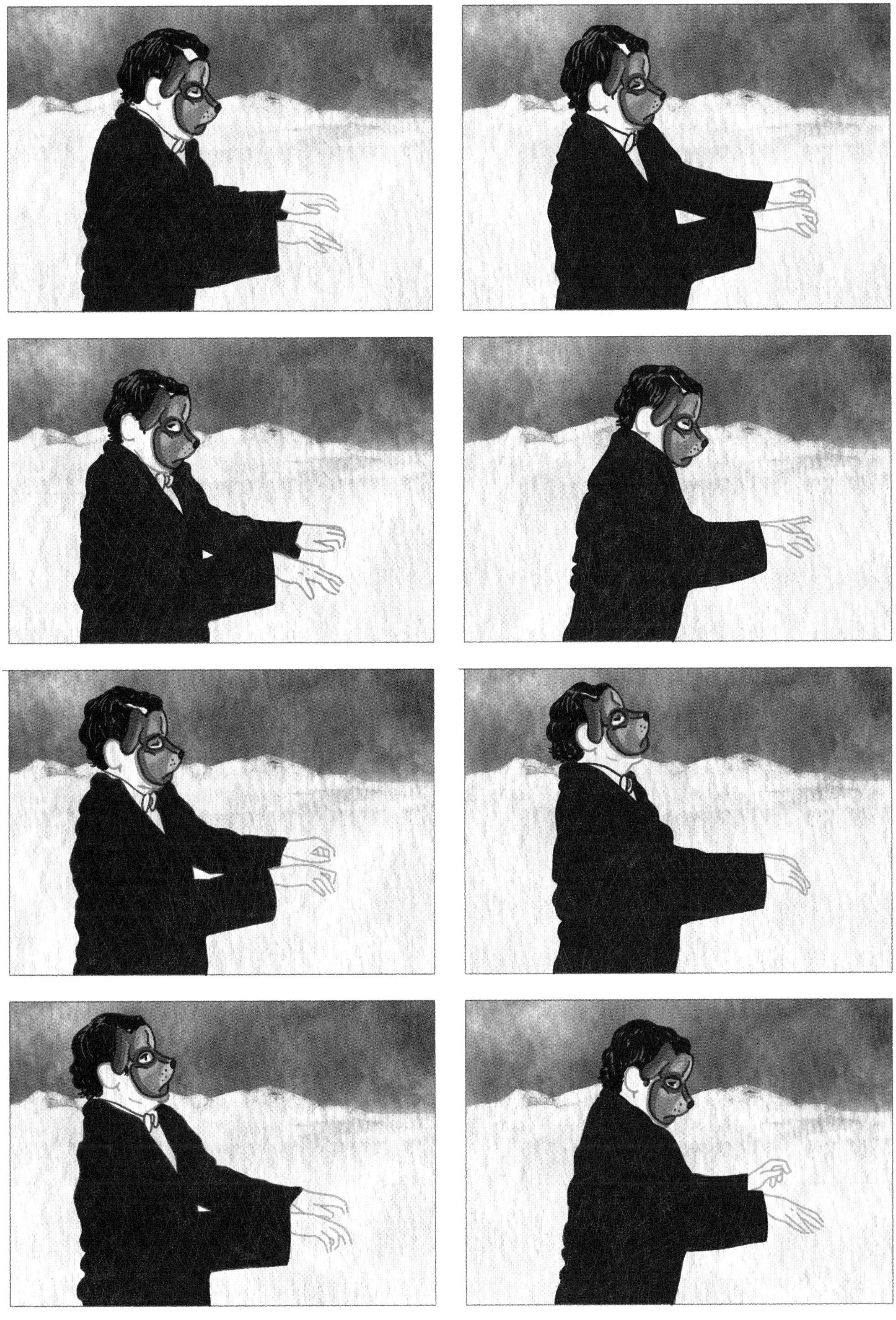

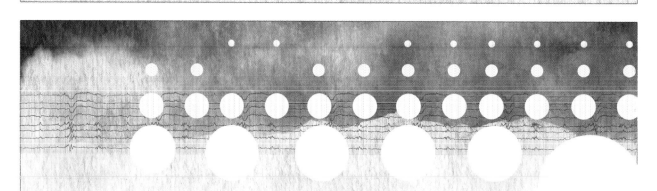

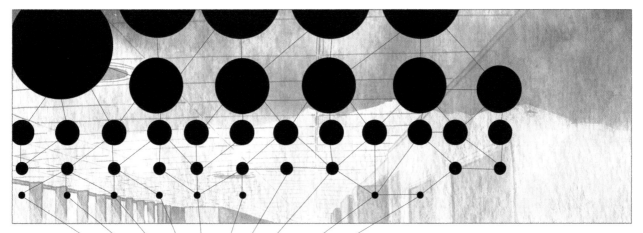
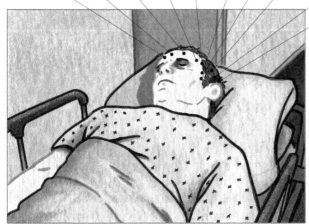
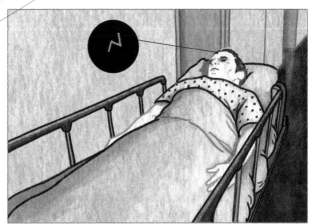

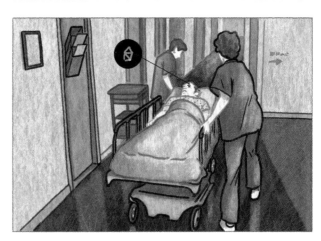

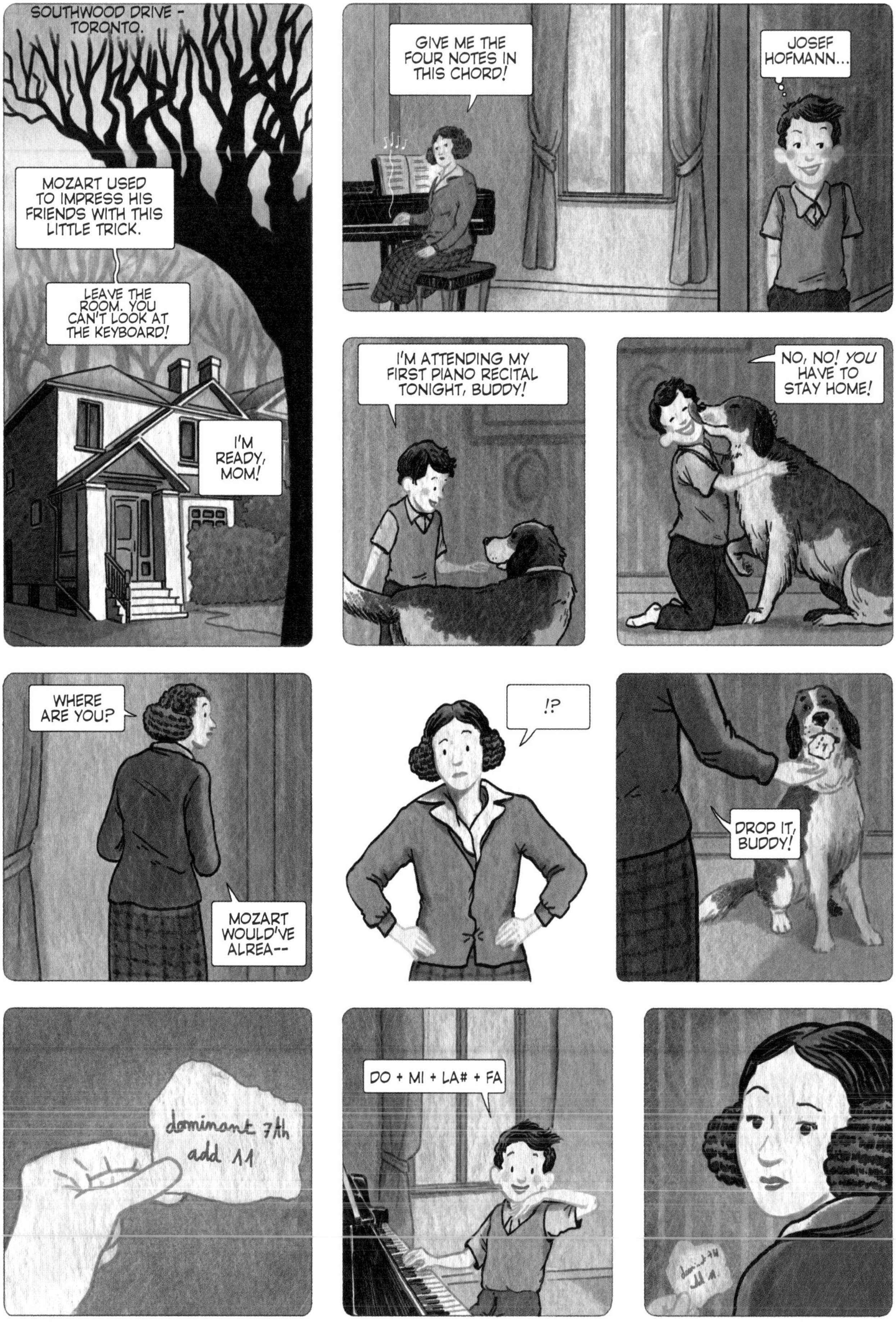
SOUTHWOOD DRIVE - TORONTO.
MOZART USED TO IMPRESS HIS FRIENDS WITH THIS LITTLE TRICK.
LEAVE THE ROOM. YOU CAN'T LOOK AT THE KEYBOARD!
I'M READY, MOM!
GIVE ME THE FOUR NOTES IN THIS CHORD!
JOSEF HOFMANN...
I'M ATTENDING MY FIRST PIANO RECITAL TONIGHT, BUDDY!
NO, NO! YOU HAVE TO STAY HOME!
WHERE ARE YOU?
MOZART WOULD'VE ALREA--
!?
DROP IT, BUDDY!
dominant 7th add 11
DO + MI + LA# + FA

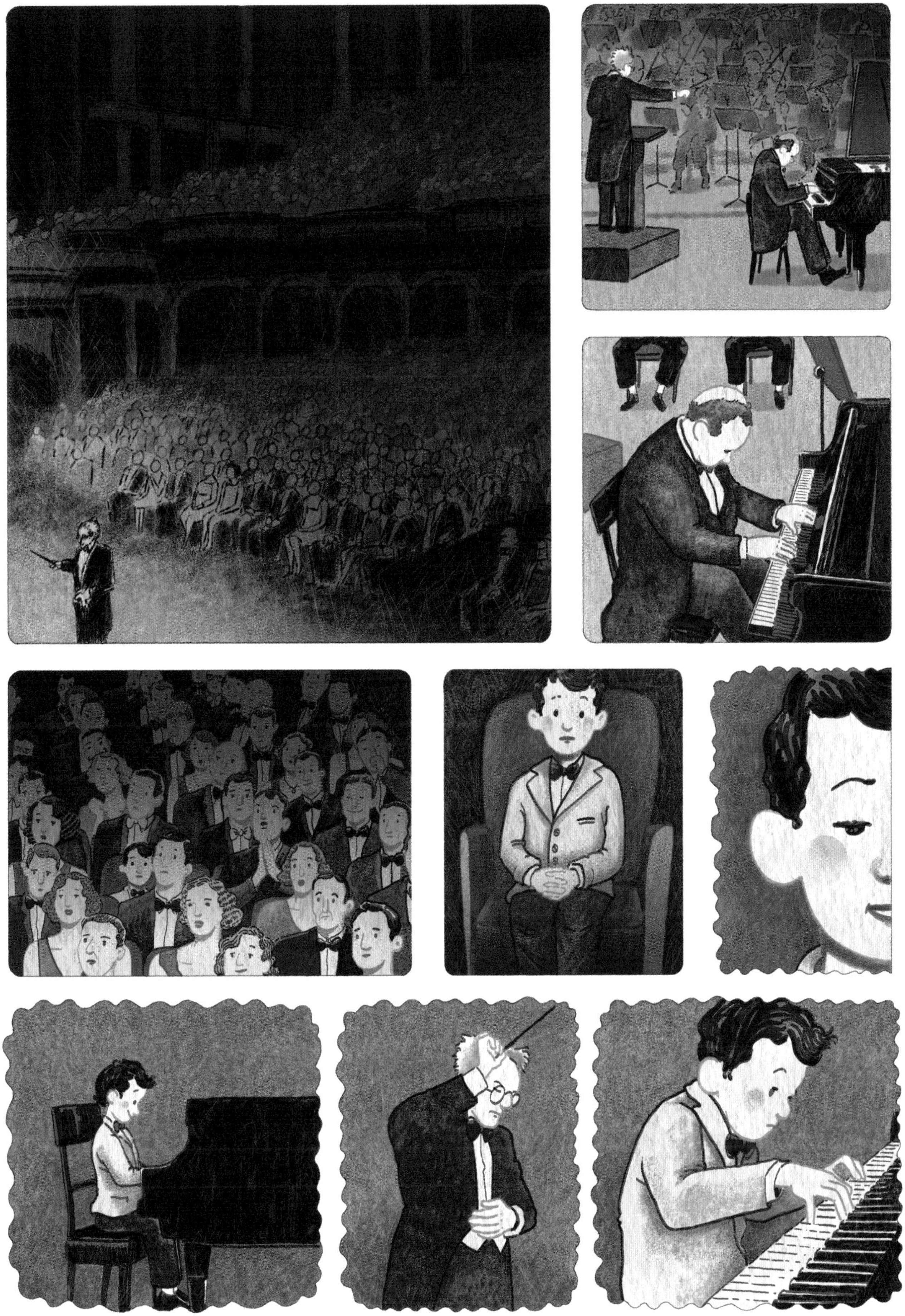

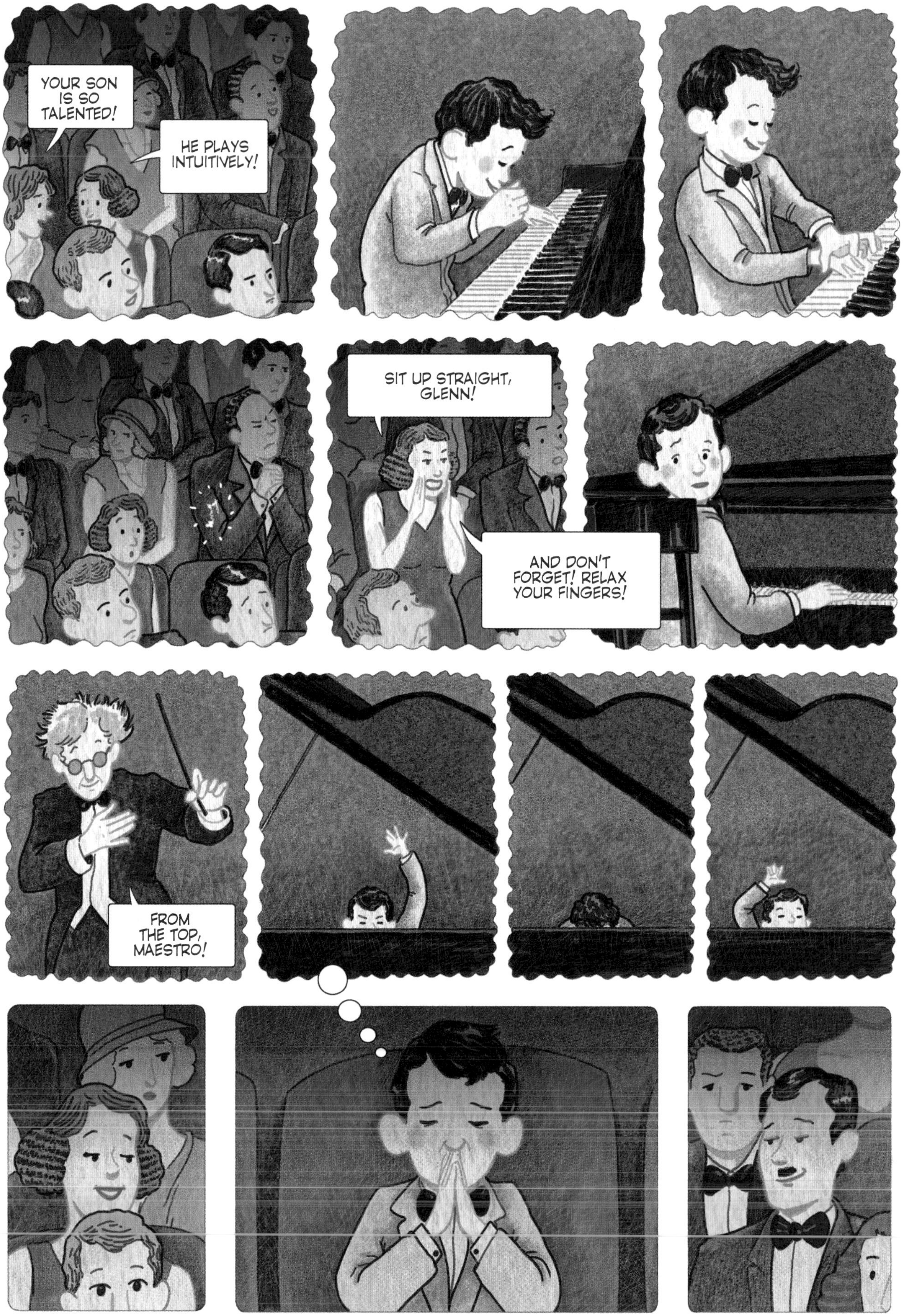
YOUR SON IS SO TALENTED!
HE PLAYS INTUITIVELY!
SIT UP STRAIGHT, GLENN!
AND DON'T FORGET! RELAX YOUR FINGERS!
FROM THE TOP, MAESTRO!

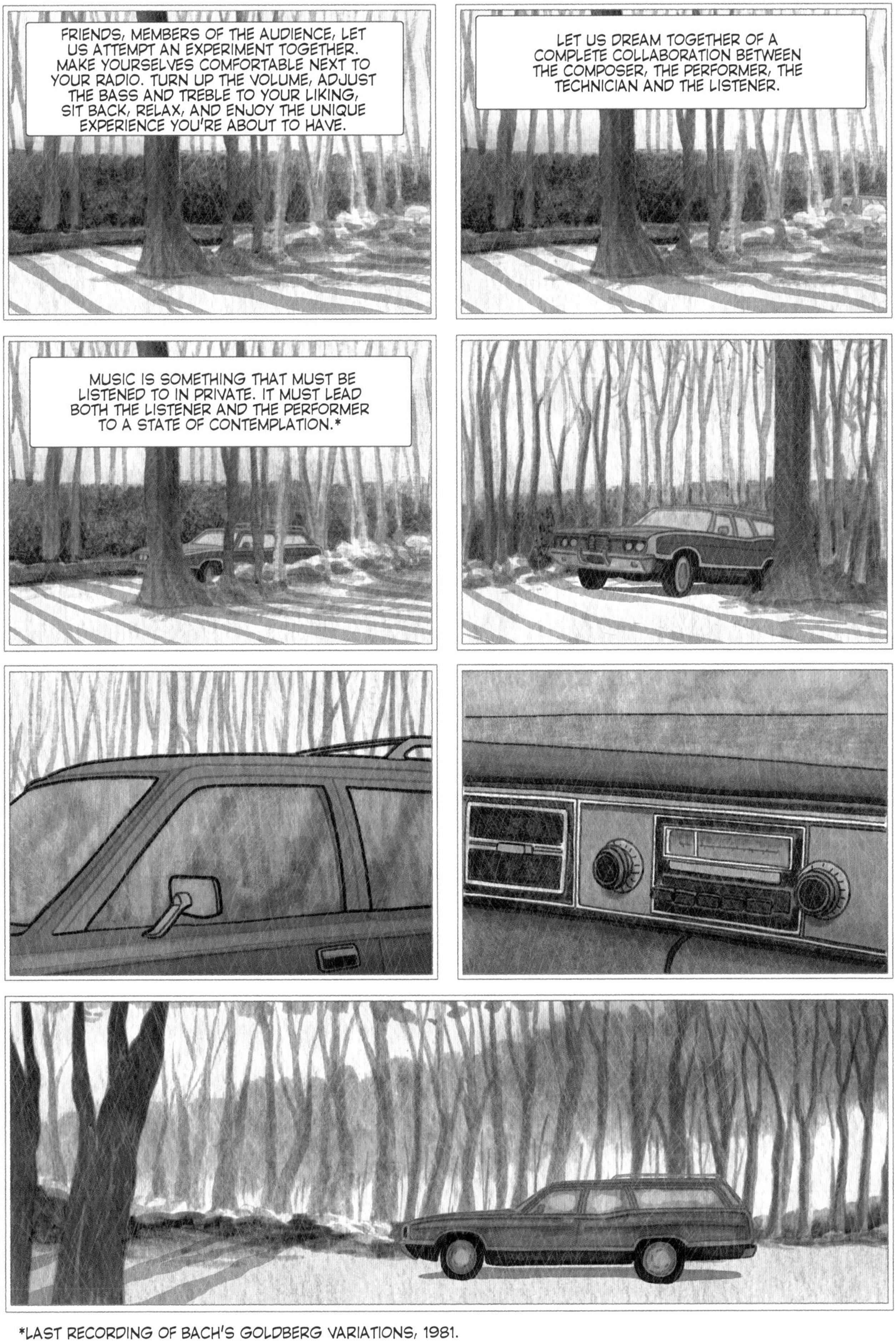
FRIENDS, MEMBERS OF THE AUDIENCE, LET US ATTEMPT AN EXPERIMENT TOGETHER. MAKE YOURSELVES COMFORTABLE NEXT TO YOUR RADIO. TURN UP THE VOLUME, ADJUST THE BASS AND TREBLE TO YOUR LIKING, SIT BACK, RELAX, AND ENJOY THE UNIQUE EXPERIENCE YOU'RE ABOUT TO HAVE.
LET US DREAM TOGETHER OF A COMPLETE COLLABORATION BETWEEN THE COMPOSER, THE PERFORMER, THE TECHNICIAN AND THE LISTENER.
MUSIC IS SOMETHING THAT MUST BE LISTENED TO IN PRIVATE. IT MUST LEAD BOTH THE LISTENER AND THE PERFORMER TO A STATE OF CONTEMPLATION.*

*LAST RECORDING OF BACH'S GOLDBERG VARIATIONS, 1981.

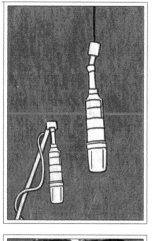

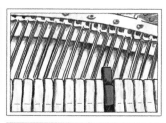

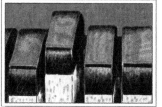

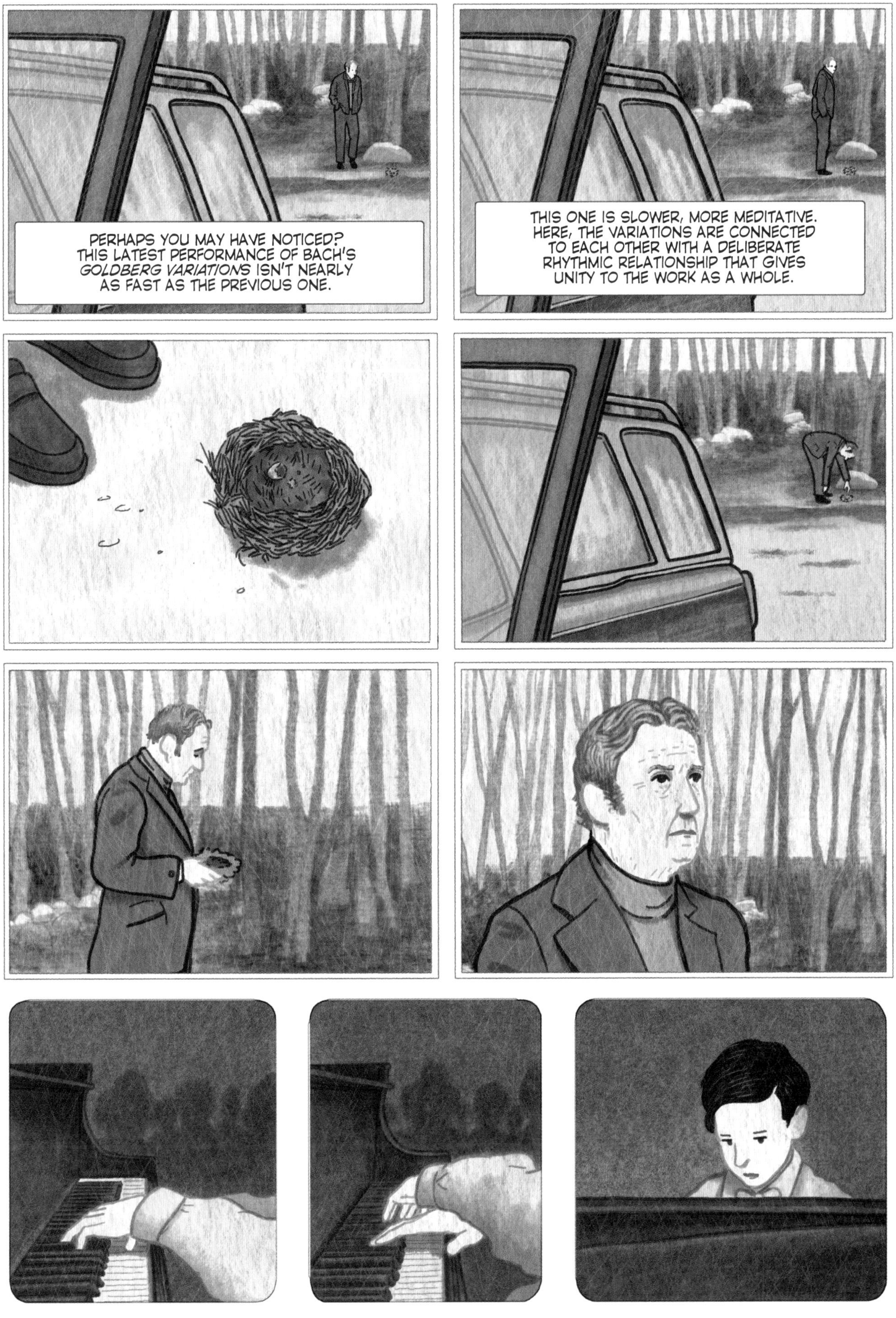
PERHAPS YOU MAY HAVE NOTICED? THIS LATEST PERFORMANCE OF BACH'S *GOLDBERG VARIATIONS* ISN'T NEARLY AS FAST AS THE PREVIOUS ONE.
THIS ONE IS SLOWER, MORE MEDITATIVE. HERE, THE VARIATIONS ARE CONNECTED TO EACH OTHER WITH A DELIBERATE RHYTHMIC RELATIONSHIP THAT GIVES UNITY TO THE WORK AS A WHOLE.

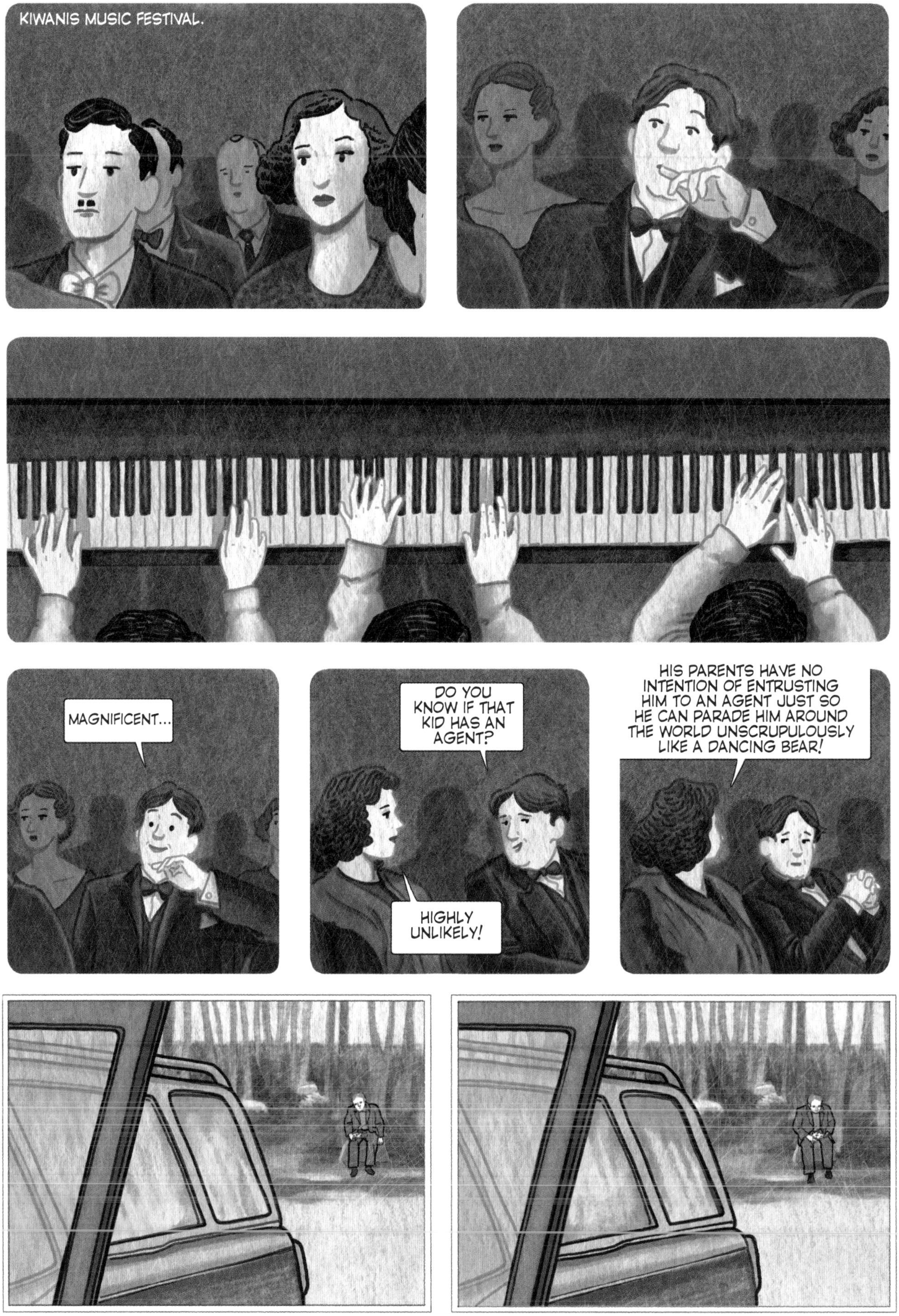
KIWANIS MUSIC FESTIVAL.
MAGNIFICENT...
DO YOU KNOW IF THAT KID HAS AN AGENT?
HIGHLY UNLIKELY!
HIS PARENTS HAVE NO INTENTION OF ENTRUSTING HIM TO AN AGENT JUST SO HE CAN PARADE HIM AROUND THE WORLD UNSCRUPULOUSLY LIKE A DANCING BEAR!

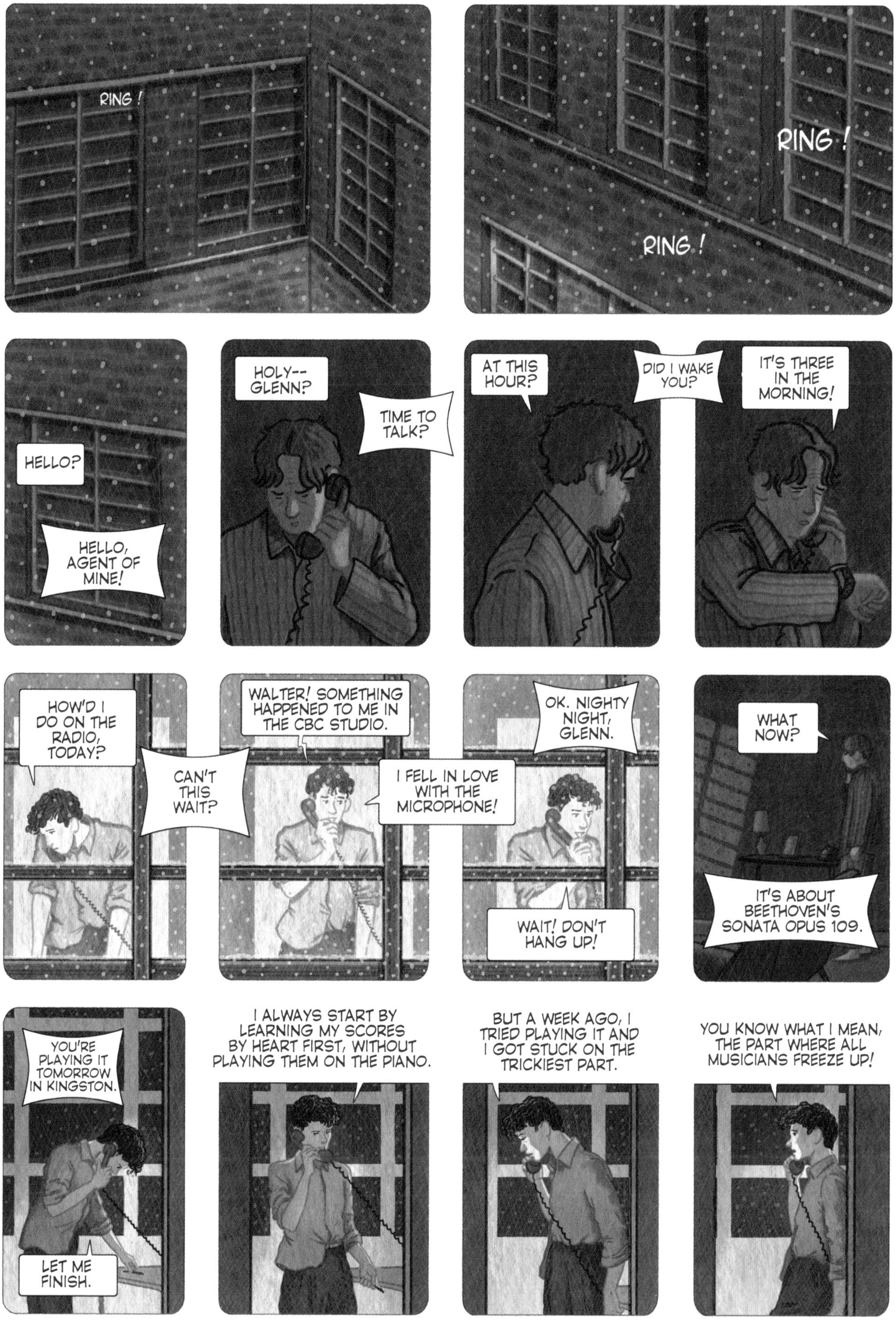
RING !
RING !
RING !
HELLO?
HELLO, AGENT OF MINE!
HOLY-- GLENN?
TIME TO TALK?
AT THIS HOUR?
DID I WAKE YOU?
IT'S THREE IN THE MORNING!
HOW'D I DO ON THE RADIO, TODAY?
CAN'T THIS WAIT?
WALTER! SOMETHING HAPPENED TO ME IN THE CBC STUDIO.
I FELL IN LOVE WITH THE MICROPHONE!
OK. NIGHTY NIGHT, GLENN.
WAIT! DON'T HANG UP!
WHAT NOW?
IT'S ABOUT BEETHOVEN'S SONATA OPUS 109.
YOU'RE PLAYING IT TOMORROW IN KINGSTON.
LET ME FINISH.
I ALWAYS START BY LEARNING MY SCORES BY HEART FIRST, WITHOUT PLAYING THEM ON THE PIANO.
BUT A WEEK AGO, I TRIED PLAYING IT AND I GOT STUCK ON THE TRICKIEST PART.
YOU KNOW WHAT I MEAN, THE PART WHERE ALL MUSICIANS FREEZE UP!

AND I JUST COULDN'T GET UNSTUCK!

IT'S TOO LATE TO CHANGE THE PROGRAM AND DROP THIS PIECE.

YOU WANT TO HEAR THE REST OF THE STORY?

GLENN...

I'M ON THE VERGE OF A NERVOUS BREAKDOWN WHEN OUR CLEANING LADY STARTS RUNNING THE VACUUM IN THE LIVING ROOM.

BINGO! DESPITE THE VACUUM, I GET THROUGH THE WHOLE OPUS WITHOUT STUMBLING ON THAT ONE DAMN PART.

AND THEN I FIGURED IT OUT.

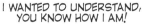

I REPEATED THE EXPERIMENT, PLACING A BLARING RADIO AND TV SET AT EITHER ENDS OF THE PIANO.

!?

AGAIN, I GOT THROUGH THE WHOLE PIECE WITHOUT TRIPPING UP.

I WANTED TO UNDERSTAND, YOU KNOW HOW I AM!

NOT BEING ABLE TO HEAR MYSELF OR NOTICE MY OWN WEAKNESSES HAD A COMPLETELY ANESTHETIC EFFECT ON THE PROBLEM, WHICH NOW NO LONGER EXISTS.

I FOUND OUT THERE'S AN AMERICAN DENTIST DESPERATELY LOOKING FOR VOLUNTEERS TO TEST THIS NEW METHOD OF ANESTHESIA.

IF IT WORKS WITH A PIANO, IT'S BOUND TO WORK WITH A DRILL!

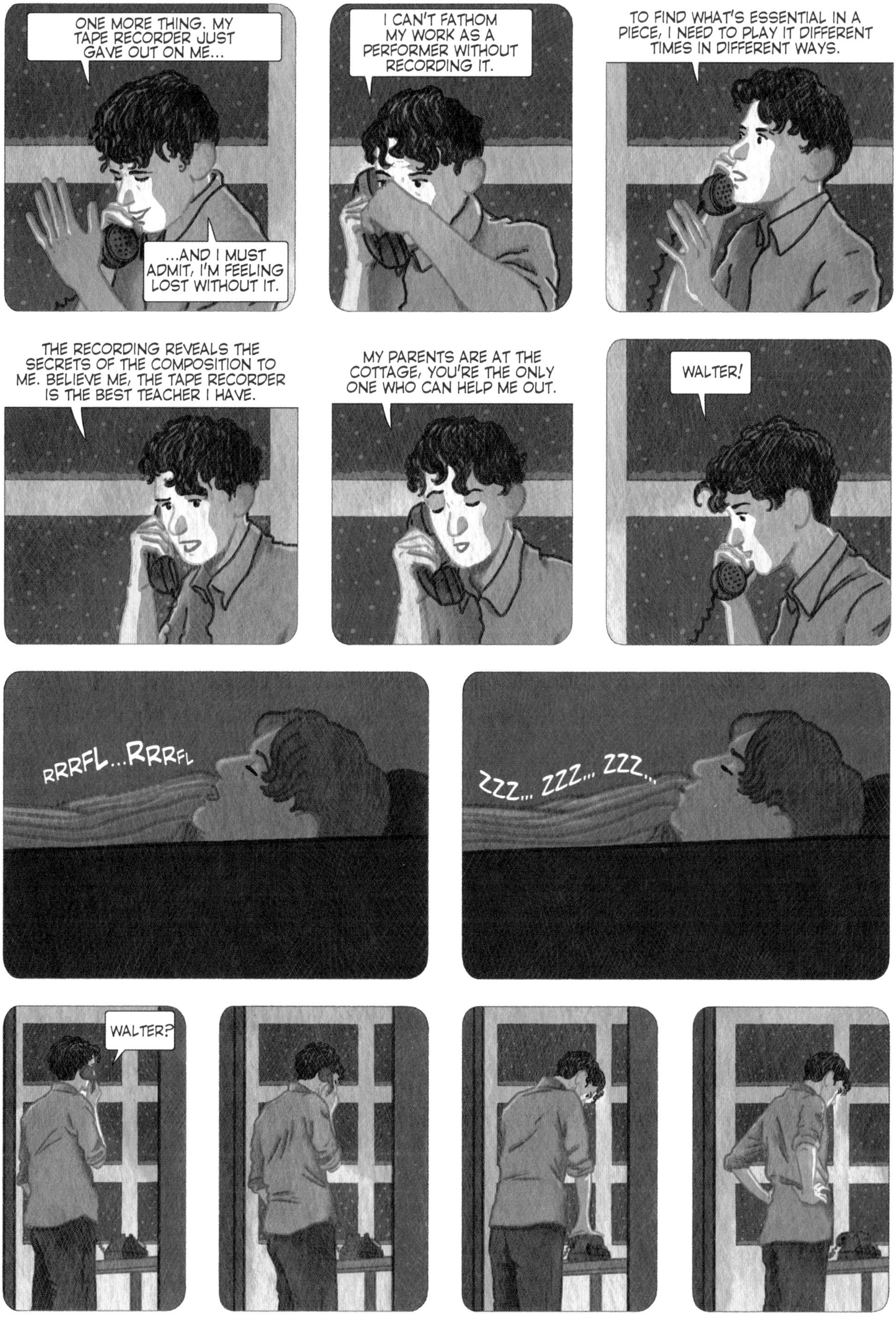
ONE MORE THING. MY TAPE RECORDER JUST GAVE OUT ON ME...
...AND I MUST ADMIT, I'M FEELING LOST WITHOUT IT.
I CAN'T FATHOM MY WORK AS A PERFORMER WITHOUT RECORDING IT.
TO FIND WHAT'S ESSENTIAL IN A PIECE, I NEED TO PLAY IT DIFFERENT TIMES IN DIFFERENT WAYS.
THE RECORDING REVEALS THE SECRETS OF THE COMPOSITION TO ME. BELIEVE ME, THE TAPE RECORDER IS THE BEST TEACHER I HAVE.
MY PARENTS ARE AT THE COTTAGE, YOU'RE THE ONLY ONE WHO CAN HELP ME OUT.
WALTER!
RRRFL...RRRFL
ZZZ... ZZZ... ZZZ...
WALTER?

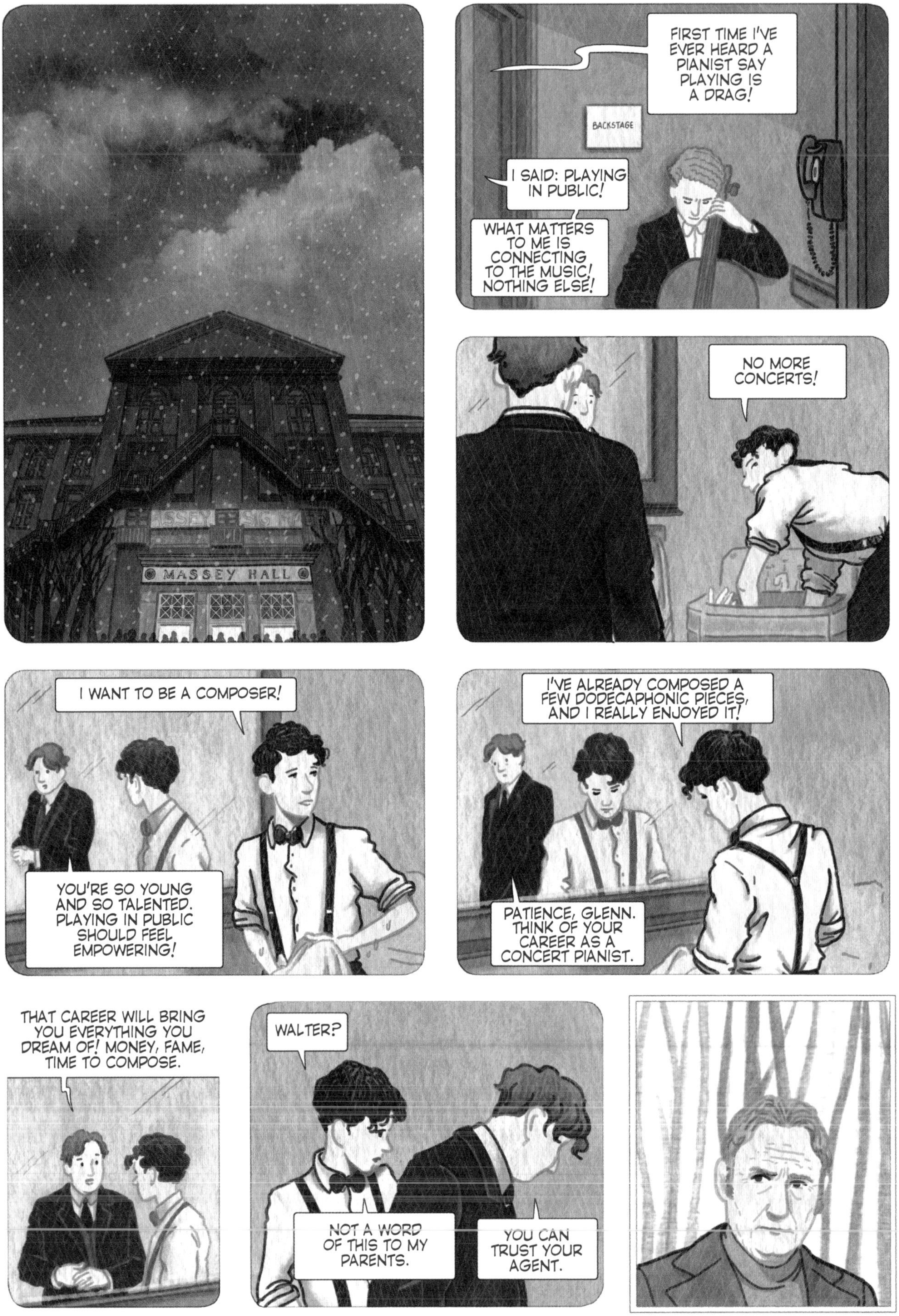
MASSEY HALL
FIRST TIME I'VE EVER HEARD A PIANIST SAY PLAYING IS A DRAG!
BACKSTAGE
I SAID: PLAYING IN PUBLIC!
WHAT MATTERS TO ME IS CONNECTING TO THE MUSIC! NOTHING ELSE!
NO MORE CONCERTS!
I WANT TO BE A COMPOSER!
YOU'RE SO YOUNG AND SO TALENTED. PLAYING IN PUBLIC SHOULD FEEL EMPOWERING!
I'VE ALREADY COMPOSED A FEW DODECAPHONIC PIECES, AND I REALLY ENJOYED IT!
PATIENCE, GLENN. THINK OF YOUR CAREER AS A CONCERT PIANIST.
THAT CAREER WILL BRING YOU EVERYTHING YOU DREAM OF! MONEY, FAME, TIME TO COMPOSE.
WALTER?
NOT A WORD OF THIS TO MY PARENTS.
YOU CAN TRUST YOUR AGENT.

DOCTOR?

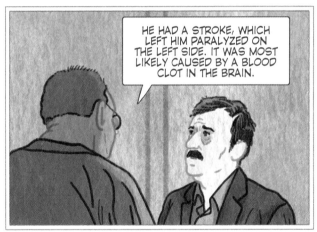

RAY ROBERTS. I DROVE MR. GOULD TO THE EMERGENCY ROOM EARLIER.

HOW IS HE?

ARE YOU FAMILY?

I'M HIS AGENT.

HE'S CONSCIOUS. HE RESPONDS TO TOUCH AND TO PAIN.

HE HAD A STROKE, WHICH LEFT HIM PARALYZED ON THE LEFT SIDE. IT WAS MOST LIKELY CAUSED BY A BLOOD CLOT IN THE BRAIN.

WE'VE TRANSFERRED HIM TO NEUROLOGY FOR FURTHER TESTING.

CALL HIS FAMILY. WE'LL KNOW MORE TOMORROW.

THANK YOU, DOCTOR. I'LL CALL HIS COUSIN JESSIE.

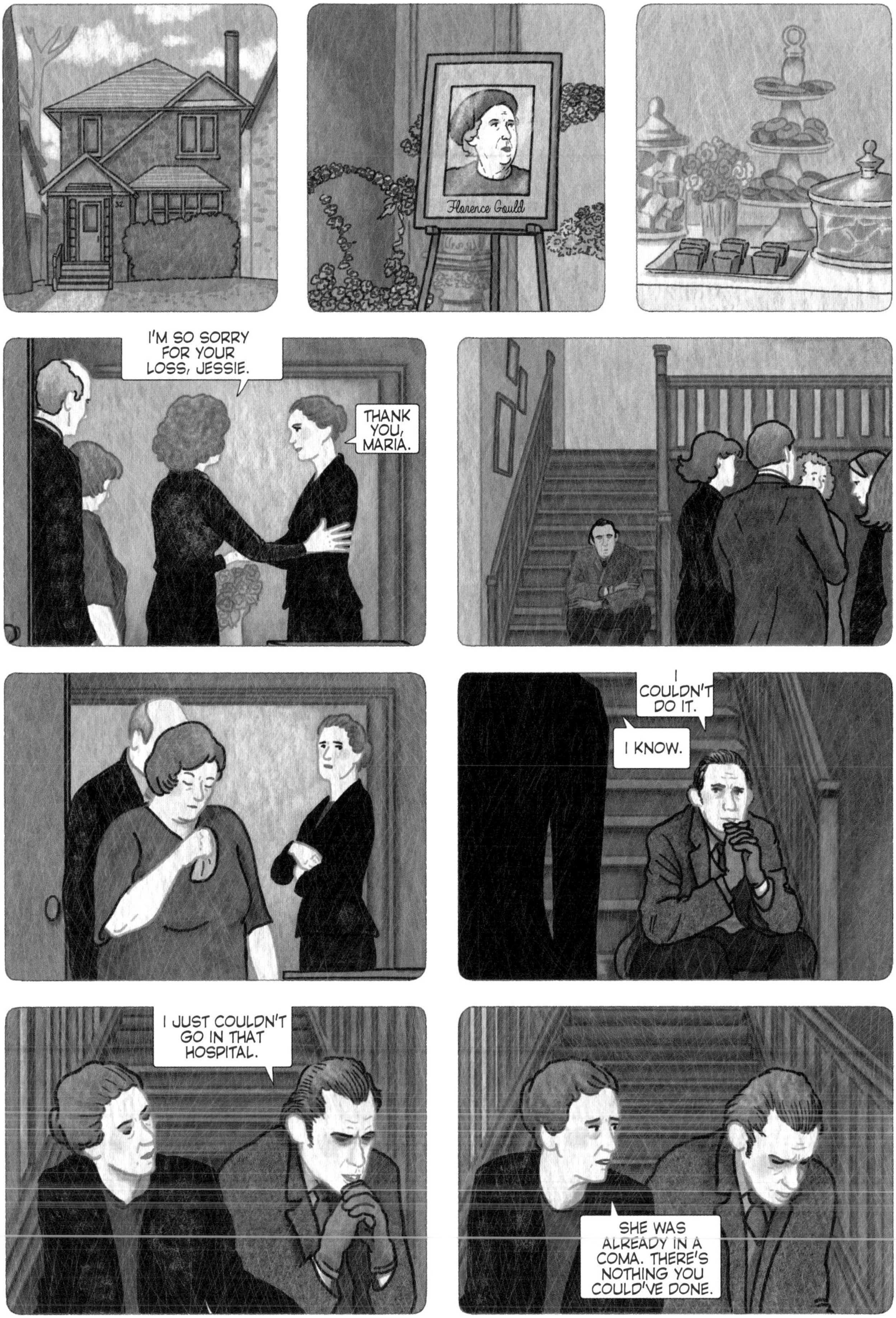
Florence Gould
I'M SO SORRY FOR YOUR LOSS, JESSIE.
THANK YOU, MARIA.
I COULDN'T DO IT.
I KNOW.
I JUST COULDN'T GO IN THAT HOSPITAL.
SHE WAS ALREADY IN A COMA. THERE'S NOTHING YOU COULD'VE DONE.

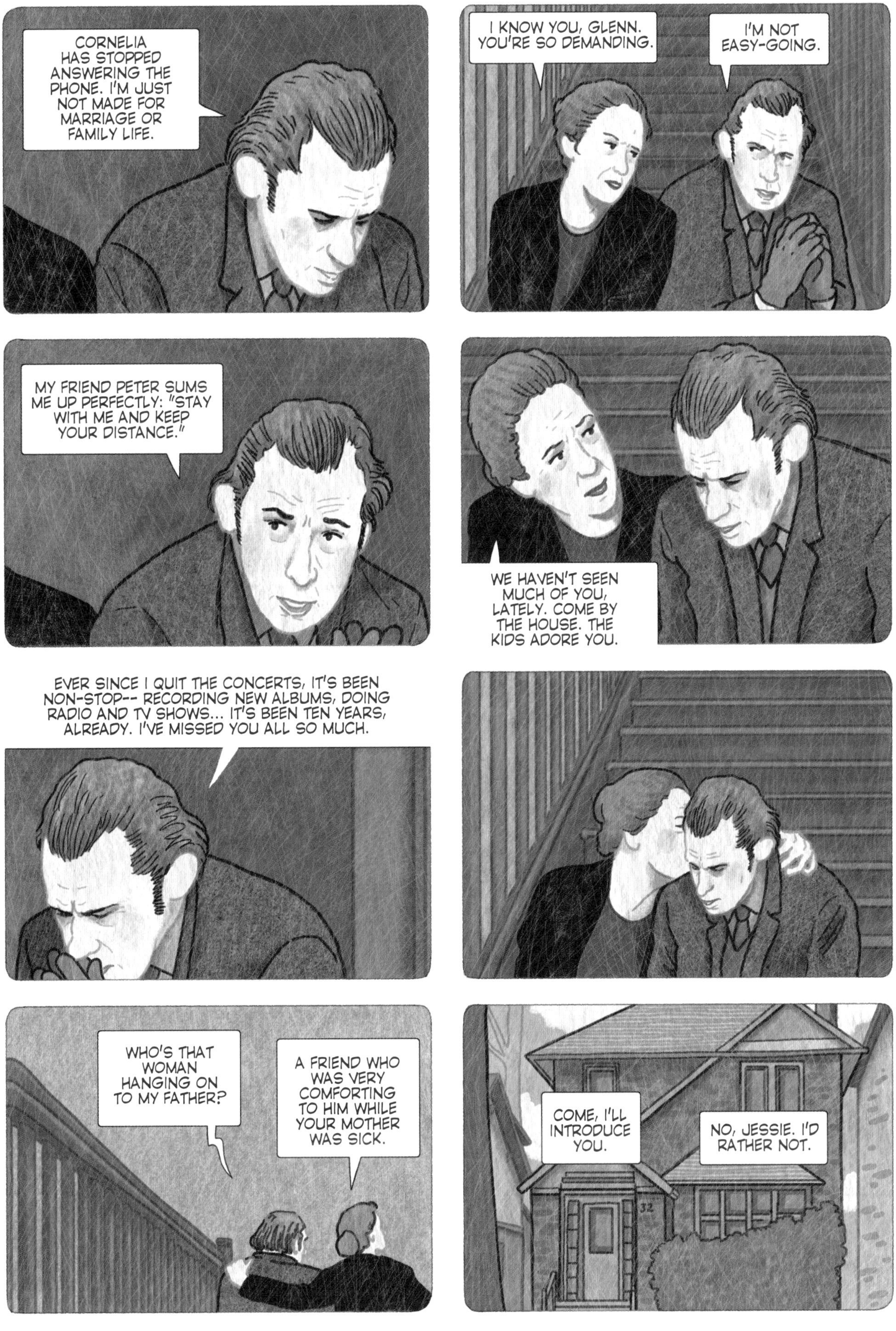

CORNELIA HAS STOPPED ANSWERING THE PHONE. I'M JUST NOT MADE FOR MARRIAGE OR FAMILY LIFE.
I KNOW YOU, GLENN. YOU'RE SO DEMANDING.
I'M NOT EASY-GOING.
MY FRIEND PETER SUMS ME UP PERFECTLY: "STAY WITH ME AND KEEP YOUR DISTANCE."
WE HAVEN'T SEEN MUCH OF YOU, LATELY. COME BY THE HOUSE. THE KIDS ADORE YOU.
EVER SINCE I QUIT THE CONCERTS, IT'S BEEN NON-STOP-- RECORDING NEW ALBUMS, DOING RADIO AND TV SHOWS... IT'S BEEN TEN YEARS, ALREADY. I'VE MISSED YOU ALL SO MUCH.
WHO'S THAT WOMAN HANGING ON TO MY FATHER?
A FRIEND WHO WAS VERY COMFORTING TO HIM WHILE YOUR MOTHER WAS SICK.
COME, I'LL INTRODUCE YOU.
NO, JESSIE. I'D RATHER NOT.
32

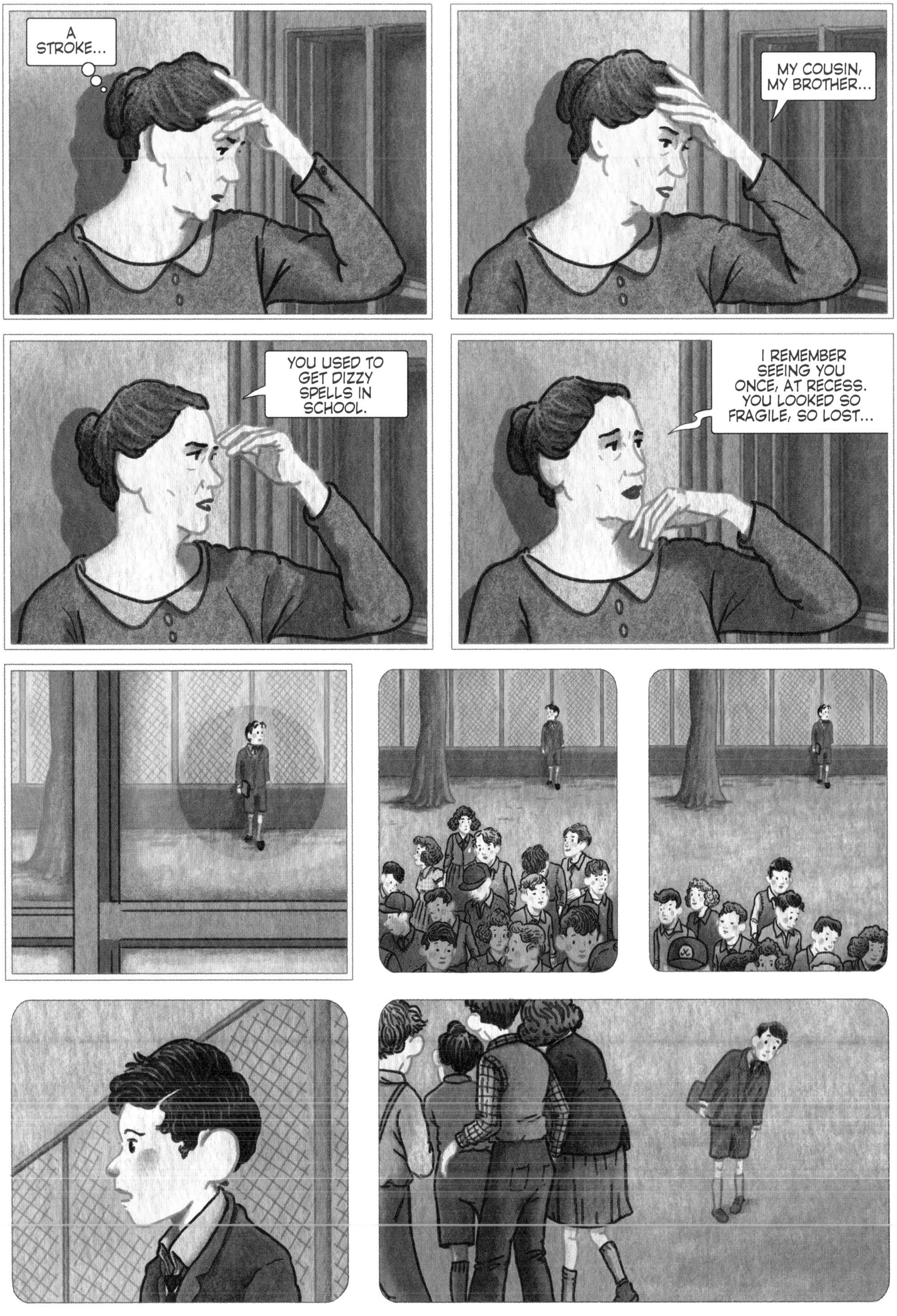
A STROKE...
MY COUSIN, MY BROTHER...
YOU USED TO GET DIZZY SPELLS IN SCHOOL.
I REMEMBER SEEING YOU ONCE, AT RECESS. YOU LOOKED SO FRAGILE, SO LOST...

BBBWWWWAARRRHHHH!

AAAAAAH!

LOSER!

HEY! LET'S CALL YOU BARF BOY!

BARF BOY!

AAA!

BARF BOY!

BARF BOY!

BARF BOY!

BARF BOY! BARF BOY! BARF BOY!

EENNN!!!

OO

EN!

WWEEEOOOOOO!!!

WWEEEOOOOOO!!! WWEE

THE GERMANS ARE ATTACKING CANADA!

IT'S JUST A DRILL. GO BACK INSIDE. QUIETLY, PLEASE!

WHAT'S WRONG WITH YOU THIS TIME, GOULD?

I DON'T FEEL VERY WELL.

AS USUAL!

WHY HIM, AND NOT ME?

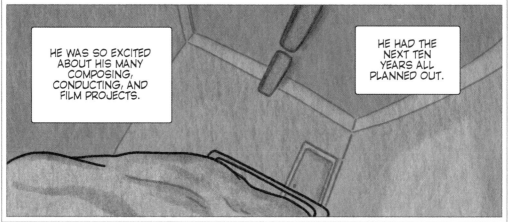

HE WAS SO EXCITED ABOUT HIS MANY COMPOSING, CONDUCTING, AND FILM PROJECTS.

HE HAD THE NEXT TEN YEARS ALL PLANNED OUT.

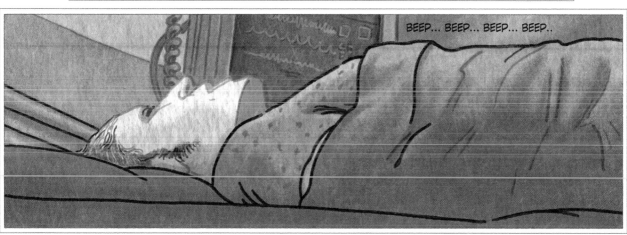

BEEP... BEEP... BEEP... BEEP..

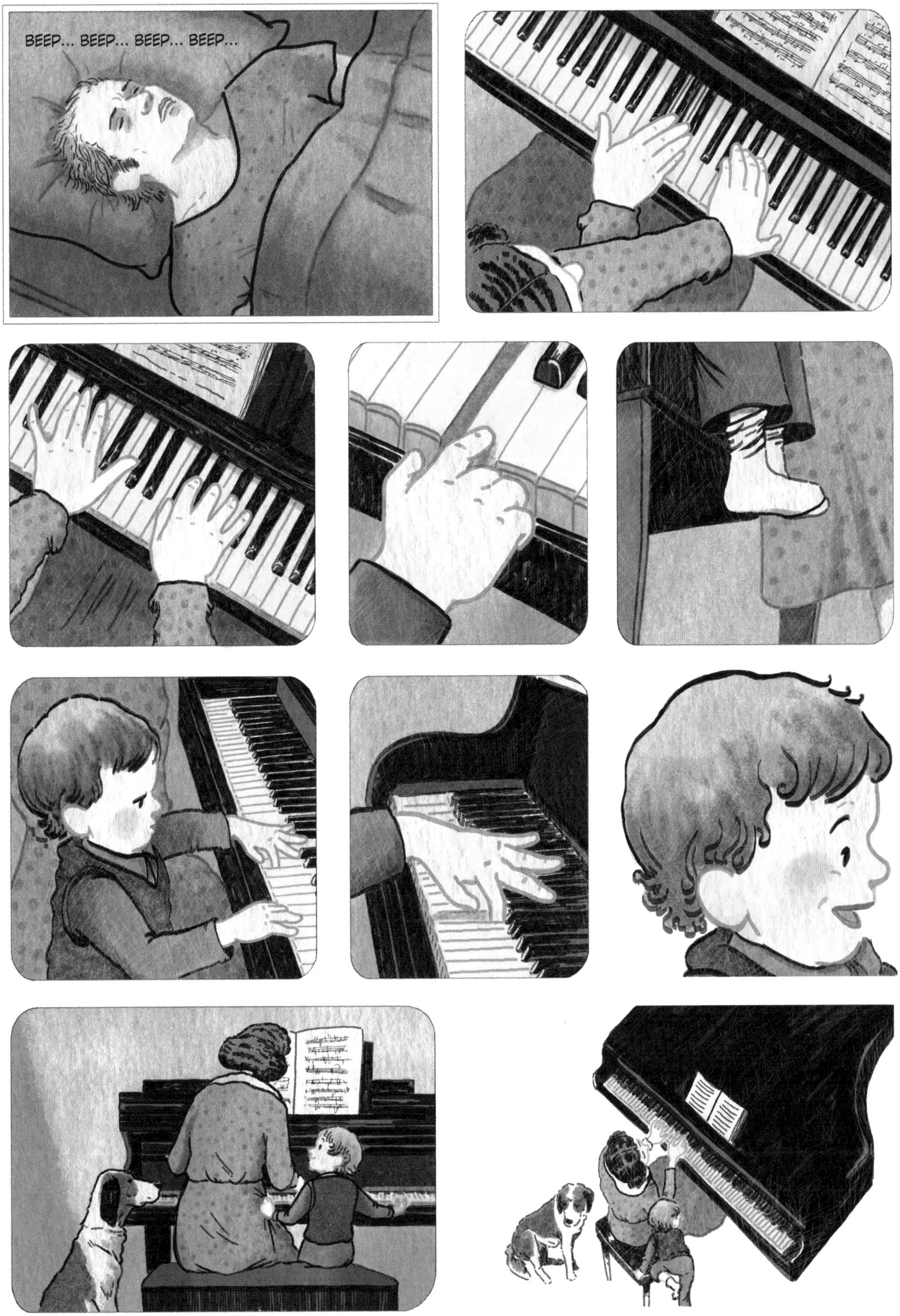
BEEP... BEEP... BEEP... BEEP...

DON'T RAISE THEM!

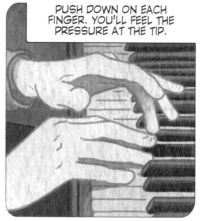

PUSH DOWN ON EACH FINGER. YOU'LL FEEL THE PRESSURE AT THE TIP.

LET THE FINGER SPRING BACK UP ON ITS OWN.

I'M GOING TO PRESS DOWN ON YOUR SHOULDERS WHILE YOU PLAY, AND YOU ARE GOING TO PUSH BACK.

GO ON, PUSH! PUSH!

CAN YOU FEEL THE DIFFERENCE?

MAINTAIN THIS POSITION AND KEEP PLAYING.

FORGET EVERYTHING YOUR MOTHER TAUGHT YOU. YOU KNOW HOW TO PLAY, BUT YOU HAVE NO TECHNIQUE!

THIS EXERCISE TEACHES YOUR FINGERS TO BE INDEPENDENT.

AND NOW, PLAY A LITTLE SCHUBERT WHILE FOLLOWING THE EXERCISE!

AGAIN!?

ARE YOU QUESTIONING MY METHODS?

I JUST MEANT THAT, TWICE A WEEK, I RELUCTANTLY GIVE OF MY TIME TO SCHUBERT, WHOM I FIND OVERLY REPETITIVE.

YOU MUST NOT INFER THAT I DISLIKE THIS COMPOSER. ON THE CONTRARY, I FIND HIM STIMULATING.

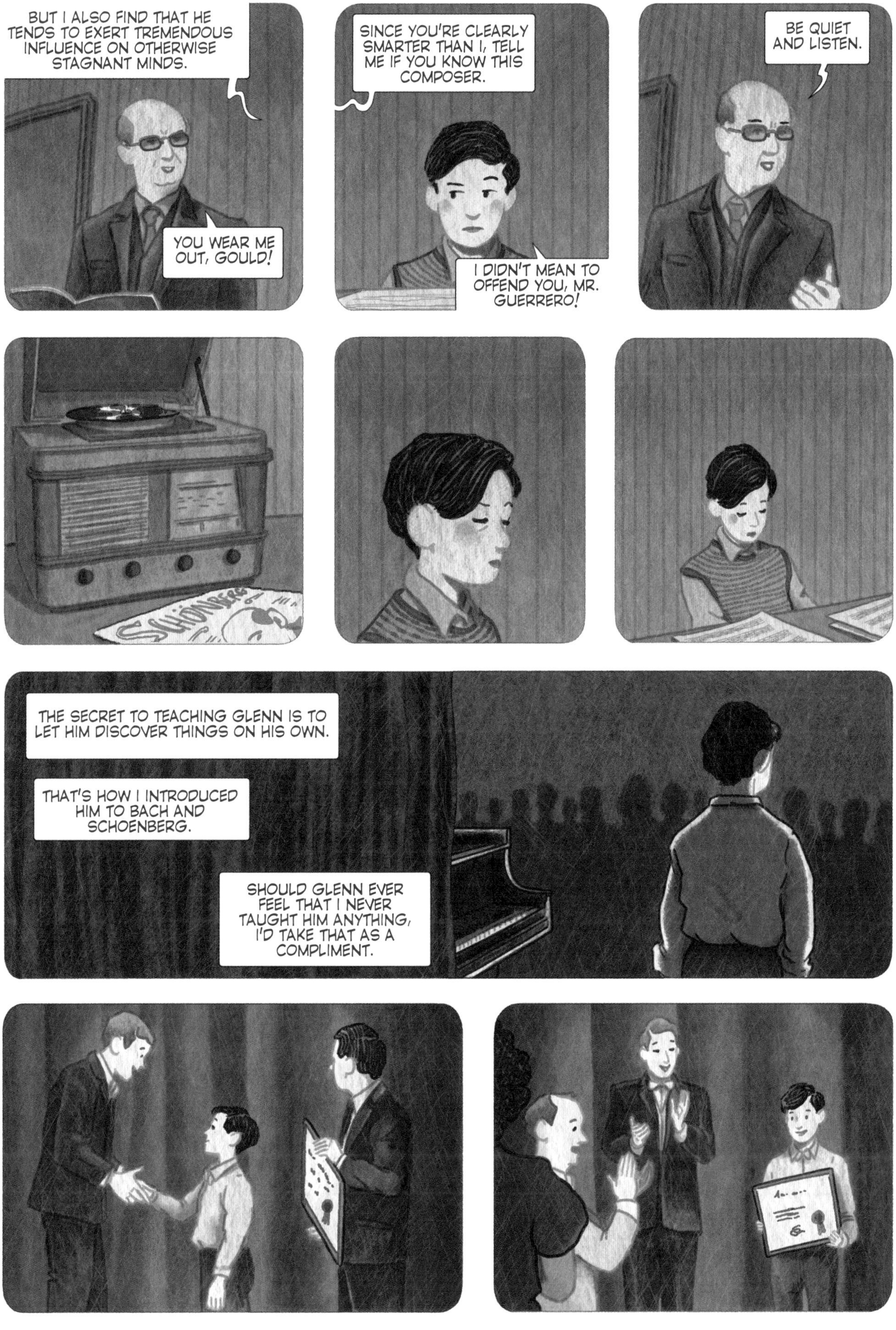
BUT I ALSO FIND THAT HE TENDS TO EXERT TREMENDOUS INFLUENCE ON OTHERWISE STAGNANT MINDS.
YOU WEAR ME OUT, GOULD!
SINCE YOU'RE CLEARLY SMARTER THAN I, TELL ME IF YOU KNOW THIS COMPOSER.
I DIDN'T MEAN TO OFFEND YOU, MR. GUERRERO!
BE QUIET AND LISTEN.
SCHÖNBERG
THE SECRET TO TEACHING GLENN IS TO LET HIM DISCOVER THINGS ON HIS OWN.
THAT'S HOW I INTRODUCED HIM TO BACH AND SCHOENBERG.
SHOULD GLENN EVER FEEL THAT I NEVER TAUGHT HIM ANYTHING, I'D TAKE THAT AS A COMPLIMENT.

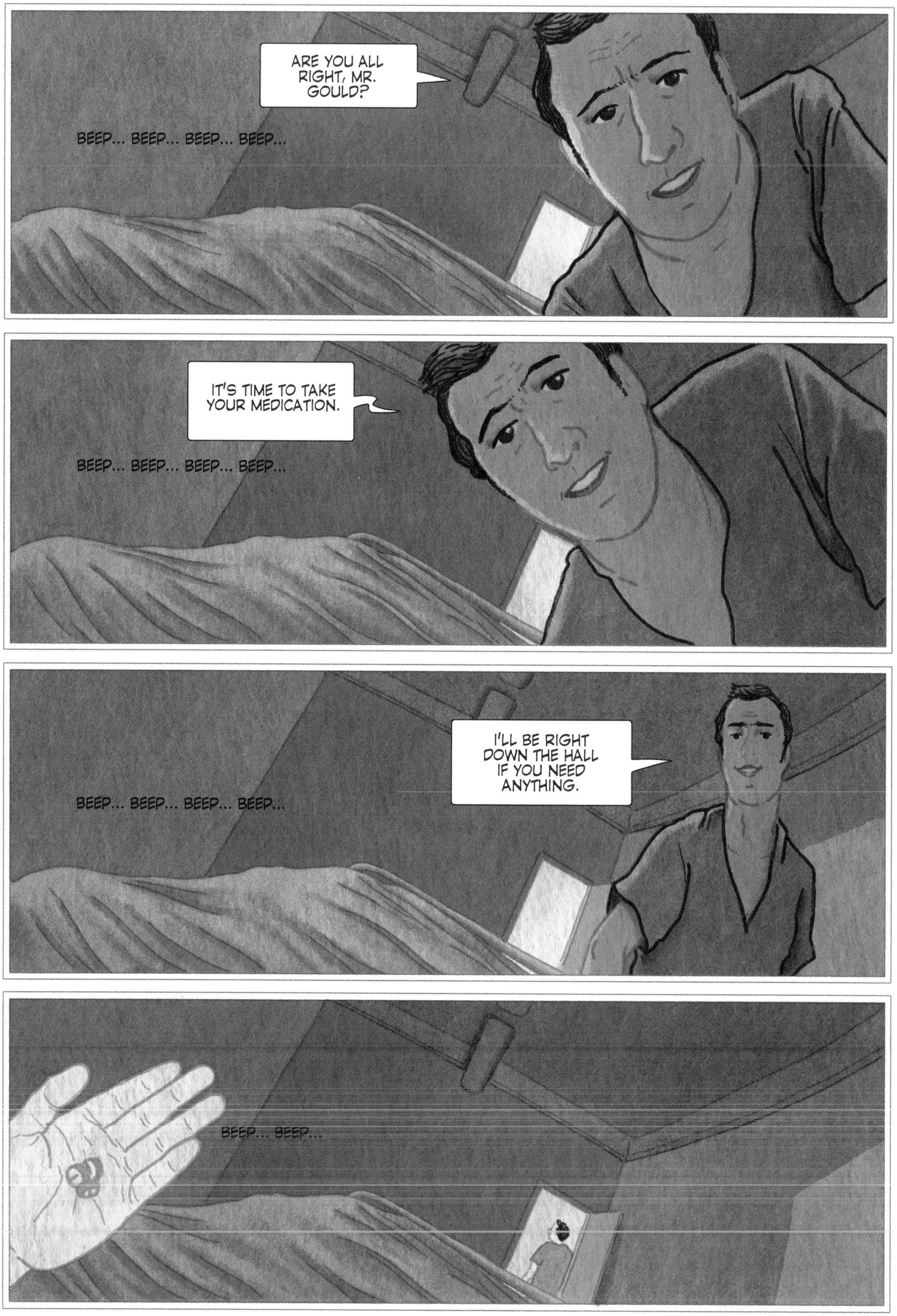
ARE YOU ALL RIGHT, MR. GOULD?
BEEP... BEEP... BEEP... BEEP...
IT'S TIME TO TAKE YOUR MEDICATION.
BEEP... BEEP... BEEP... BEEP...
BEEP... BEEP... BEEP... BEEP...
I'LL BE RIGHT DOWN THE HALL IF YOU NEED ANYTHING.
BEEP... BEEP...

MUSIC IS BECOMING AN OBSESSION.

HE ISOLATES HIMSELF MORE AND MORE.

HE'S BEEN PLAYING FOR HOURS. I CAN'T TEAR HIM AWAY FROM THAT PIANO.

IT'S SUCH A GORGEOUS DAY. YOU SHOULD INSIST.

HE WON'T HEAR OF IT.

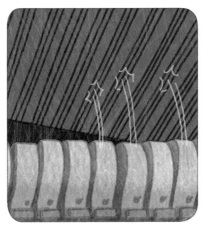

BUT YOU'RE RIGHT. THIS TIME, HE WILL LISTEN TO ME!

GLENN, COME OUT OF THIS ROOM. NOW!

IN A MINUTE!

YOU SAID THAT AN HOUR AGO. I'M DONE BELIEVING YOU!

BUT I HAVEN'T FINISHED THE FIRST BOOK OF PRELUDES AND FUGUES IN BACH'S "WELL-TEMPERED CLAVIER" YET!

DO AS I SAY, OR NO PIANO PRIVILEGES FOR A WEEK!

NO!

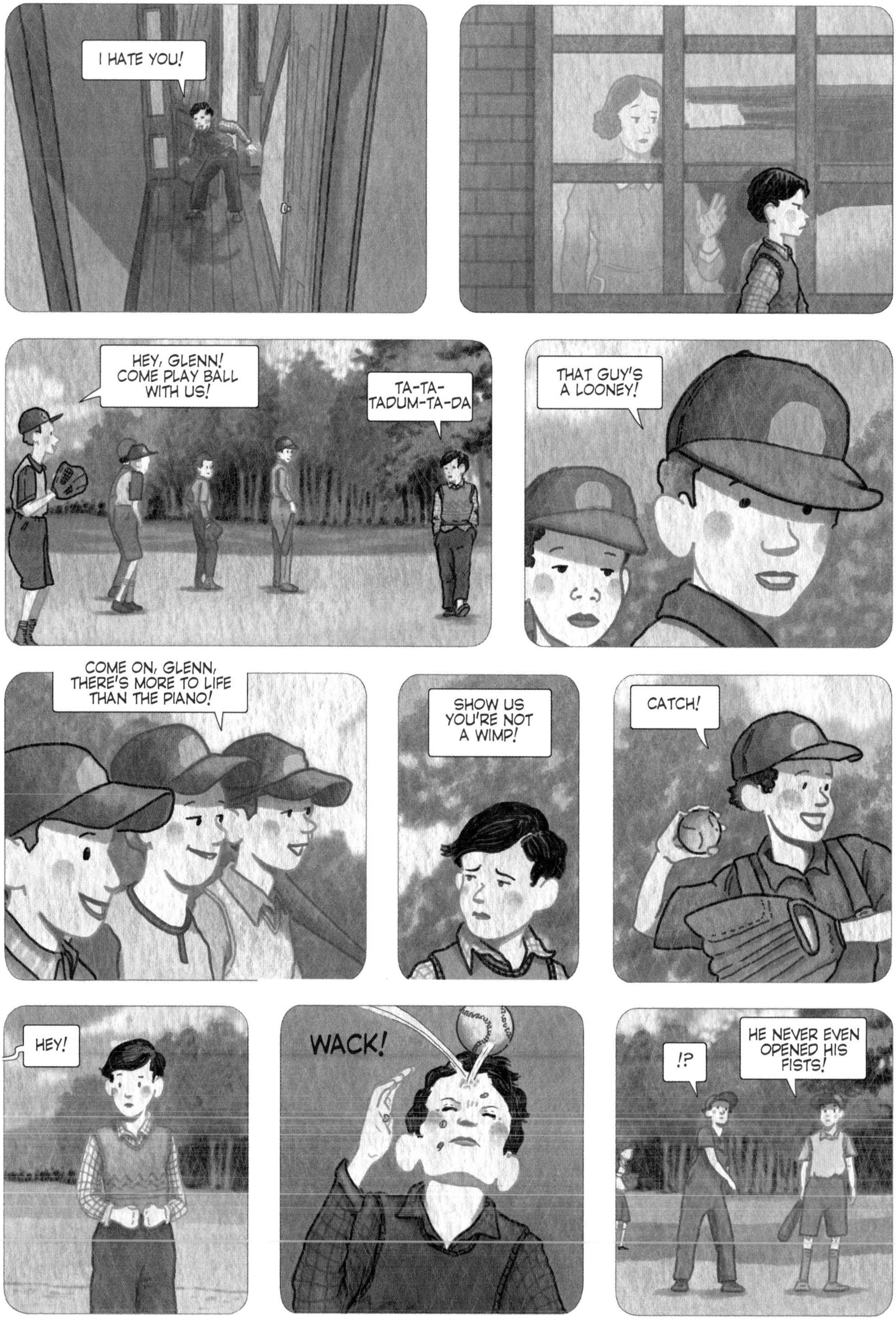
I HATE YOU!
HEY, GLENN! COME PLAY BALL WITH US!
TA-TA-TADUM-TA-DA
THAT GUY'S A LOONEY!
COME ON, GLENN, THERE'S MORE TO LIFE THAN THE PIANO!
SHOW US YOU'RE NOT A WIMP!
CATCH!
HEY!
WACK!
!?
HE NEVER EVEN OPENED HIS FISTS!

YOU ALL RIGHT, BUDDY?

MY HEAD'S SPINNING!

MY HANDS WEREN'T FREE.

HOW COME YOU DIDN'T TRY TO CATCH?

YOU SURE YOU'RE ALL RIGHT?

MY PILLS!

DID YOU LOSE SOMETHING?

THE PILLS I HAD IN MY HANDS!

ARE YOU SICK?

HEAVENS, NO!

I JUST ALWAYS HAVE THEM ON ME IN CASE I GET NAUSEOUS!

FORGET THAT NUT JOB, LET'S GO!

SORRY AGAIN.

TA-DA-DUM TA-DA

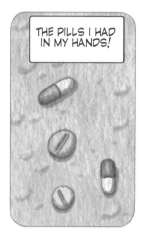

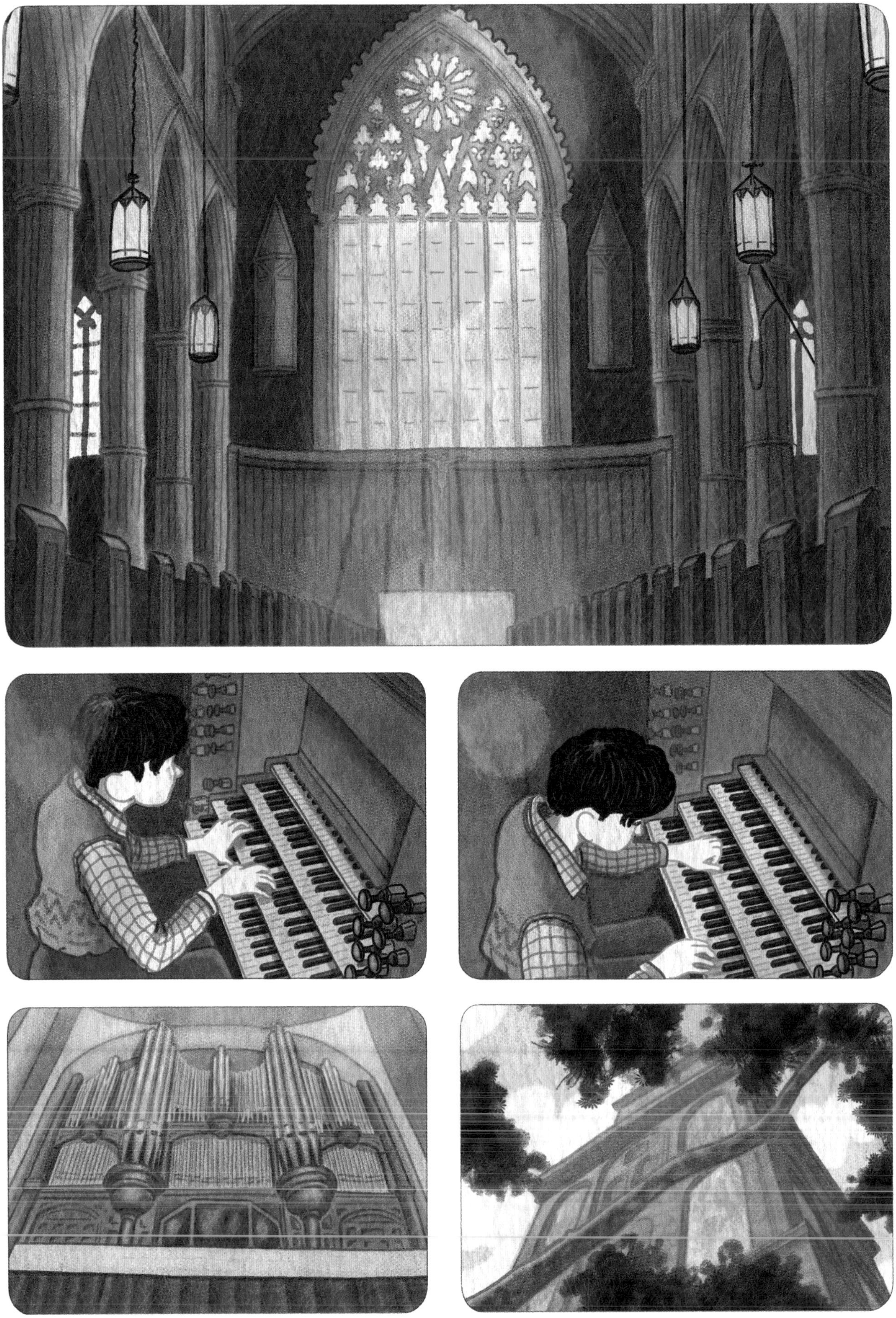

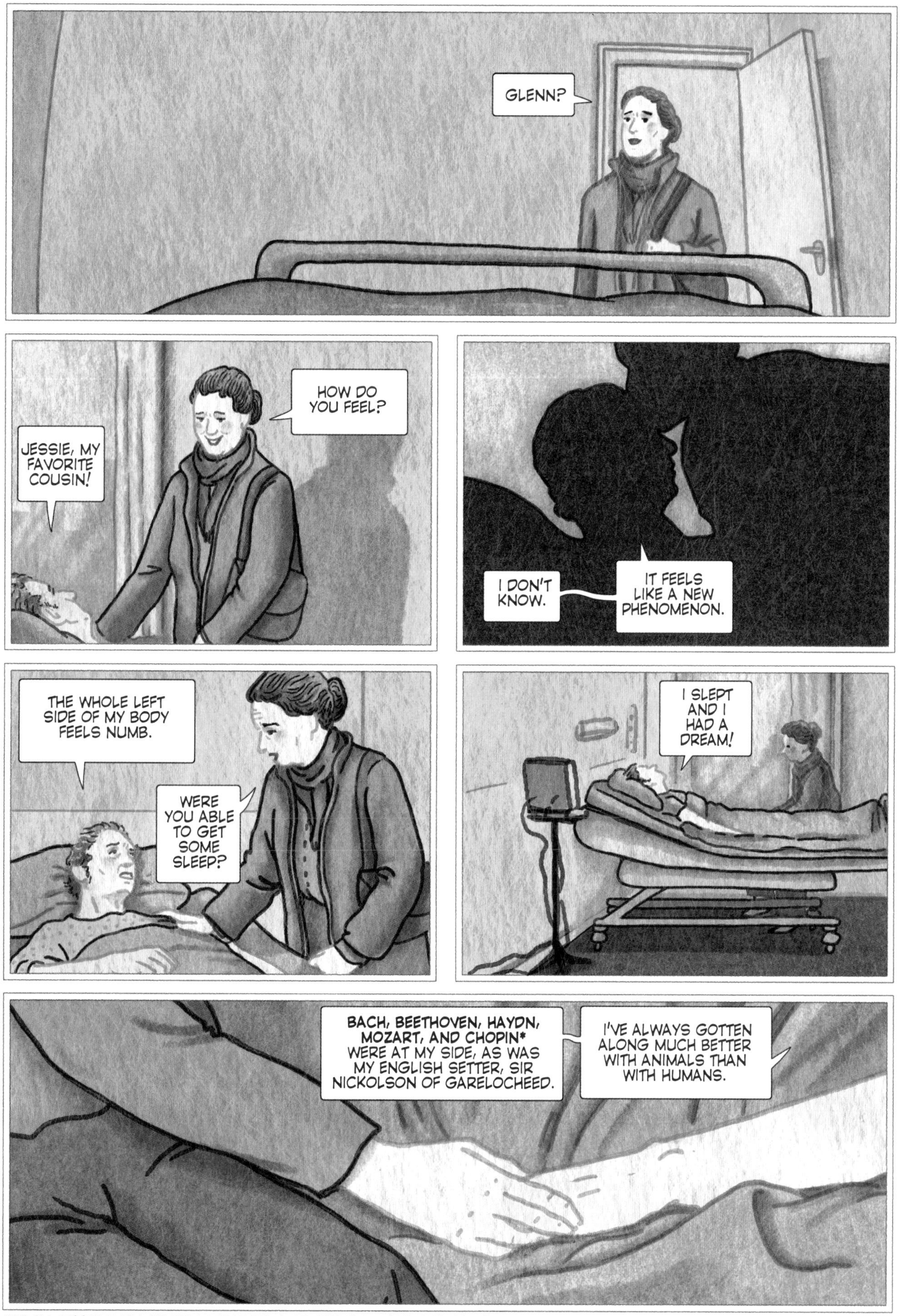
GLENN?
JESSIE, MY FAVORITE COUSIN!
HOW DO YOU FEEL?
I DON'T KNOW.
IT FEELS LIKE A NEW PHENOMENON.
THE WHOLE LEFT SIDE OF MY BODY FEELS NUMB.
WERE YOU ABLE TO GET SOME SLEEP?
I SLEPT AND I HAD A DREAM!
BACH, BEETHOVEN, HAYDN, MOZART, AND CHOPIN* WERE AT MY SIDE, AS WAS MY ENGLISH SETTER, SIR NICKOLSON OF GARELOCHEED.
I'VE ALWAYS GOTTEN ALONG MUCH BETTER WITH ANIMALS THAN WITH HUMANS.

*BACH, BEETHOVEN, HAYDN, MOZART, AND CHOPIN WERE THE NAMES OF HIS TWO DOGS, TWO RABBITS, FOUR GOLDFISH AND PARAKEET.

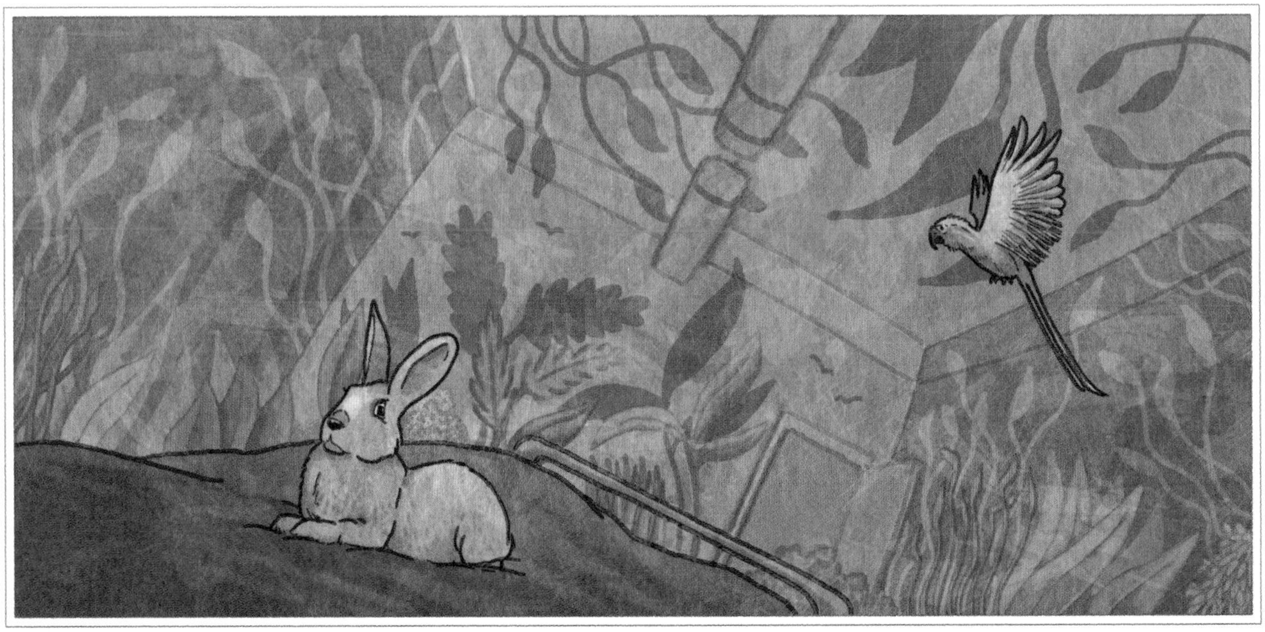
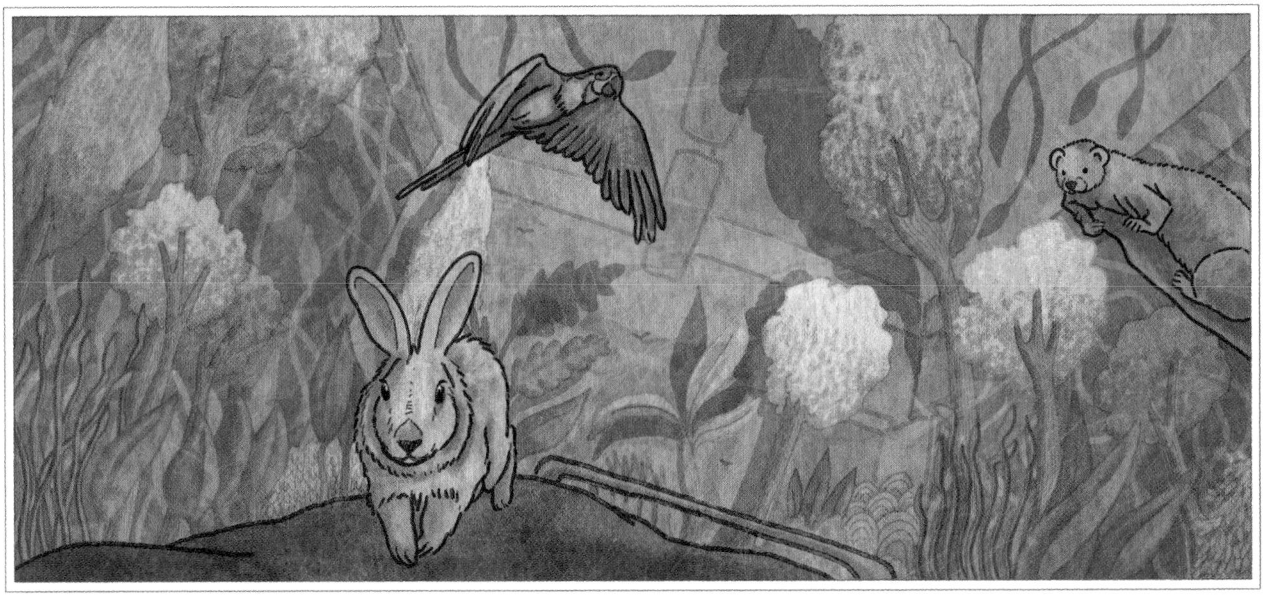
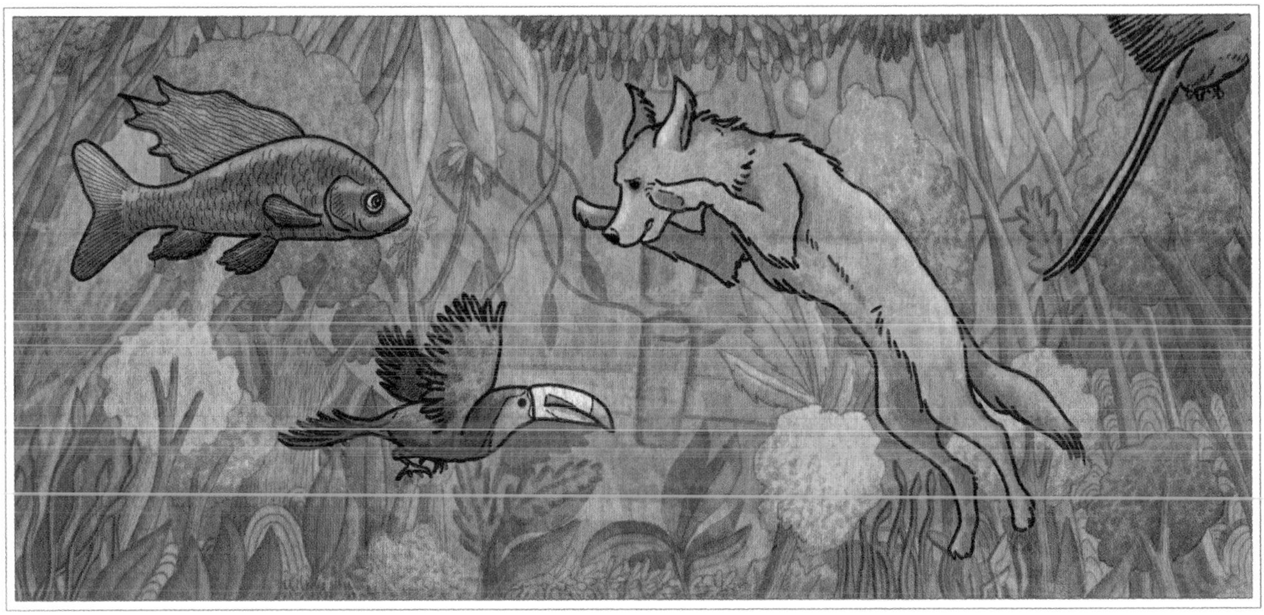

UPTERGROVE,
ONTARIO.

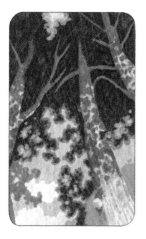

IT'S SO NICE
TO BE BACK AT
THE COTTAGE.

HEY, GLENN!

YOU WANNA GO
FISHING ON THE
LAKE?

I DON'T KNOW
HOW TO
FISH.

IT'S NOT
THAT HARD,
YOU'LL SEE!

CAN I GO WITH
THEM, MOUSE?

PLEASE?

LET HIM GO HAVE
FUN WITH THE
NEIGHBORS. HE'S
ON VACATION!

DON'T STAY OUT
TOO LATE, AND
NO SWIMMING! I
DON'T WANT YOU
GETTING SICK.

OK,
MOUSE!

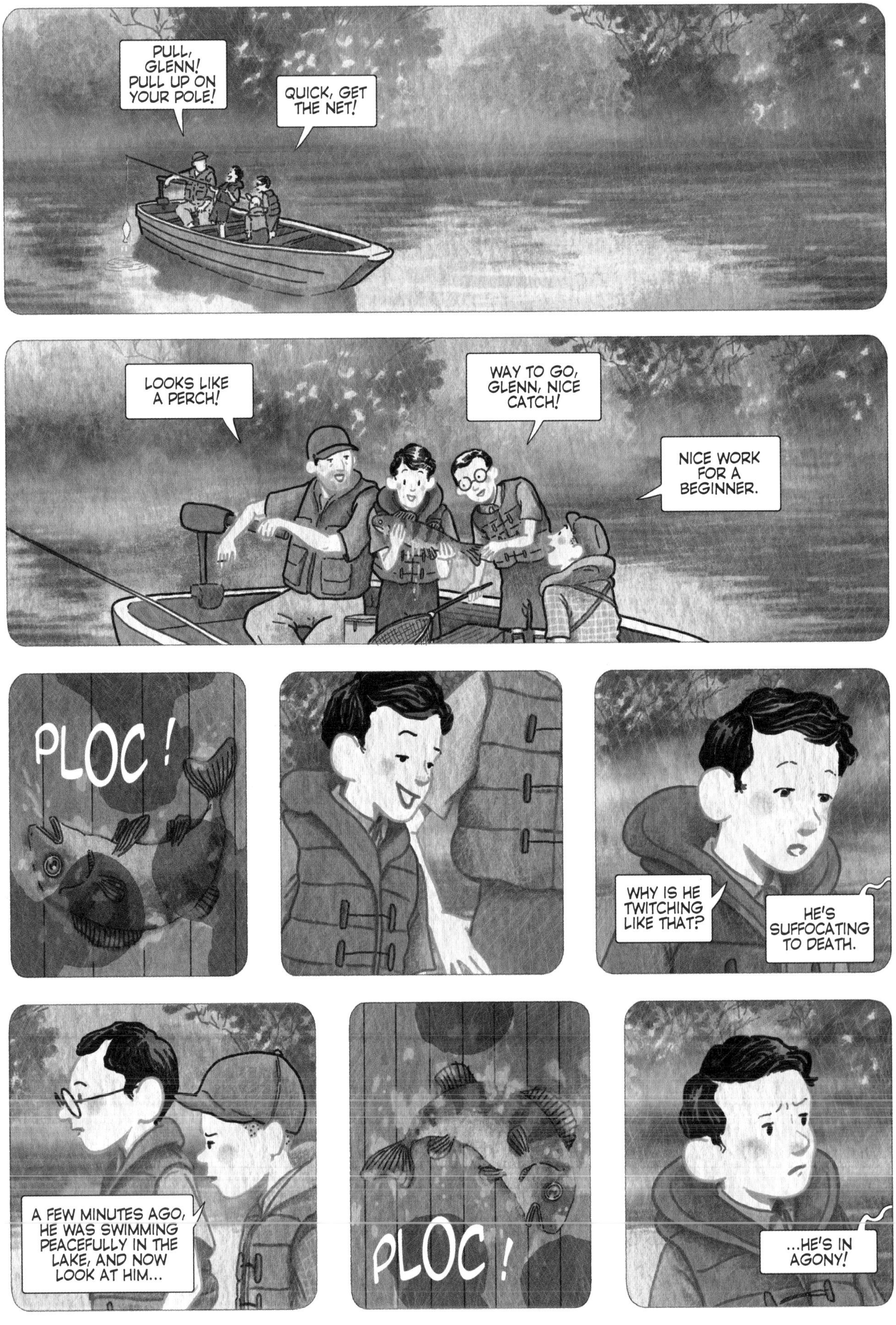
PULL, GLENN! PULL UP ON YOUR POLE!
QUICK, GET THE NET!
LOOKS LIKE A PERCH!
WAY TO GO, GLENN, NICE CATCH!
NICE WORK FOR A BEGINNER.
PLOC!
WHY IS HE TWITCHING LIKE THAT?
HE'S SUFFOCATING TO DEATH.
A FEW MINUTES AGO, HE WAS SWIMMING PEACEFULLY IN THE LAKE, AND NOW LOOK AT HIM...
PLOC!
...HE'S IN AGONY!

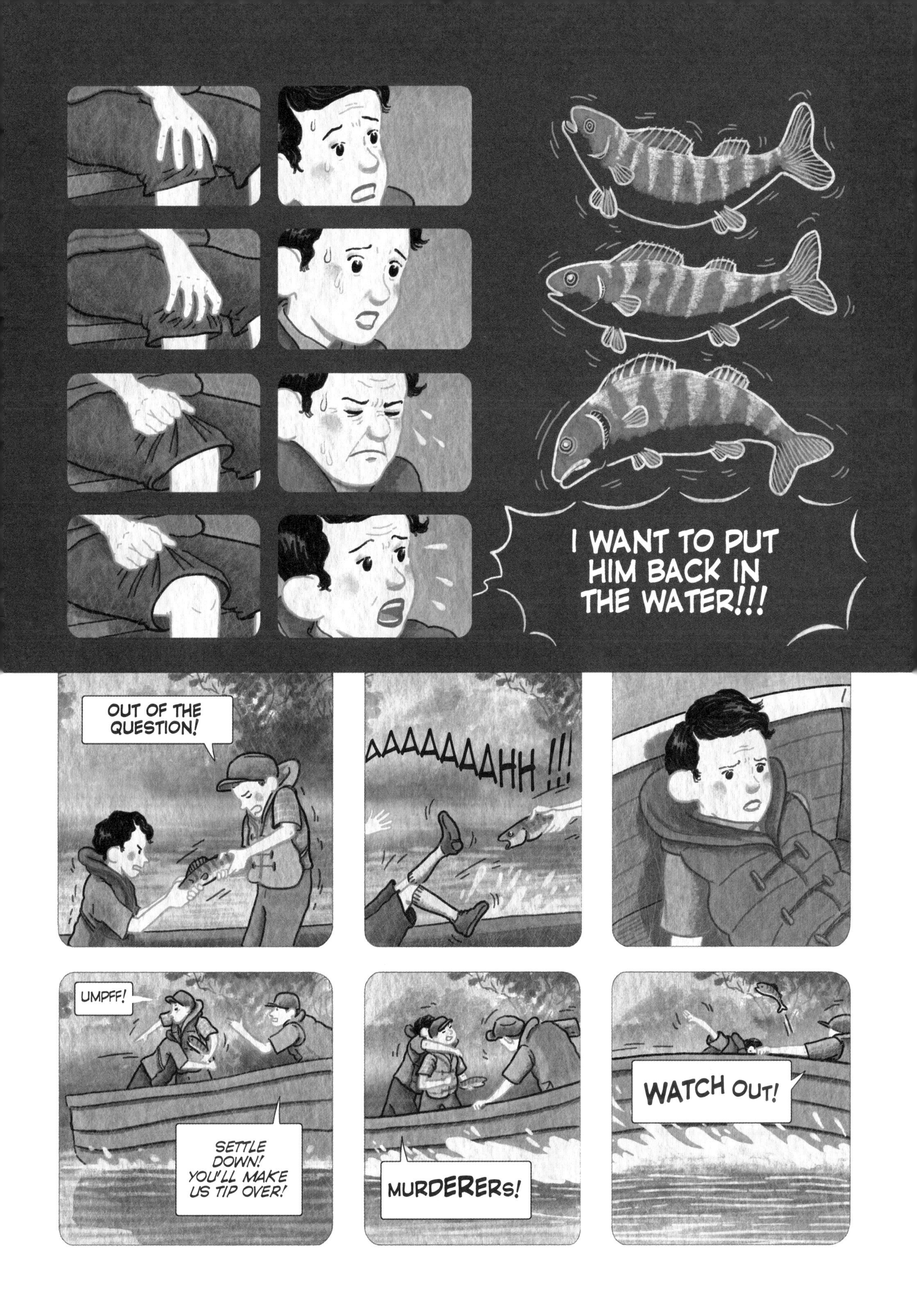
I WANT TO PUT HIM BACK IN THE WATER!!!
OUT OF THE QUESTION!
AAAAAAAAHH!!!
UMPFF!
SETTLE DOWN! YOU'LL MAKE US TIP OVER!
MURDERERS!
WATCH OUT!

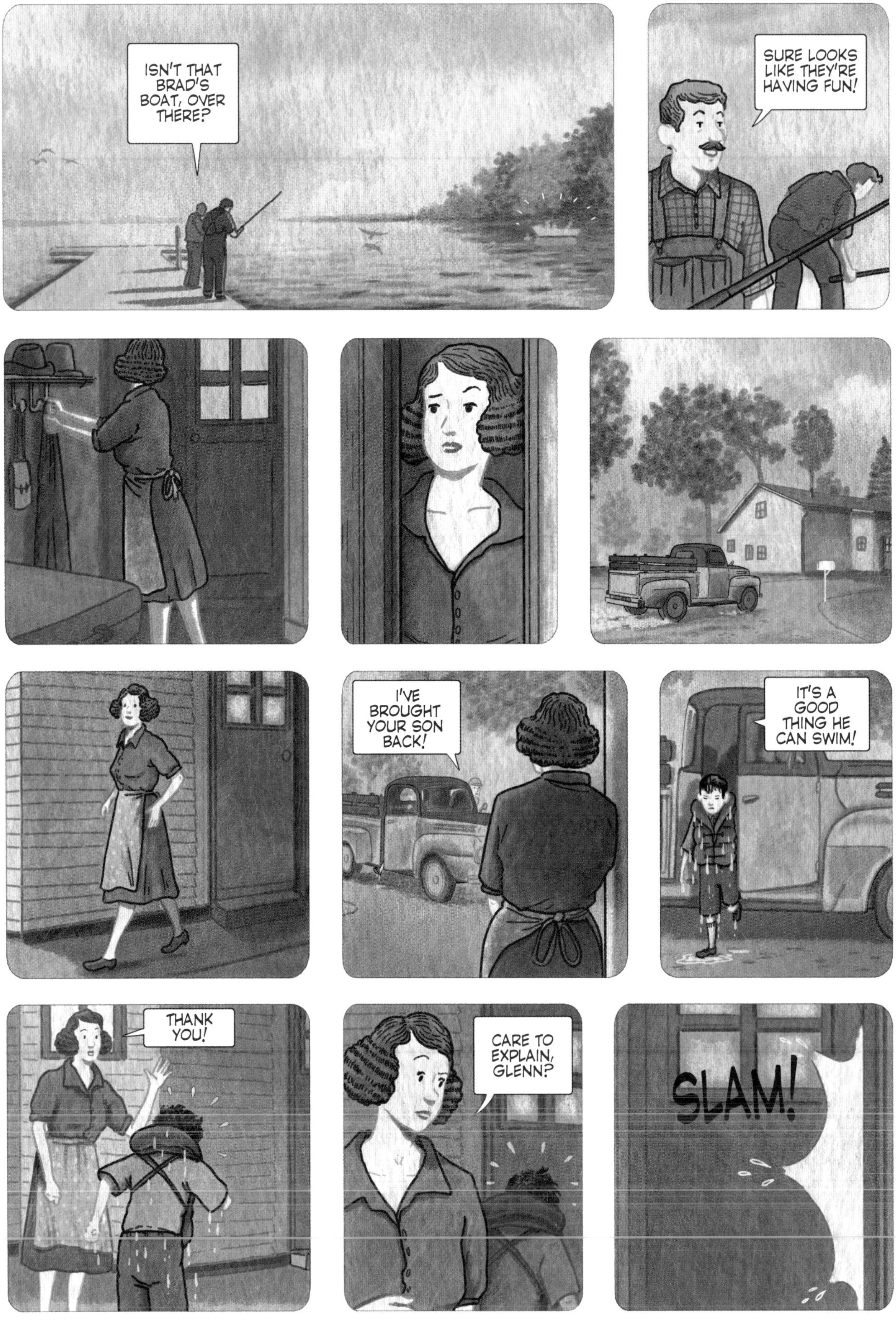

ISN'T THAT BRAD'S BOAT, OVER THERE?
SURE LOOKS LIKE THEY'RE HAVING FUN!
I'VE BROUGHT YOUR SON BACK!
IT'S A GOOD THING HE CAN SWIM!
THANK YOU!
CARE TO EXPLAIN, GLENN?
SLAM!

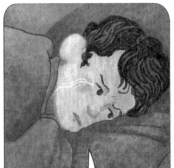

I DON'T WANT DAD TO GO FISHING ANYMORE AND I WANT YOU TO STOP WEARING FUR COATS!

WHEN I GROW UP, I'M BUYING A FARM WHERE I'LL TAKE IN ALL THE ABANDONED ANIMALS.

DOGS, CATS, COWS, HORSES, INSECTS, FISH...

HOW IS HE?

HE FELL ASLEEP.

HOW WILL HE REACT WHEN HE FINDS OUT YOU SELL FURS?

HE'S SO SENSITIVE!

WHAT ARE YOU THINKING ABOUT?
ABOUT MY ABIDING HATRED FOR FISHING!
EVER SINCE MY STROKE, ALL SORTS OF MEMORIES HAVE BEEN PLAYING OUT IN MY MIND.
GLENN?
I CALLED YOUR FATHER. I TOLD HIM YOU WERE IN THE HOSPITAL.
KNOWING HIM, HE'LL BE WORRIED SICK!
MY PARENTS WERE ALWAYS OVERPROTECTIVE.
WHICH CERTAINLY EXPLAINS A LOT.

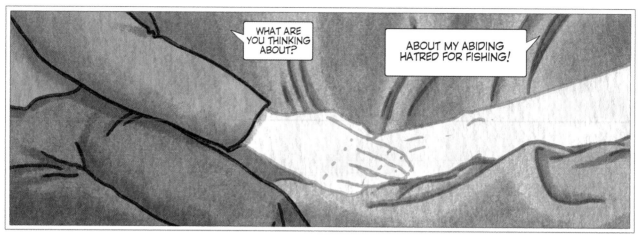

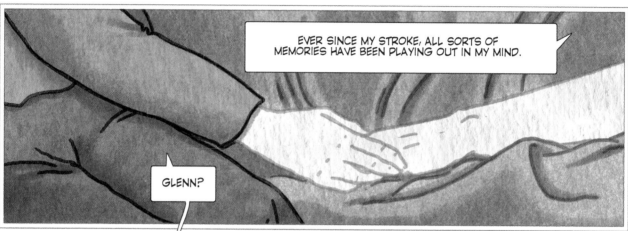

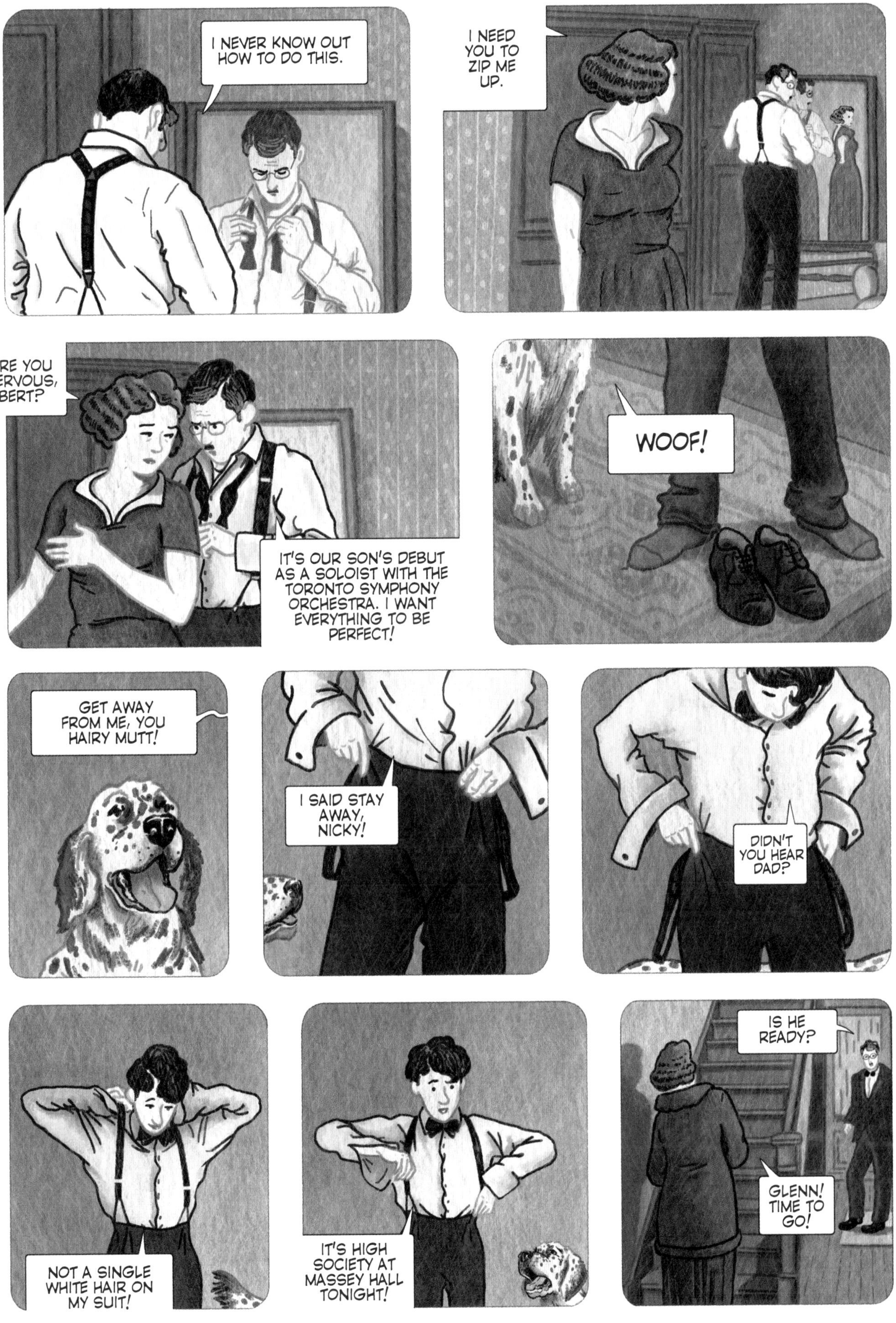
I NEVER KNOW OUT HOW TO DO THIS.
I NEED YOU TO ZIP ME UP.
ARE YOU NERVOUS, BERT?
IT'S OUR SON'S DEBUT AS A SOLOIST WITH THE TORONTO SYMPHONY ORCHESTRA. I WANT EVERYTHING TO BE PERFECT!
WOOF!
GET AWAY FROM ME, YOU HAIRY MUTT!
I SAID STAY AWAY, NICKY!
DIDN'T YOU HEAR DAD?
NOT A SINGLE WHITE HAIR ON MY SUIT!
IT'S HIGH SOCIETY AT MASSEY HALL TONIGHT!
IS HE READY?
GLENN! TIME TO GO!

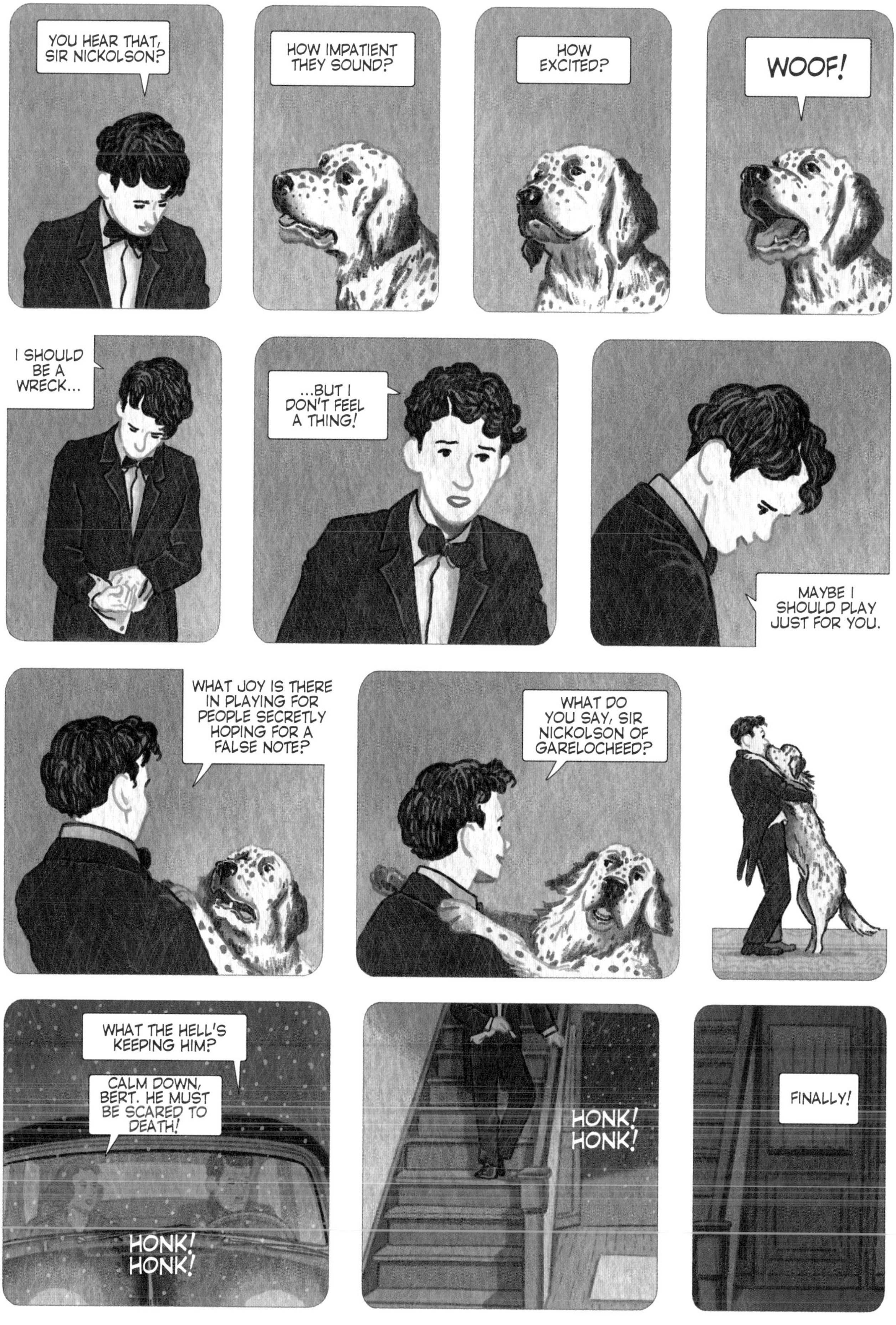
YOU HEAR THAT, SIR NICKOLSON?
HOW IMPATIENT THEY SOUND?
HOW EXCITED?
WOOF!
I SHOULD BE A WRECK...
...BUT I DON'T FEEL A THING!
MAYBE I SHOULD PLAY JUST FOR YOU.
WHAT JOY IS THERE IN PLAYING FOR PEOPLE SECRETLY HOPING FOR A FALSE NOTE?
WHAT DO YOU SAY, SIR NICKOLSON OF GARELOCHEED?
WHAT THE HELL'S KEEPING HIM?
CALM DOWN, BERT. HE MUST BE SCARED TO DEATH!
HONK! HONK!
HONK! HONK!
FINALLY!

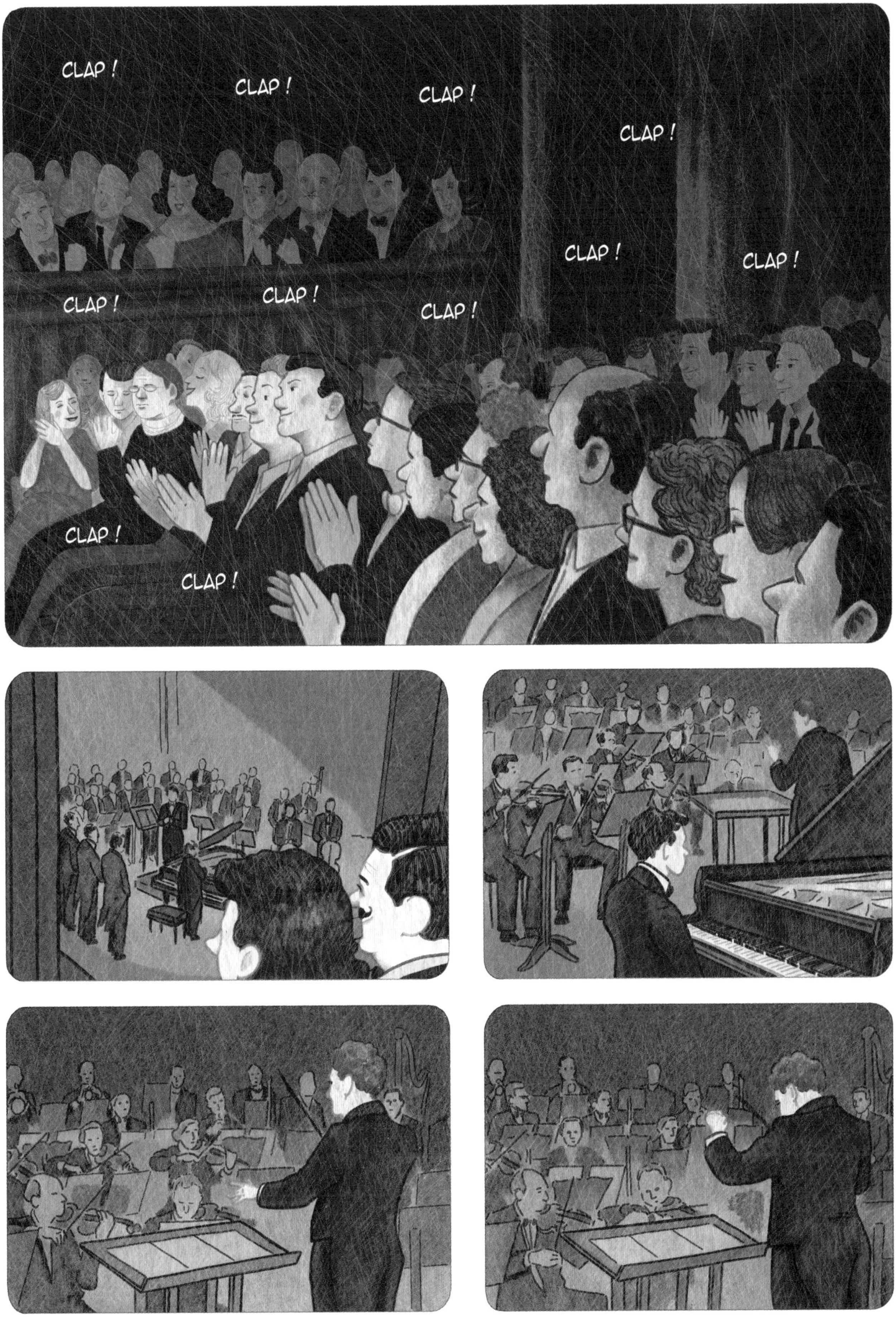
CLAP !
CLAP !
CLAP !
CLAP !
CLAP !
CLAP !
CLAP !
CLAP !
CLAP !
CLAP !
CLAP !

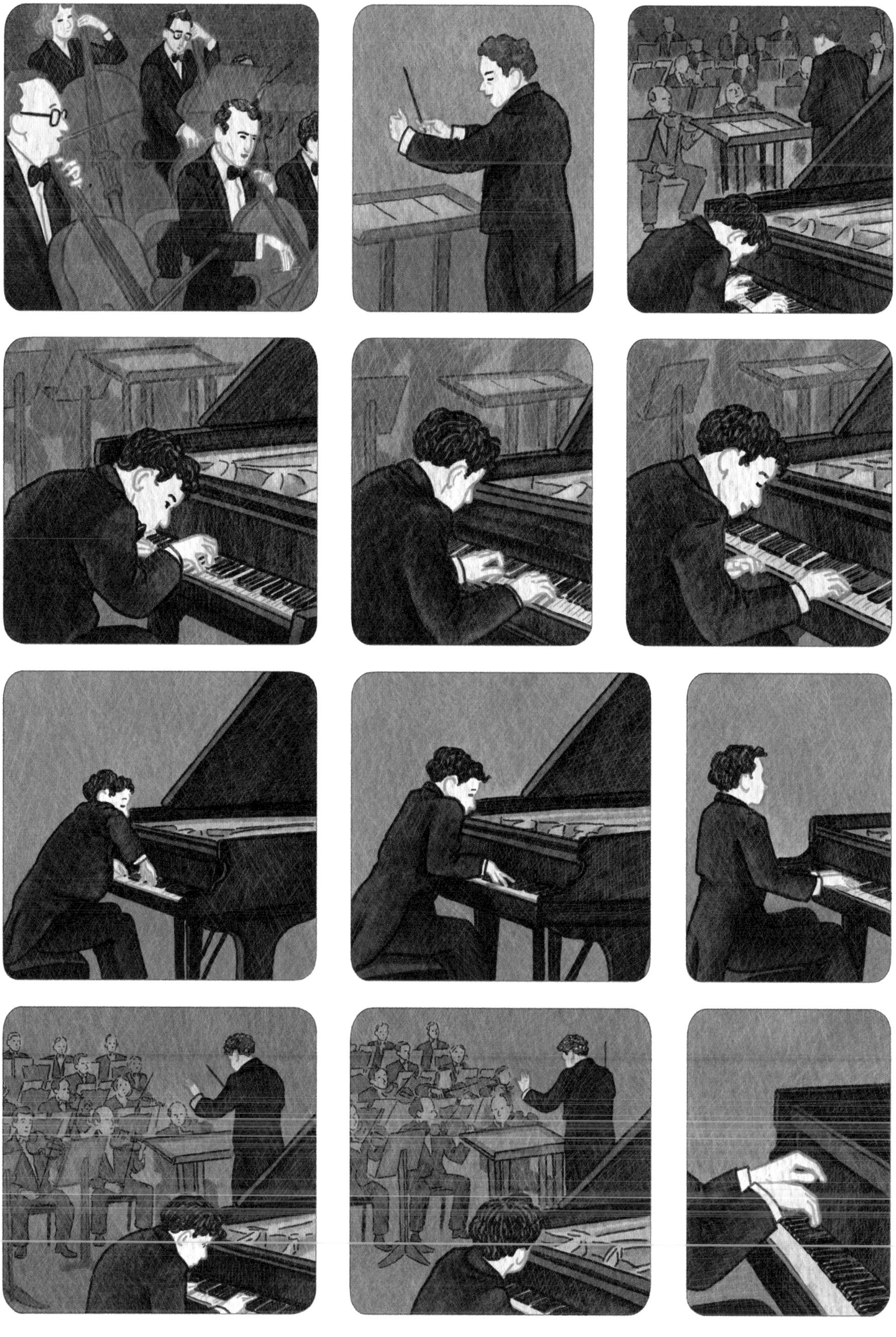

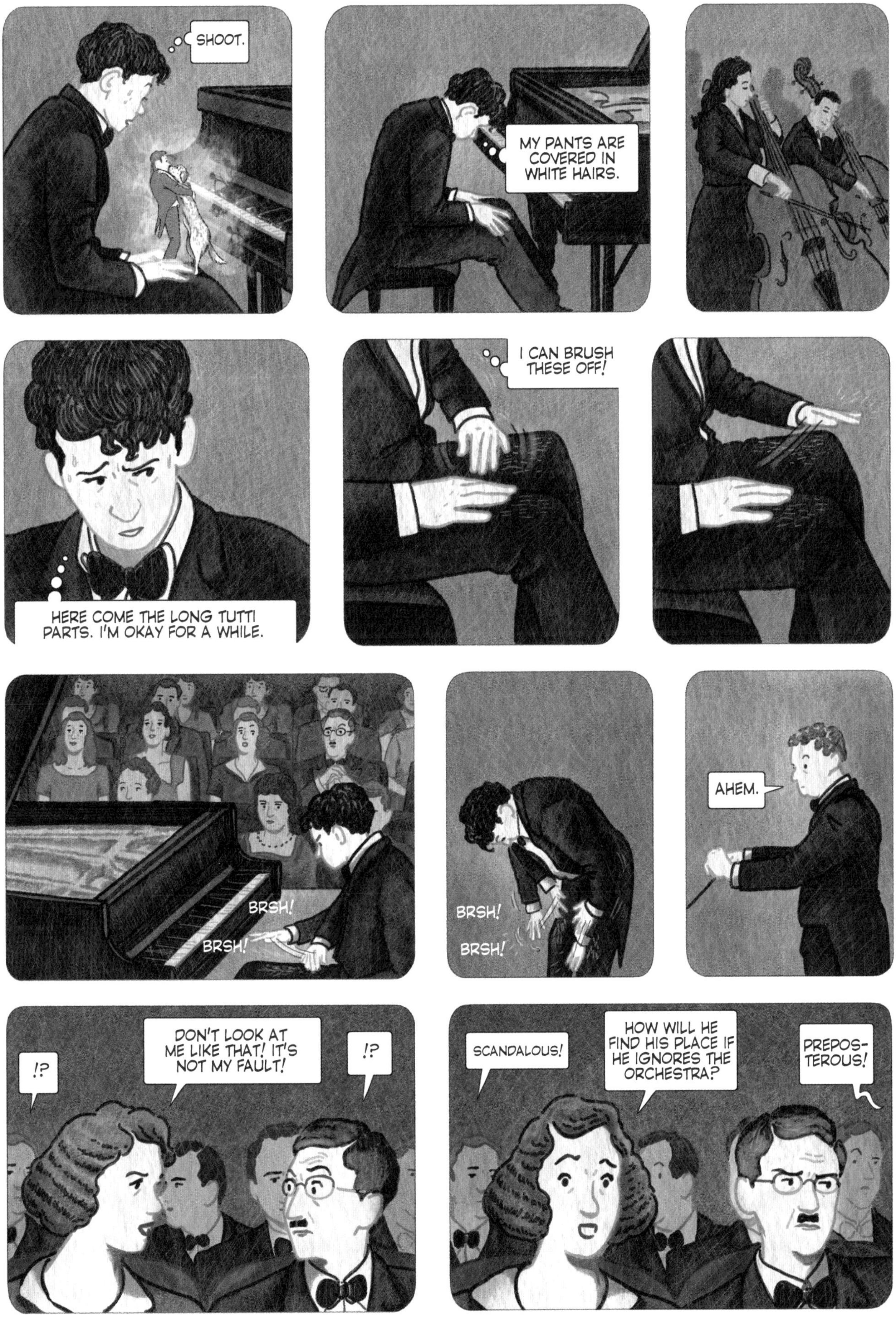
SHOOT.
MY PANTS ARE COVERED IN WHITE HAIRS.
HERE COME THE LONG TUTTI PARTS. I'M OKAY FOR A WHILE.
I CAN BRUSH THESE OFF!
BRSH!
BRSH!
BRSH!
BRSH!
AHEM.
!?
DON'T LOOK AT ME LIKE THAT! IT'S NOT MY FAULT!
!?
SCANDALOUS!
HOW WILL HE FIND HIS PLACE IF HE IGNORES THE ORCHESTRA?
PREPOS-TEROUS!

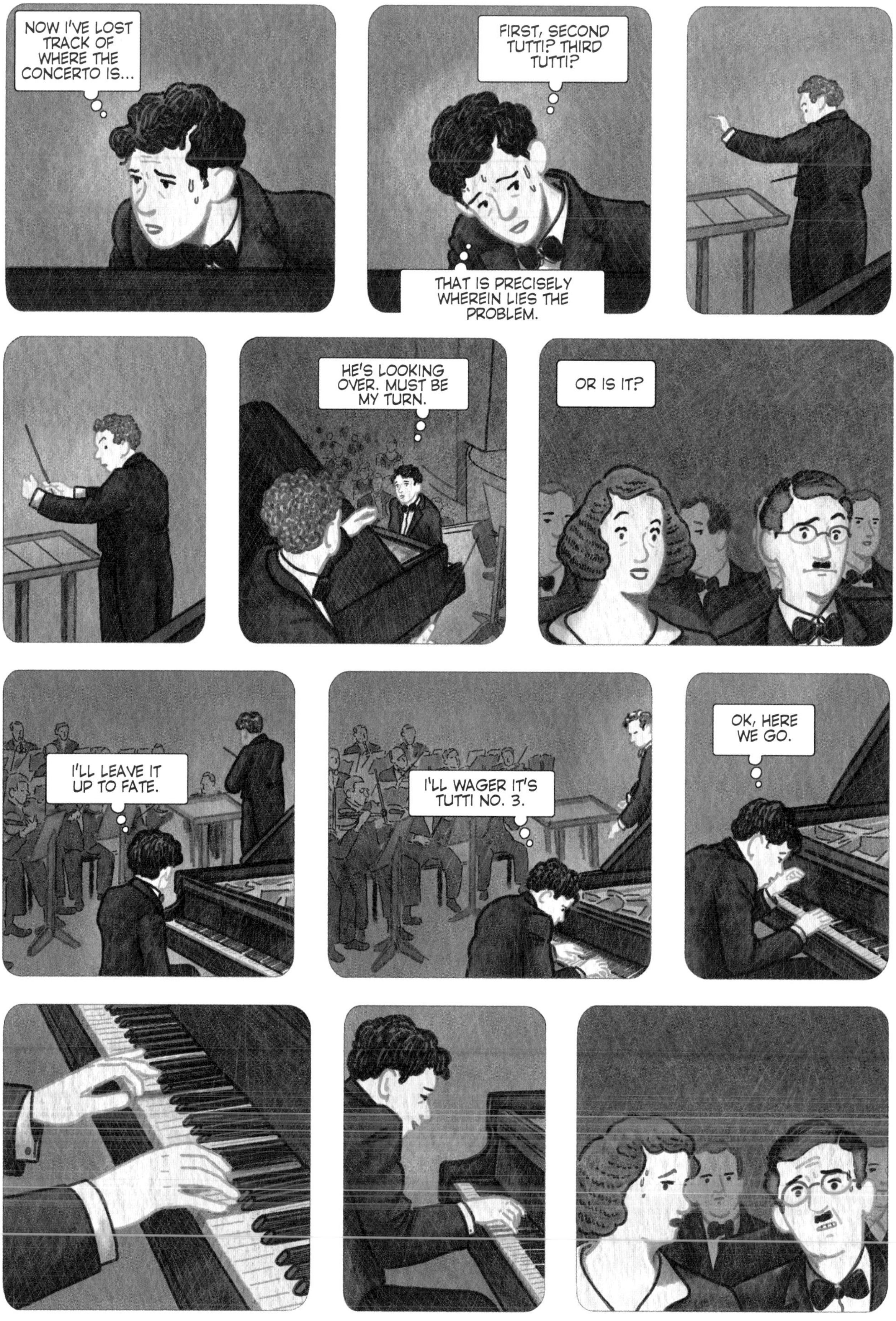
NOW I'VE LOST TRACK OF WHERE THE CONCERTO IS...
FIRST, SECOND TUTTI? THIRD TUTTI?
THAT IS PRECISELY WHEREIN LIES THE PROBLEM.
HE'S LOOKING OVER. MUST BE MY TURN.
OR IS IT?
I'LL LEAVE IT UP TO FATE.
I'LL WAGER IT'S TUTTI NO. 3.
OK, HERE WE GO.

ARE YOU PROUD OF YOURSELF?

YOUR MOTHER AND I DIDN'T APPRECIATE THAT ONE BIT!

WELL?

ARE YOU GOING TO PUNISH NICKY?

GOOD-NESS, GLENN!

WE JUST SKIRTED DISASTER!

RULE NO. 1: A SOLOIST MUST NEVER IGNORE THE OTHER MUSICIANS. HE MUST BE THINKING ABOUT THE ORCHESTRA AND NOTHING ELSE!

IF THIS HAD BEEN ON THE RADIO, NOBODY WOULD HAVE NOTICED THE INCIDENT AND THAT WOULD'VE BEEN THAT.

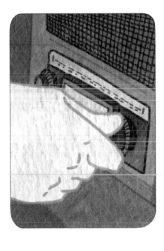

YOU ARE LISTENING TO CBC, THE CANADIAN RADIO THAT BRINGS YOU THE ARTISTS OF TOMORROW.

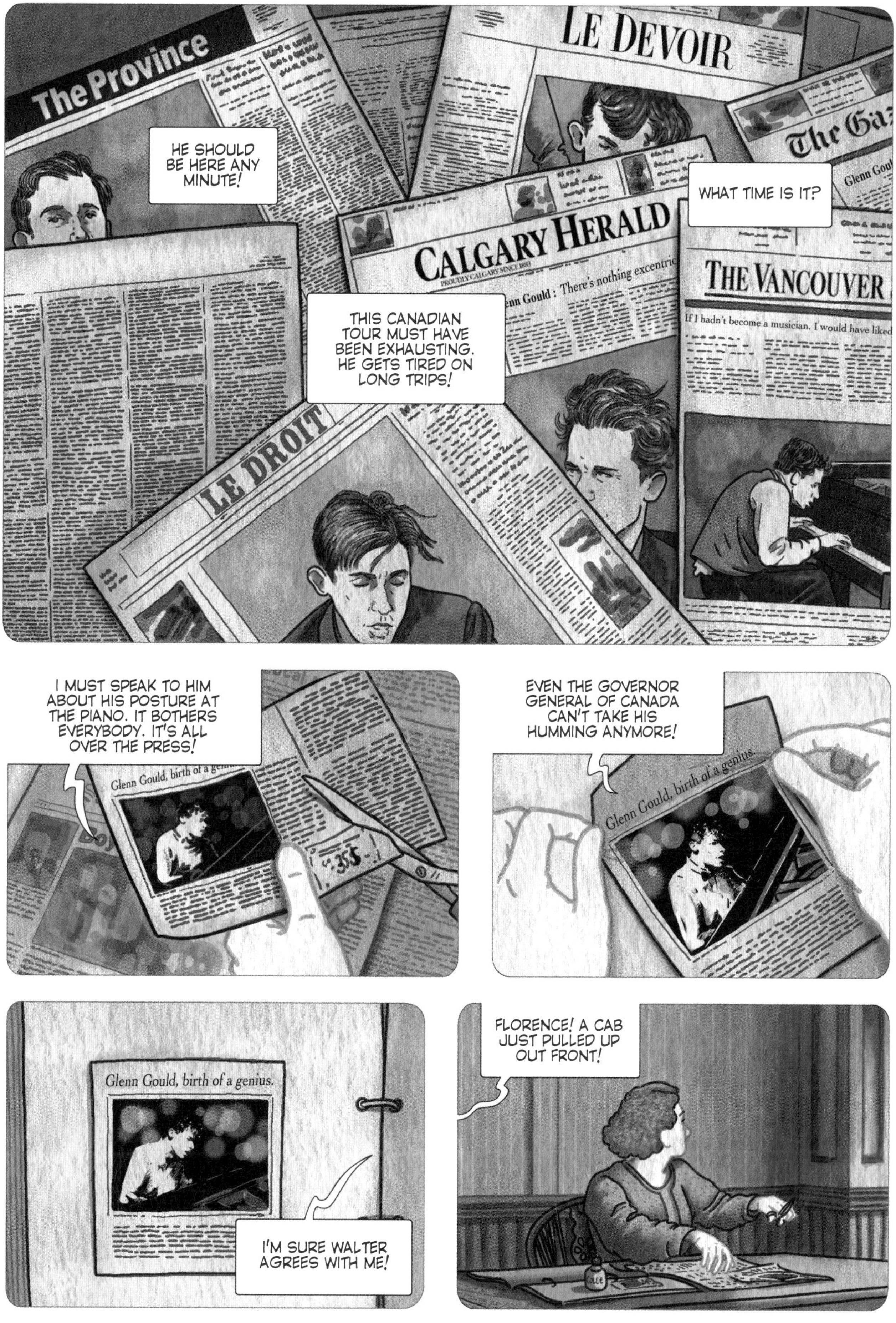
The Province
LE DEVOIR
HE SHOULD BE HERE ANY MINUTE!
CALGARY HERALD
WHAT TIME IS IT?
THE VANCOUVER
If I hadn't become a musician, I would have liked
THIS CANADIAN TOUR MUST HAVE BEEN EXHAUSTING. HE GETS TIRED ON LONG TRIPS!
LE DROIT
I MUST SPEAK TO HIM ABOUT HIS POSTURE AT THE PIANO. IT BOTHERS EVERYBODY. IT'S ALL OVER THE PRESS!
EVEN THE GOVERNOR GENERAL OF CANADA CAN'T TAKE HIS HUMMING ANYMORE!
Glenn Gould, birth of a genius.
Glenn Gould, birth of a genius.
I'M SURE WALTER AGREES WITH ME!
FLORENCE! A CAB JUST PULLED UP OUT FRONT!

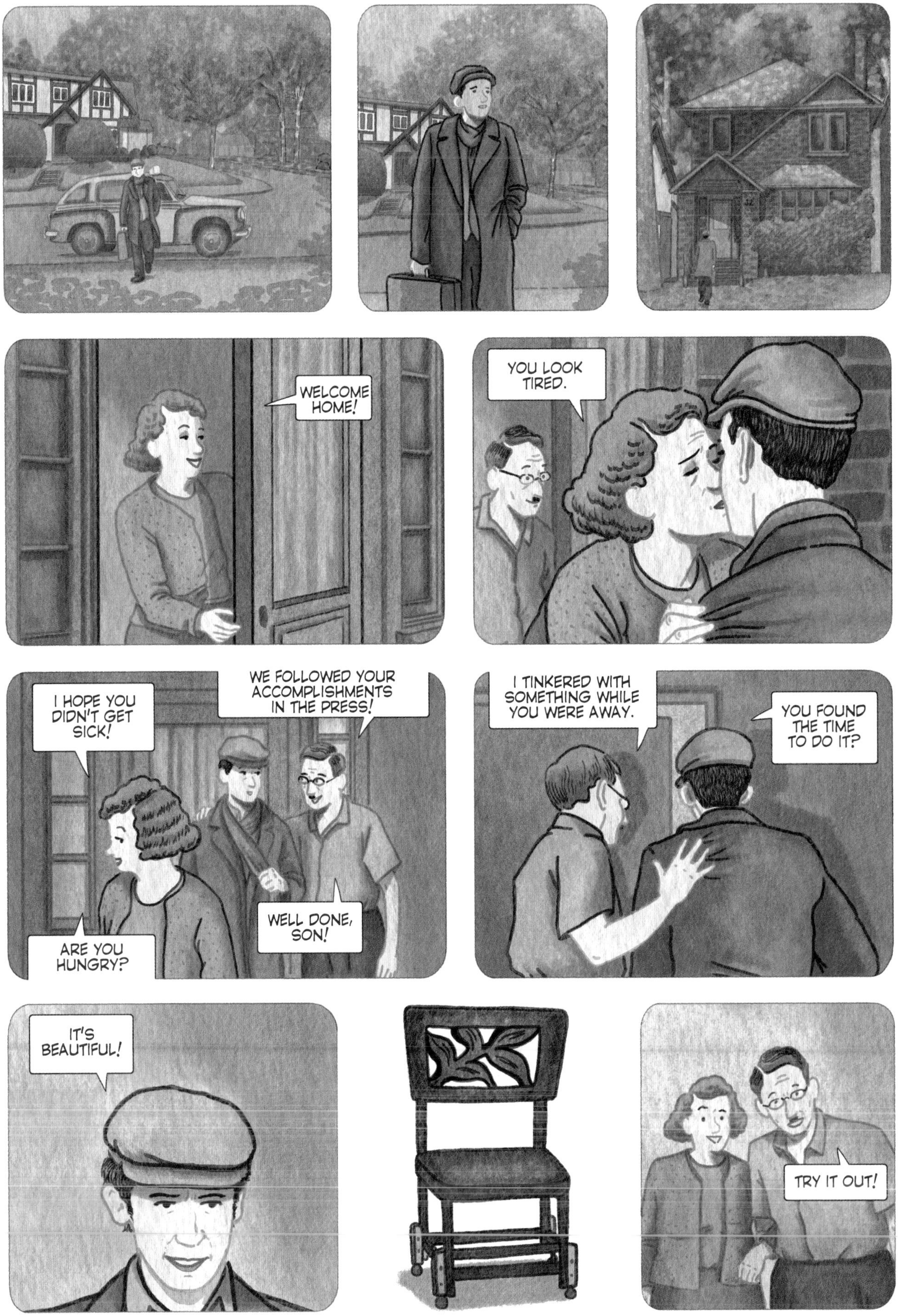
WELCOME HOME!
YOU LOOK TIRED.
I HOPE YOU DIDN'T GET SICK!
WE FOLLOWED YOUR ACCOMPLISHMENTS IN THE PRESS!
ARE YOU HUNGRY?
WELL DONE, SON!
I TINKERED WITH SOMETHING WHILE YOU WERE AWAY.
YOU FOUND THE TIME TO DO IT?
IT'S BEAUTIFUL!
TRY IT OUT!

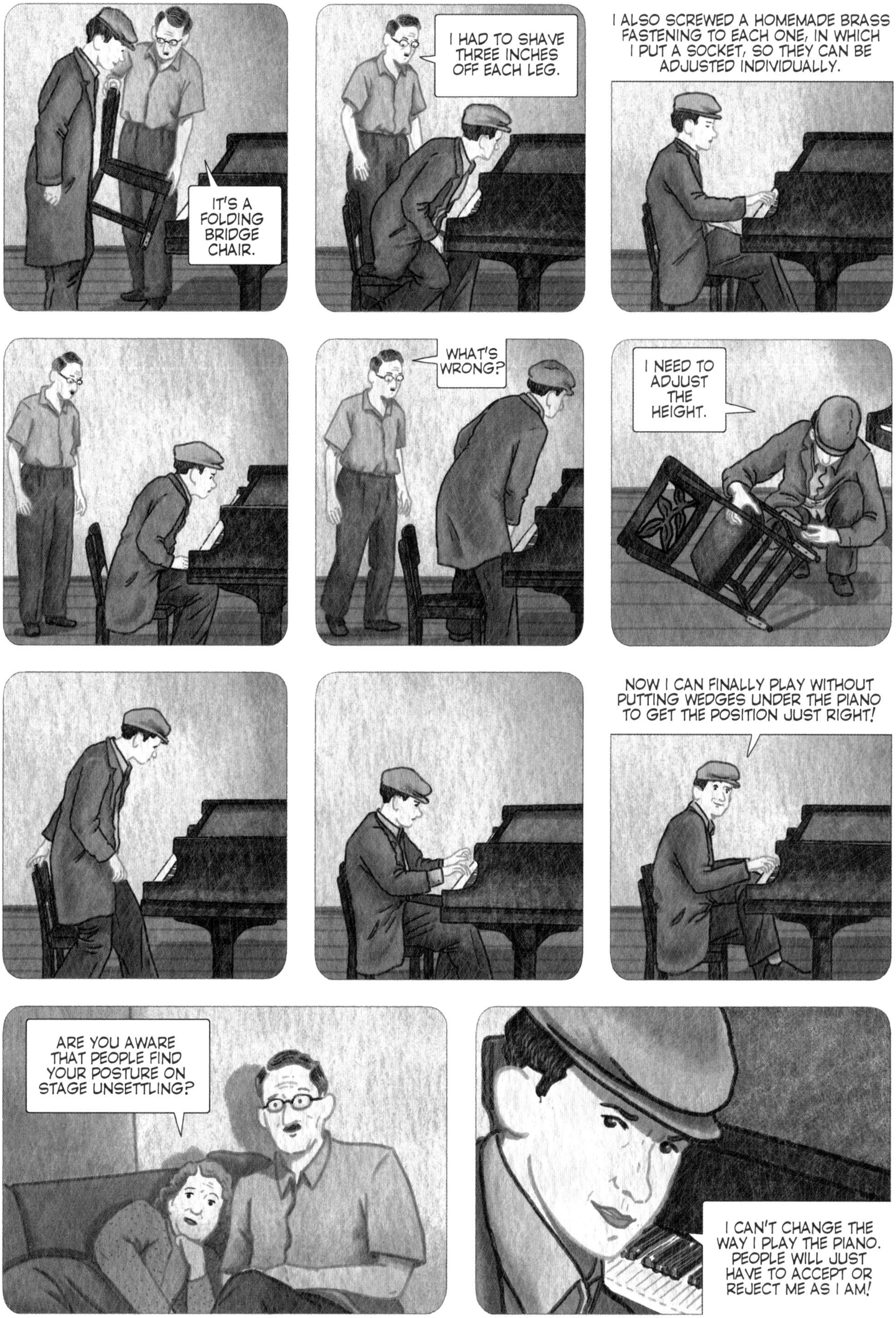
IT'S A FOLDING BRIDGE CHAIR.
I HAD TO SHAVE THREE INCHES OFF EACH LEG.
I ALSO SCREWED A HOMEMADE BRASS FASTENING TO EACH ONE, IN WHICH I PUT A SOCKET, SO THEY CAN BE ADJUSTED INDIVIDUALLY.
WHAT'S WRONG?
I NEED TO ADJUST THE HEIGHT.
NOW I CAN FINALLY PLAY WITHOUT PUTTING WEDGES UNDER THE PIANO TO GET THE POSITION JUST RIGHT!
ARE YOU AWARE THAT PEOPLE FIND YOUR POSTURE ON STAGE UNSETTLING?
I CAN'T CHANGE THE WAY I PLAY THE PIANO. PEOPLE WILL JUST HAVE TO ACCEPT OR REJECT ME AS I AM!

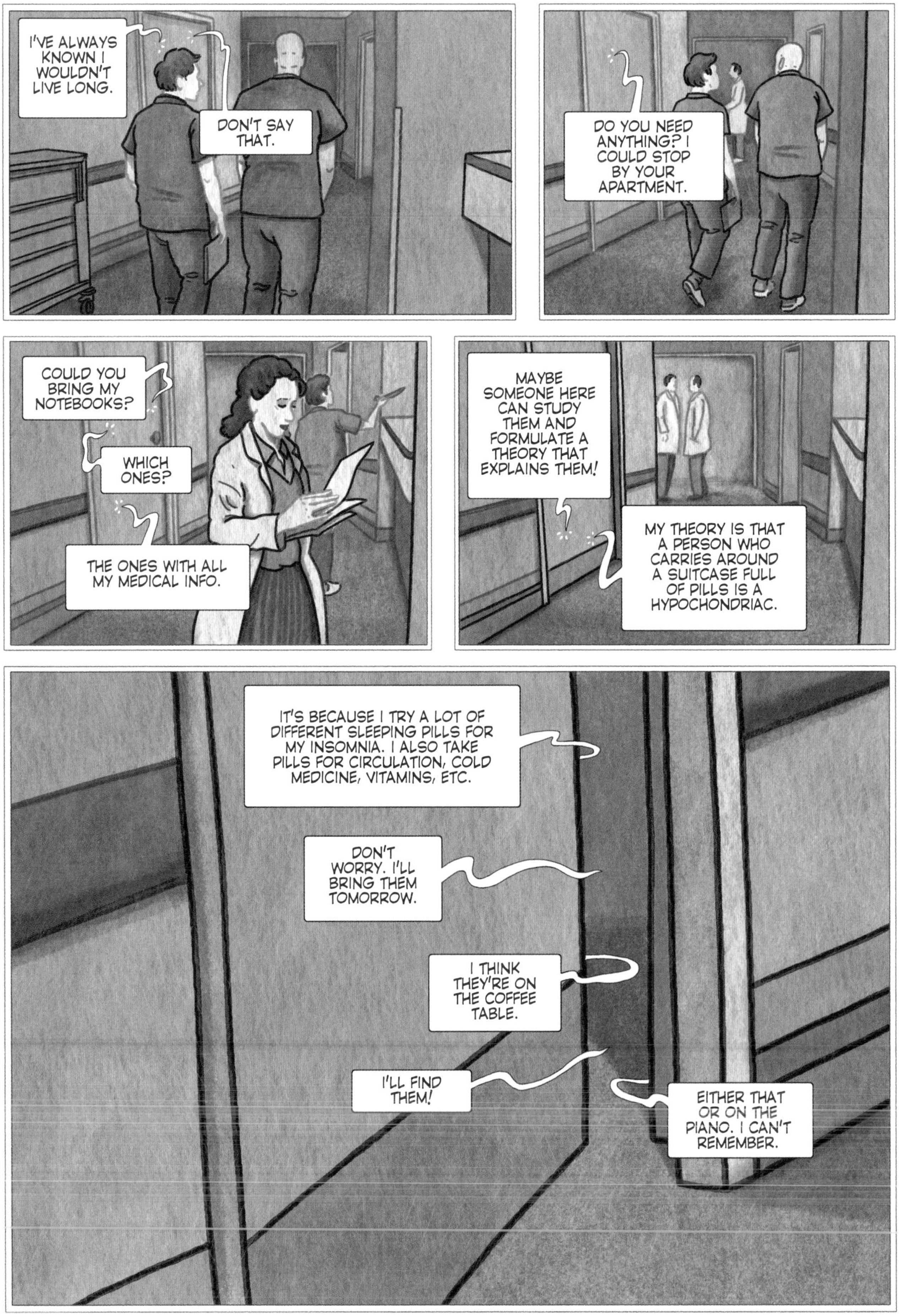
I'VE ALWAYS KNOWN I WOULDN'T LIVE LONG.
DON'T SAY THAT.
DO YOU NEED ANYTHING? I COULD STOP BY YOUR APARTMENT.
COULD YOU BRING MY NOTEBOOKS?
WHICH ONES?
THE ONES WITH ALL MY MEDICAL INFO.
MAYBE SOMEONE HERE CAN STUDY THEM AND FORMULATE A THEORY THAT EXPLAINS THEM!
MY THEORY IS THAT A PERSON WHO CARRIES AROUND A SUITCASE FULL OF PILLS IS A HYPOCHONDRIAC.
IT'S BECAUSE I TRY A LOT OF DIFFERENT SLEEPING PILLS FOR MY INSOMNIA. I ALSO TAKE PILLS FOR CIRCULATION, COLD MEDICINE, VITAMINS, ETC.
DON'T WORRY. I'LL BRING THEM TOMORROW.
I THINK THEY'RE ON THE COFFEE TABLE.
I'LL FIND THEM!
EITHER THAT OR ON THE PIANO. I CAN'T REMEMBER.

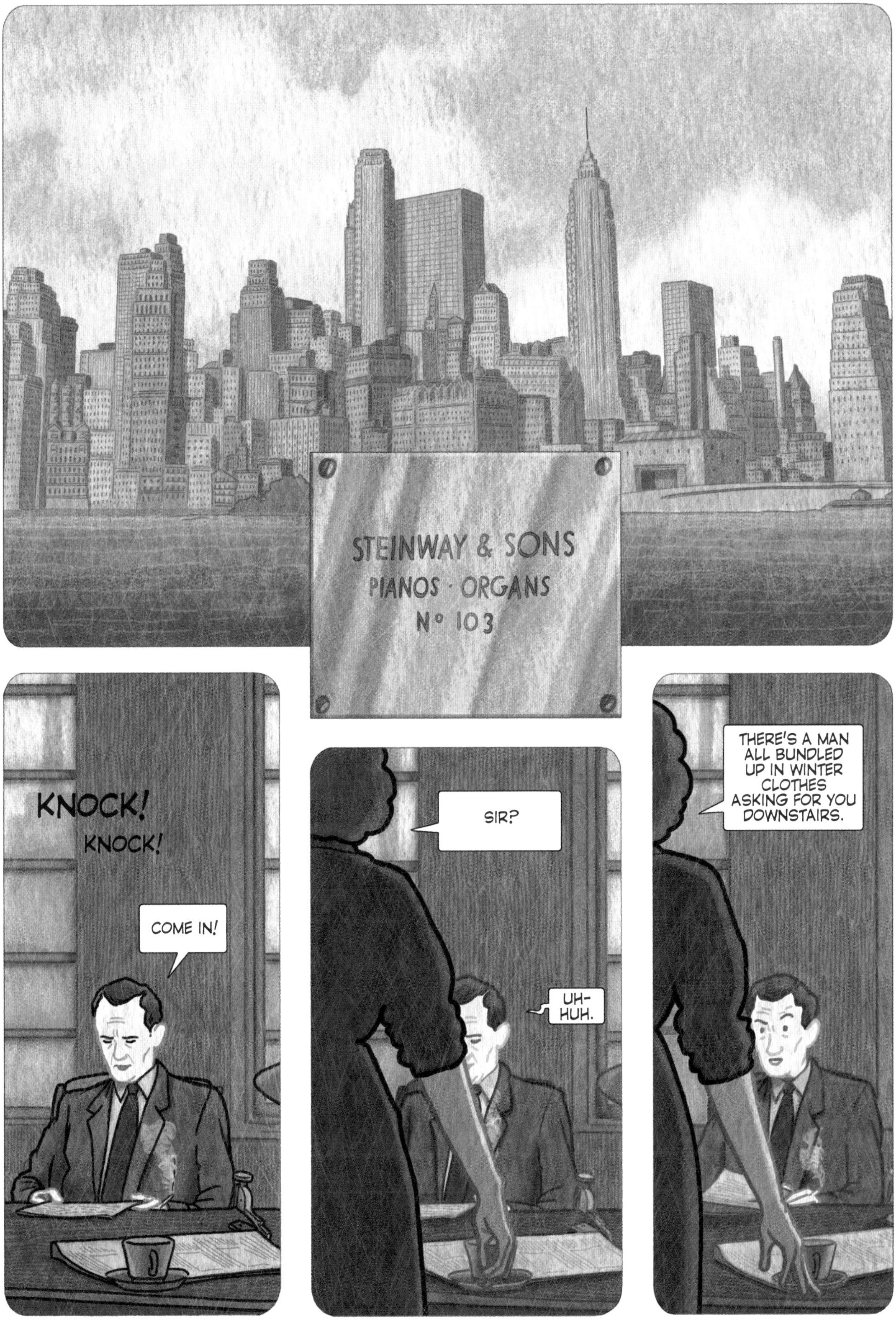
STEINWAY & SONS
PIANOS · ORGANS
Nº 103
KNOCK!
KNOCK!
COME IN!
SIR?
UH-HUH.
THERE'S A MAN ALL BUNDLED UP IN WINTER CLOTHES ASKING FOR YOU DOWNSTAIRS.

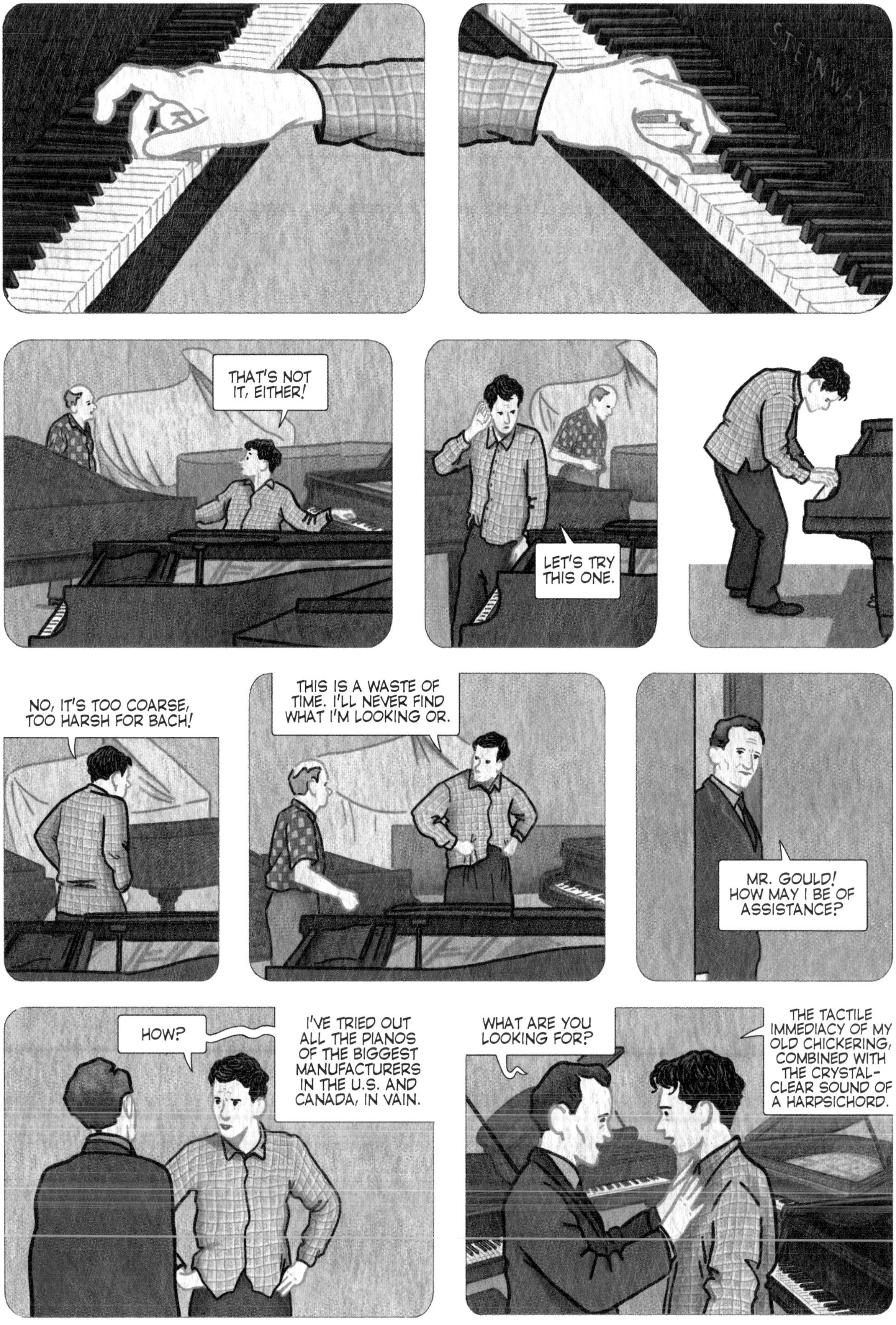
STEINWAY
THAT'S NOT IT, EITHER!
LET'S TRY THIS ONE.
NO, IT'S TOO COARSE, TOO HARSH FOR BACH!
THIS IS A WASTE OF TIME. I'LL NEVER FIND WHAT I'M LOOKING OR.
MR. GOULD! HOW MAY I BE OF ASSISTANCE?
HOW?
I'VE TRIED OUT ALL THE PIANOS OF THE BIGGEST MANUFACTURERS IN THE U.S. AND CANADA, IN VAIN.
WHAT ARE YOU LOOKING FOR?
THE TACTILE IMMEDIACY OF MY OLD CHICKERING, COMBINED WITH THE CRYSTAL-CLEAR SOUND OF A HARPSICHORD.

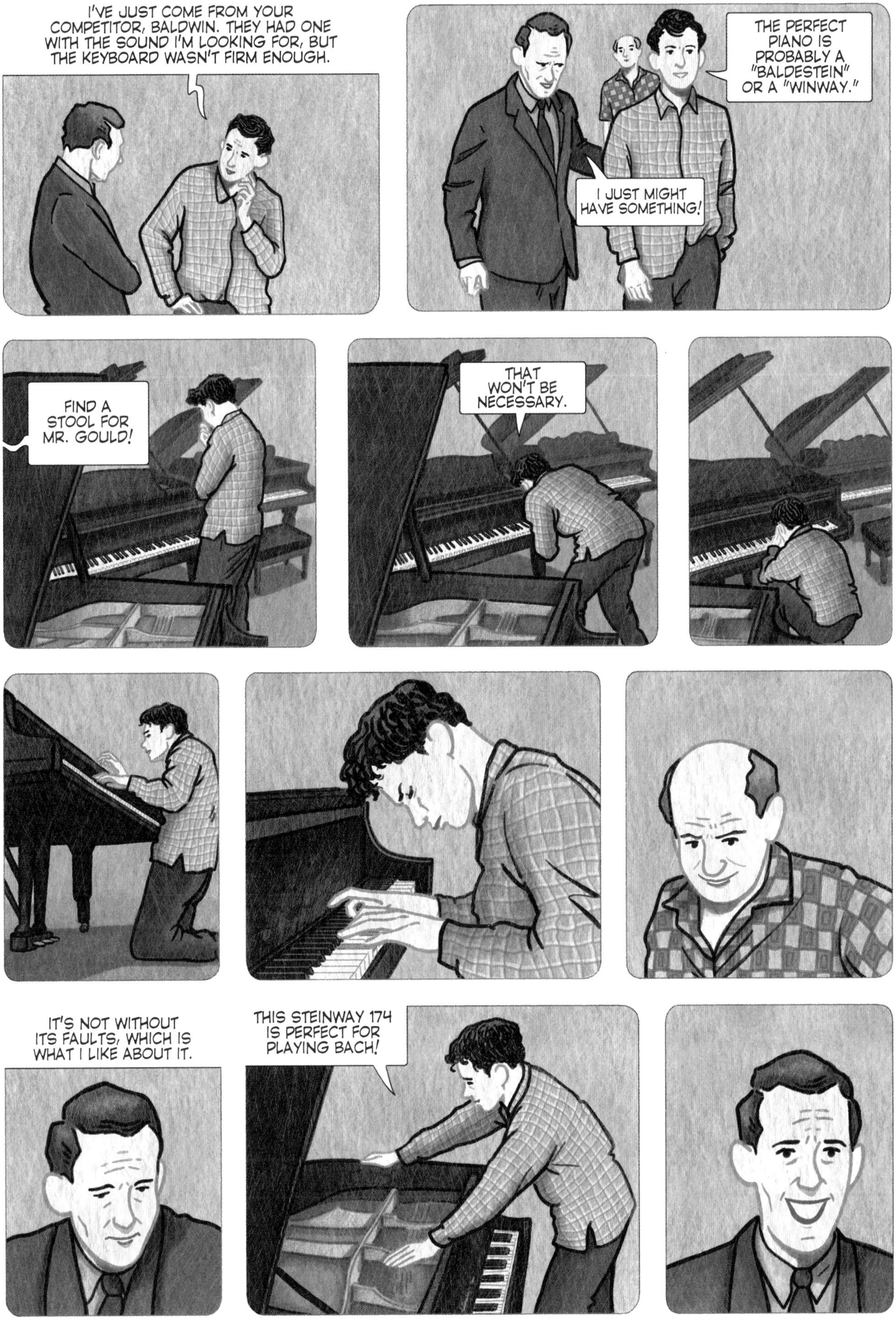
I'VE JUST COME FROM YOUR COMPETITOR, BALDWIN. THEY HAD ONE WITH THE SOUND I'M LOOKING FOR, BUT THE KEYBOARD WASN'T FIRM ENOUGH.
THE PERFECT PIANO IS PROBABLY A "BALDESTEIN" OR A "WINWAY."
I JUST MIGHT HAVE SOMETHING!
FIND A STOOL FOR MR. GOULD!
THAT WON'T BE NECESSARY.
IT'S NOT WITHOUT ITS FAULTS, WHICH IS WHAT I LIKE ABOUT IT.
THIS STEINWAY 174 IS PERFECT FOR PLAYING BACH!

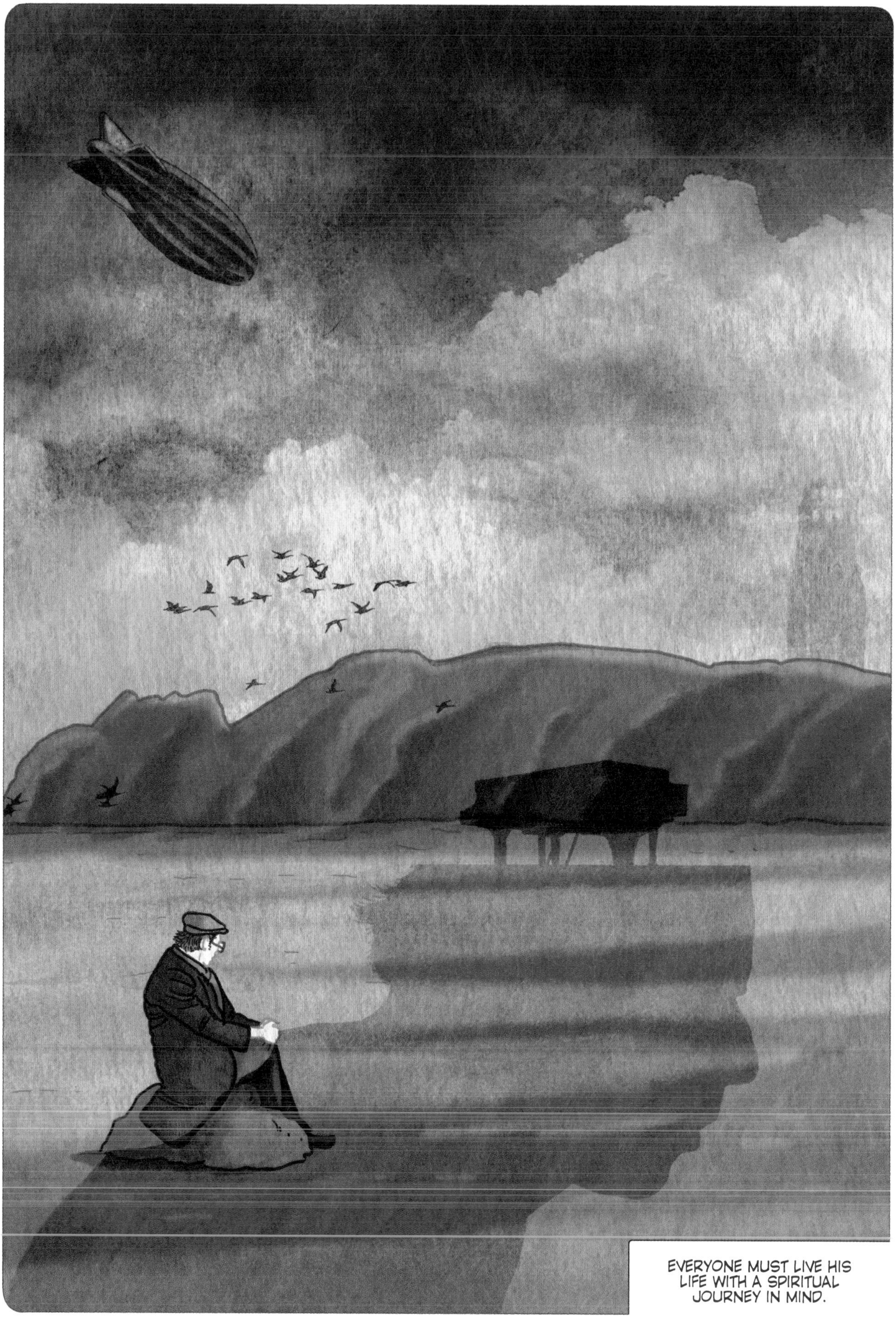
EVERYONE MUST LIVE HIS LIFE WITH A SPIRITUAL JOURNEY IN MIND.

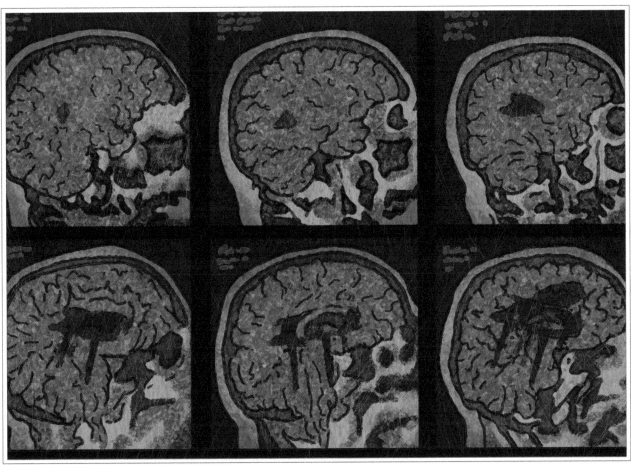

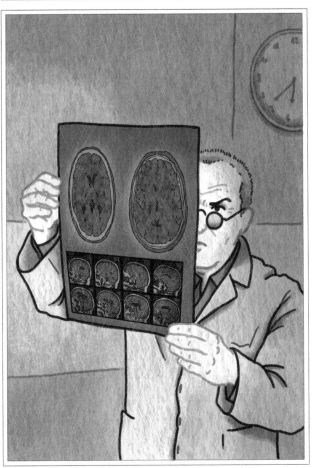

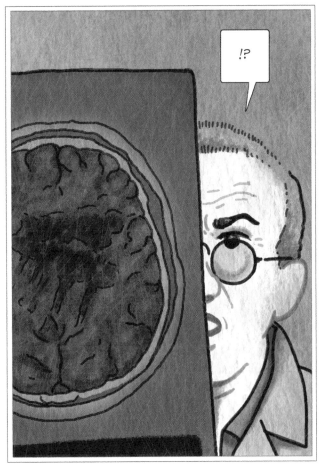

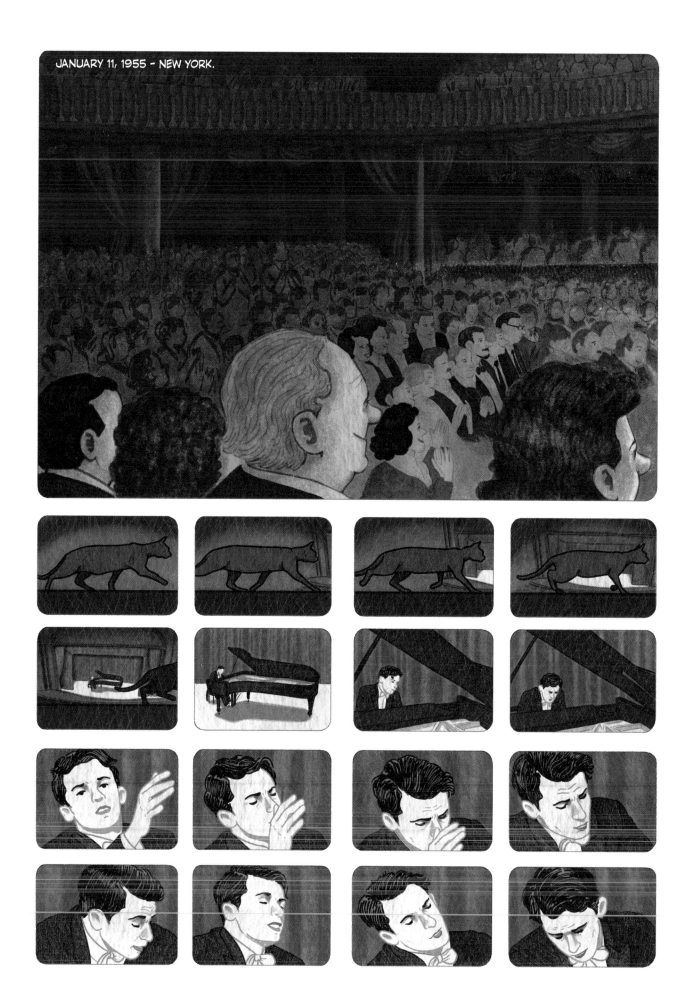

JANUARY 11, 1955 - NEW YORK.

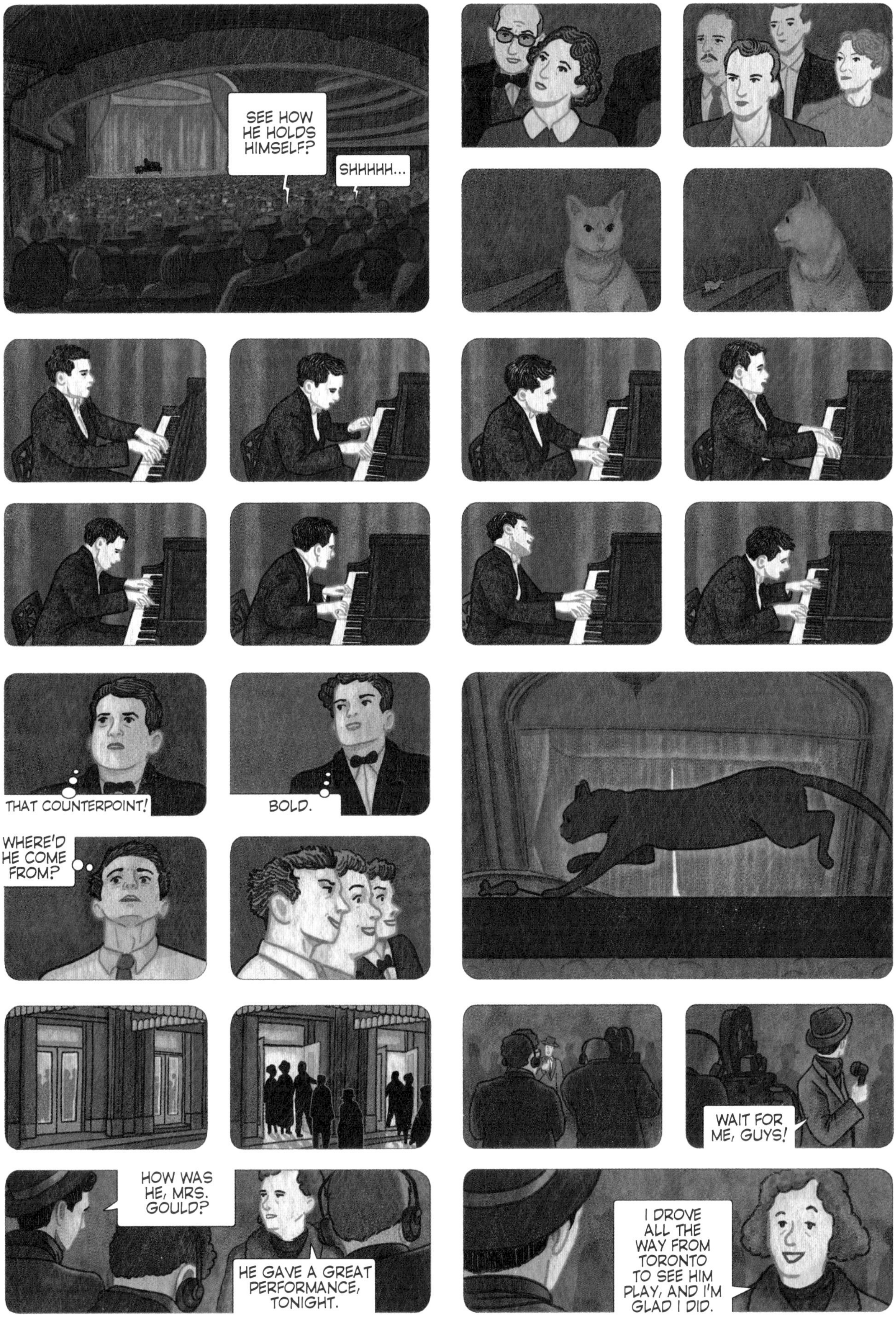
SEE HOW HE HOLDS HIMSELF?
SHHHHH...
THAT COUNTERPOINT!
BOLD.
WHERE'D HE COME FROM?
WAIT FOR ME, GUYS!
HOW WAS HE, MRS. GOULD?
HE GAVE A GREAT PERFORMANCE, TONIGHT.
I DROVE ALL THE WAY FROM TORONTO TO SEE HIM PLAY, AND I'M GLAD I DID.

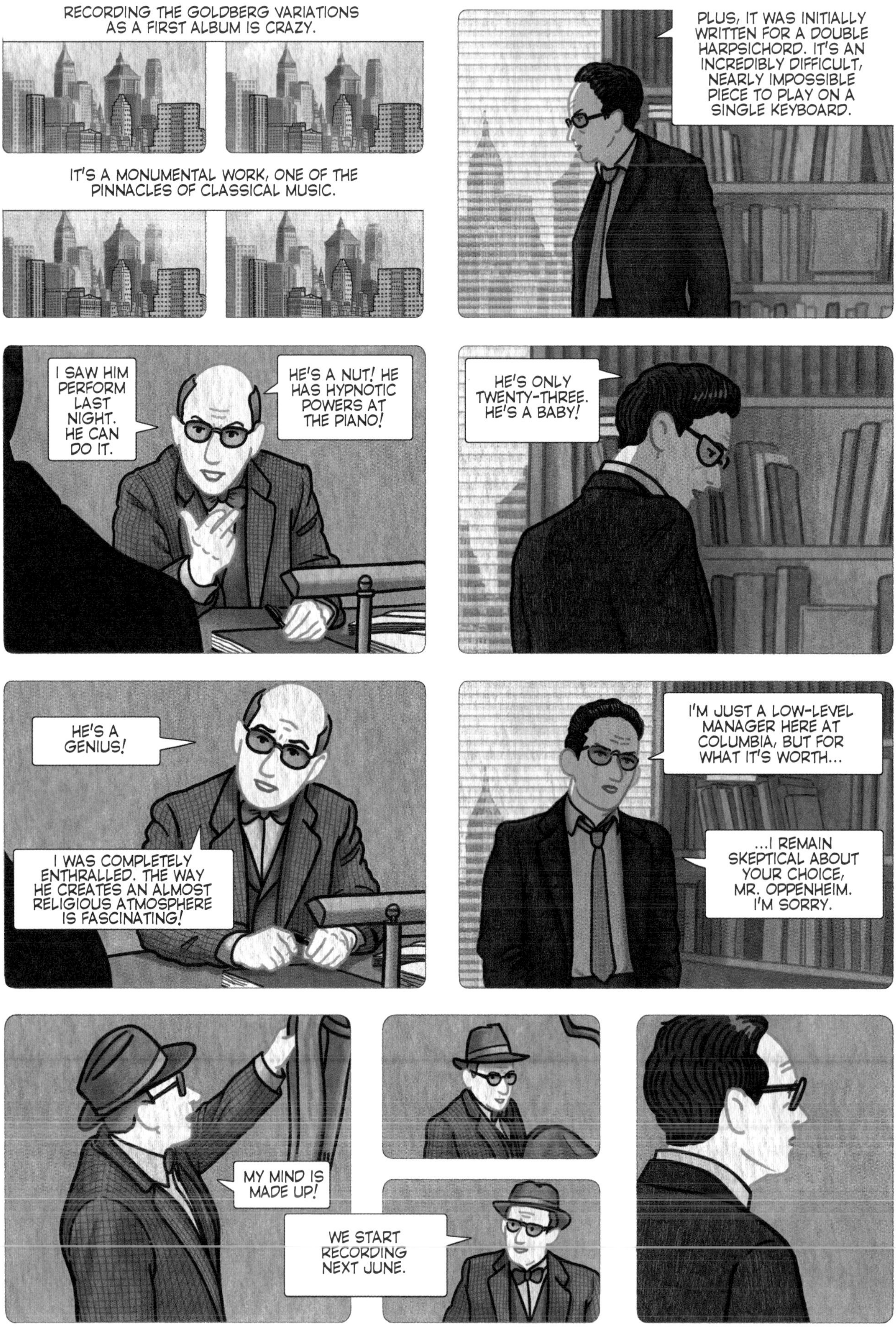
RECORDING THE GOLDBERG VARIATIONS AS A FIRST ALBUM IS CRAZY.
IT'S A MONUMENTAL WORK, ONE OF THE PINNACLES OF CLASSICAL MUSIC.
PLUS, IT WAS INITIALLY WRITTEN FOR A DOUBLE HARPSICHORD. IT'S AN INCREDIBLY DIFFICULT, NEARLY IMPOSSIBLE PIECE TO PLAY ON A SINGLE KEYBOARD.
I SAW HIM PERFORM LAST NIGHT. HE CAN DO IT.
HE'S A NUT! HE HAS HYPNOTIC POWERS AT THE PIANO!
HE'S ONLY TWENTY-THREE. HE'S A BABY!
HE'S A GENIUS!
I WAS COMPLETELY ENTHRALLED. THE WAY HE CREATES AN ALMOST RELIGIOUS ATMOSPHERE IS FASCINATING!
I'M JUST A LOW-LEVEL MANAGER HERE AT COLUMBIA, BUT FOR WHAT IT'S WORTH...
...I REMAIN SKEPTICAL ABOUT YOUR CHOICE, MR. OPPENHEIM. I'M SORRY.
MY MIND IS MADE UP!
WE START RECORDING NEXT JUNE.

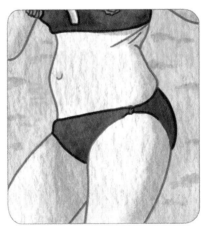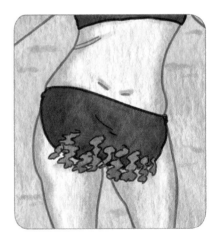

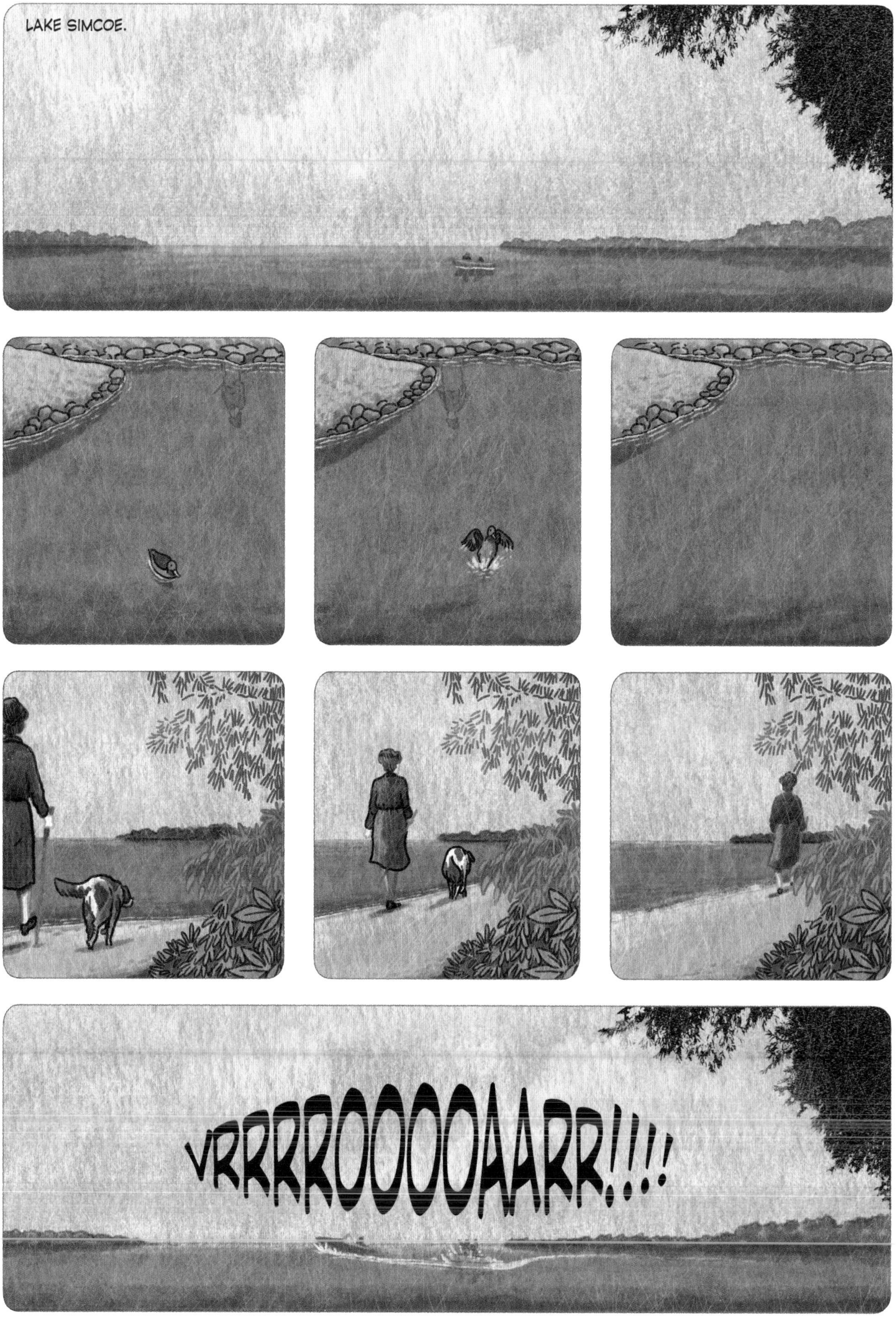
LAKE SIMCOE.
VRRRROOOOOAARR!!!!

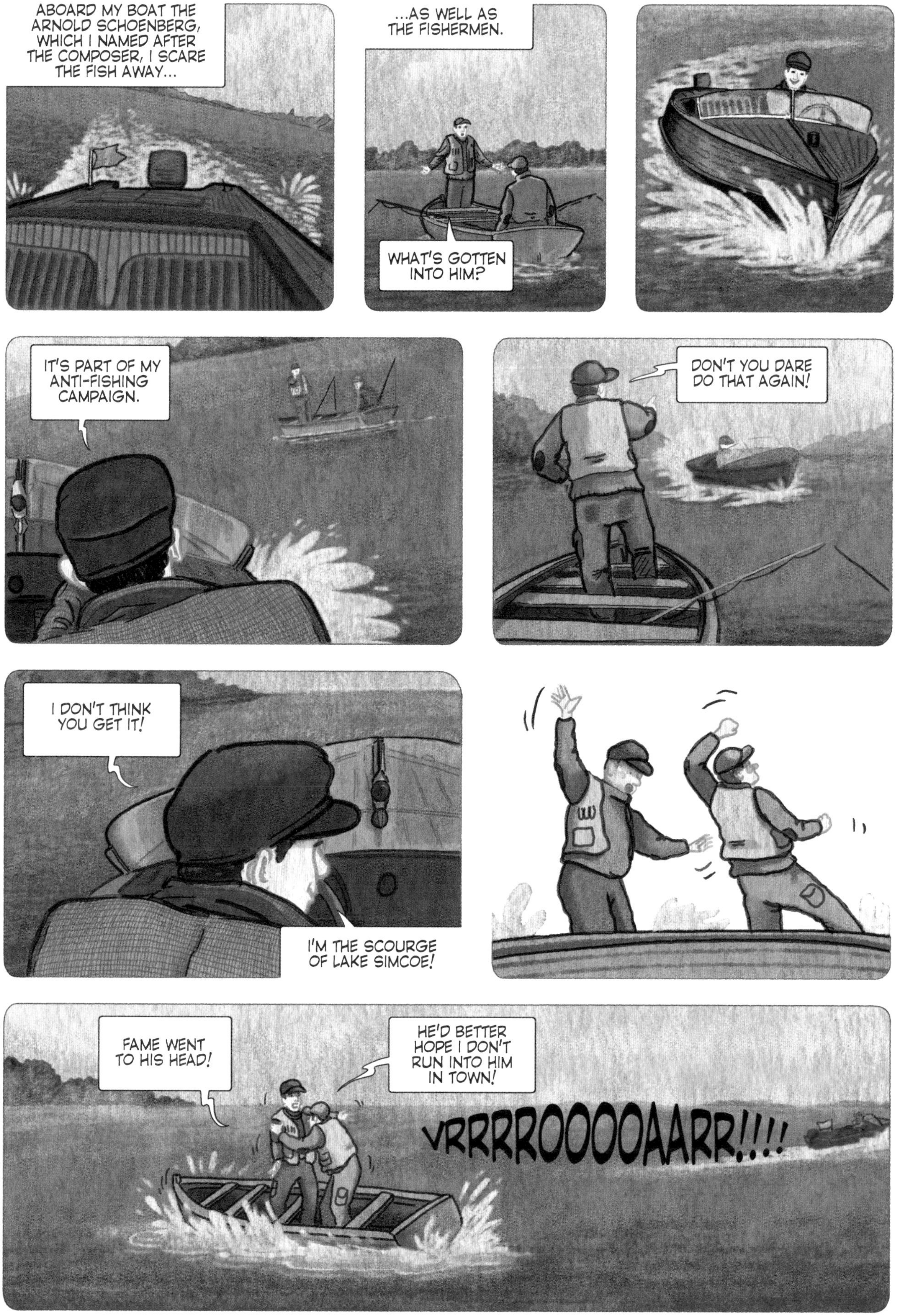
ABOARD MY BOAT THE ARNOLD SCHOENBERG, WHICH I NAMED AFTER THE COMPOSER, I SCARE THE FISH AWAY...
...AS WELL AS THE FISHERMEN.
WHAT'S GOTTEN INTO HIM?
IT'S PART OF MY ANTI-FISHING CAMPAIGN.
DON'T YOU DARE DO THAT AGAIN!
I DON'T THINK YOU GET IT!
I'M THE SCOURGE OF LAKE SIMCOE!
FAME WENT TO HIS HEAD!
HE'D BETTER HOPE I DON'T RUN INTO HIM IN TOWN!
VRRRROOOOAARR!!!!

I'M MAKING TEA. WANT SOME?

NO THANKS, JESSIE!

THE CABINETS ARE EMPTY.

NOT A SINGLE TEABAG IN SIGHT.

NOTHING BUT EGGS, MILK, CRACKERS, AND...

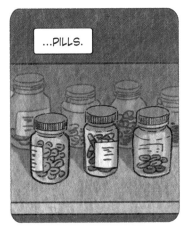

...PILLS.

LOTS OF PILLS.

POM POM POM...

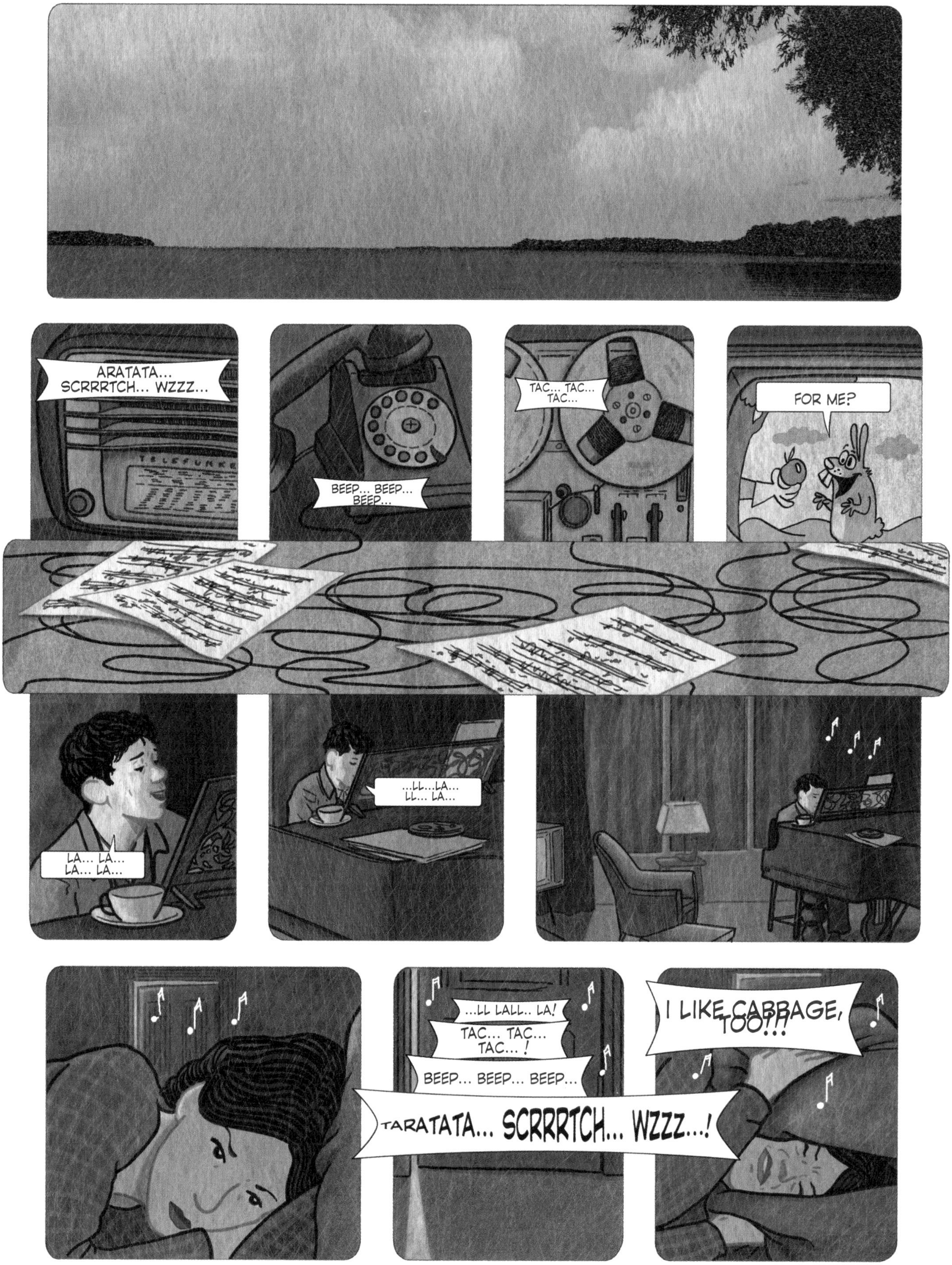
ARATATA... SCRRRTCH... WZZZ...
BEEP... BEEP... BEEP...
TAC... TAC... TAC...
FOR ME?
LA... LA... LA... LA...
...LL...LA... LL... LA...
...LL LALL.. LA!
TAC... TAC... TAC... !
BEEP... BEEP... BEEP...
TARATATA... SCRRRTCH... WZZZ...!
I LIKE CABBAGE, TOO!!!

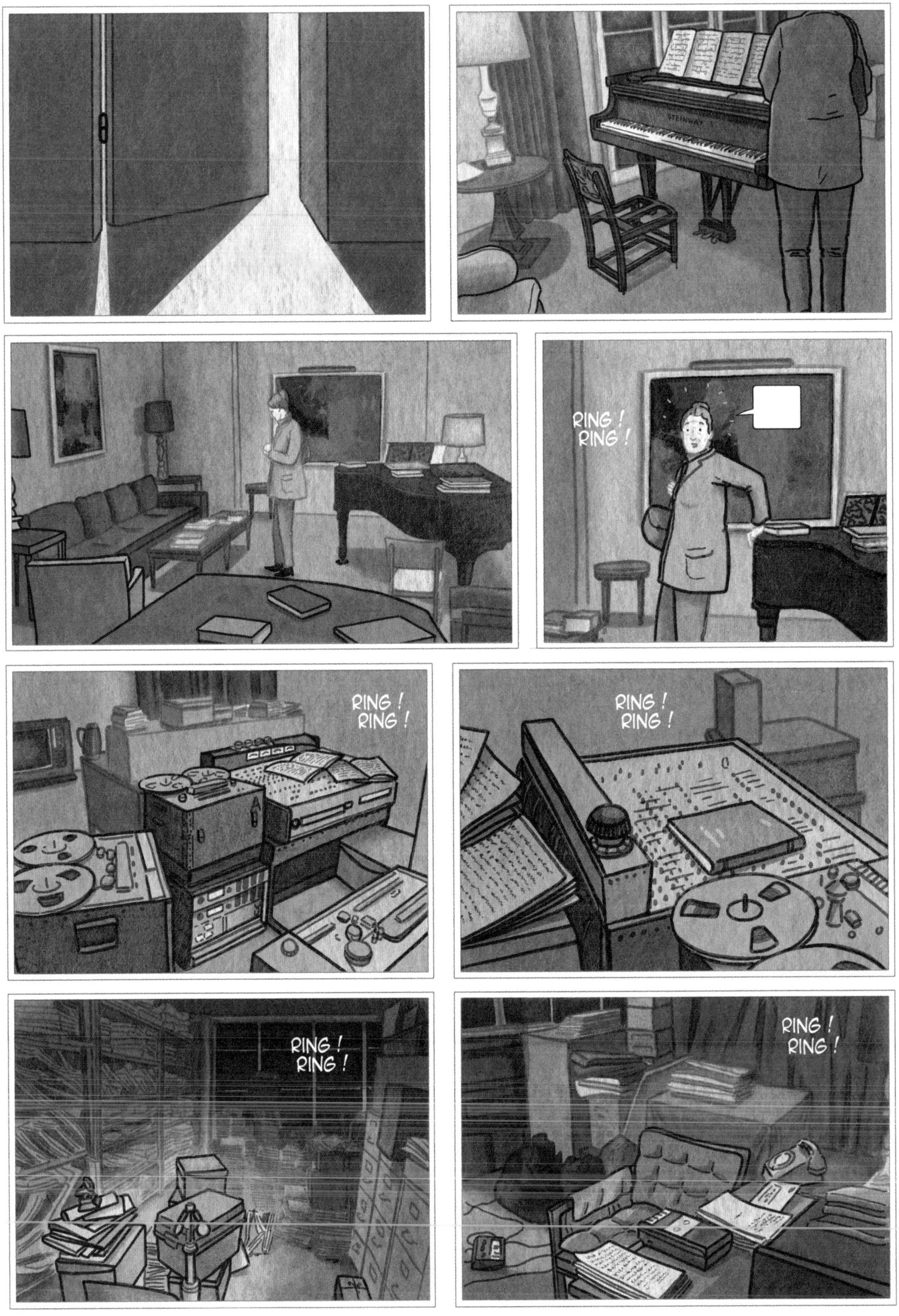
RING! RING!
RING! RING!
RING! RING!
RING! RING!
RING! RING!

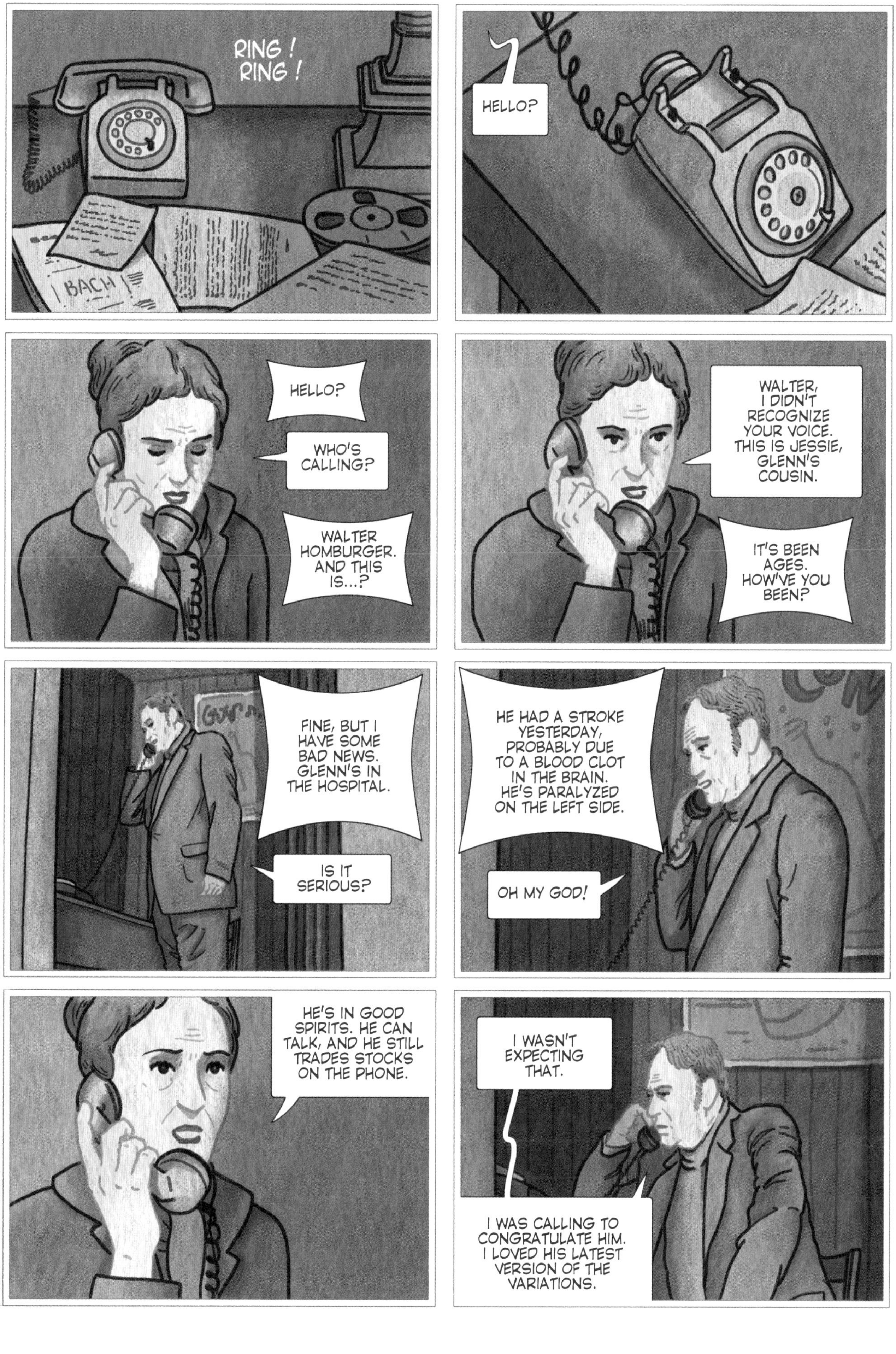
RING ! RING !
BACH
HELLO?
HELLO?
WHO'S CALLING?
WALTER HOMBURGER. AND THIS IS...?
WALTER, I DIDN'T RECOGNIZE YOUR VOICE. THIS IS JESSIE, GLENN'S COUSIN.
IT'S BEEN AGES. HOW'VE YOU BEEN?
FINE, BUT I HAVE SOME BAD NEWS. GLENN'S IN THE HOSPITAL.
IS IT SERIOUS?
HE HAD A STROKE YESTERDAY, PROBABLY DUE TO A BLOOD CLOT IN THE BRAIN. HE'S PARALYZED ON THE LEFT SIDE.
OH MY GOD!
HE'S IN GOOD SPIRITS. HE CAN TALK, AND HE STILL TRADES STOCKS ON THE PHONE.
I WASN'T EXPECTING THAT.
I WAS CALLING TO CONGRATULATE HIM. I LOVED HIS LATEST VERSION OF THE VARIATIONS.

WILL YOU COME AND VISIT HIM? HE'S AT TORONTO GENERAL. BUT DON'T WAIT TOO LONG, HIS CONDITION COULD DETERIORATE RAPIDLY.

UNFORTUNATELY, I'M NOWHERE NEAR TORONTO. PLEASE KEEP ME POSTED, JESSIE!

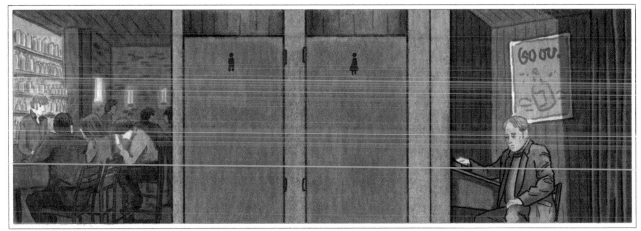

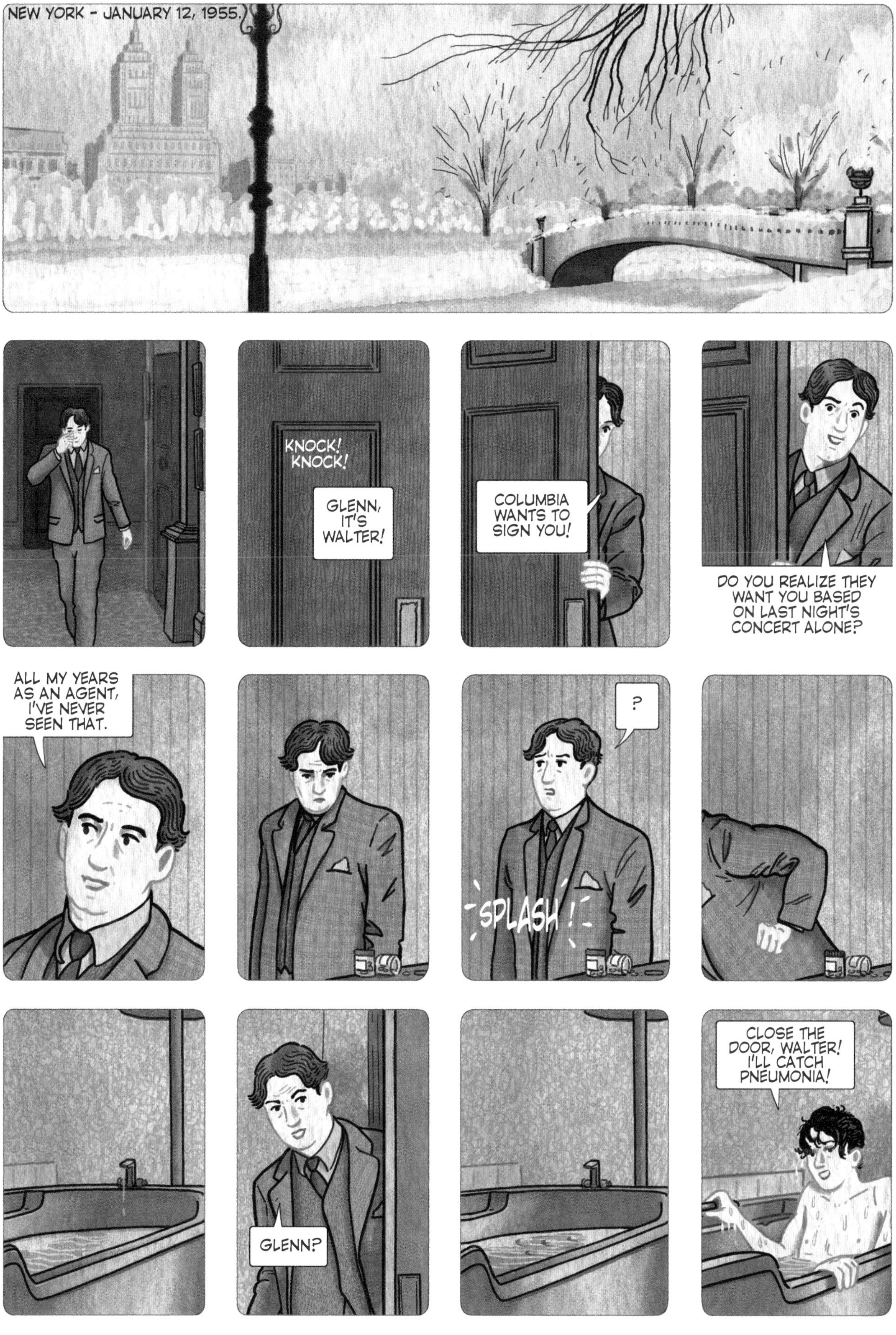
NEW YORK - JANUARY 12, 1955.
KNOCK! KNOCK!
GLENN, IT'S WALTER!
COLUMBIA WANTS TO SIGN YOU!
DO YOU REALIZE THEY WANT YOU BASED ON LAST NIGHT'S CONCERT ALONE?
ALL MY YEARS AS AN AGENT, I'VE NEVER SEEN THAT.
?
SPLASH!
GLENN?
CLOSE THE DOOR, WALTER! I'LL CATCH PNEUMONIA!

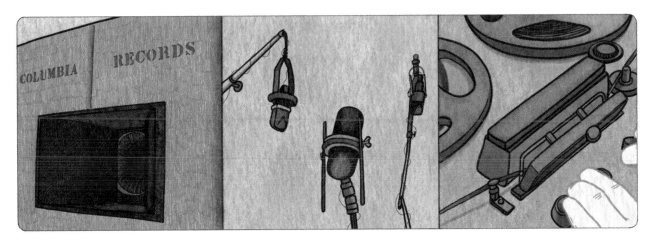

UM...

HOW WAS IT?

WHAT DO YOU THINK?

I THINK HAVING THE HEAT ON IN JUNE IS PURE TORTURE!

HIS WISHES ARE OUR ORDERS!

FROM THE TOP AGAIN?

WHAT TIME IS IT?

I'M SUFFOCATING IN HERE!

LET'S TAKE FIVE.

GLENN, WE HAVE A SLIGHT PROBLEM. SORRY, MAKE THAT A BIG PROBLEM!

COMING!

WHAT'S GOING ON?

A FEW DETAILS TO GO OVER WITH YOU.

WE'RE CONCERNED ABOUT--

OUCH!!

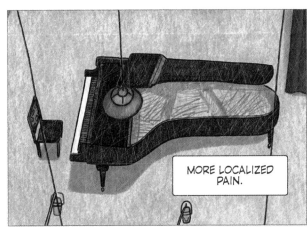

MORE LOCALIZED PAIN.

I HATE TO SAY THIS, BUT YOU LOOK FINE.

I'LL GO LIE DOWN IN MY DRESSING ROOM FOR A FEW MINUTES.

GLENN, WE REALLY NEED TO FIND A SOLUTION FOR THE SQUEAKING SOUND YOUR CHAIR MAKES. AND THEN THERE'S THE HUMMING...

AND THE SOUND OF YOUR FEET, KEEPING THE BEAT.

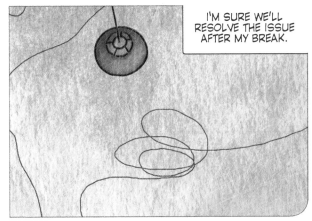

I'M SURE WE'LL RESOLVE THE ISSUE AFTER MY BREAK.

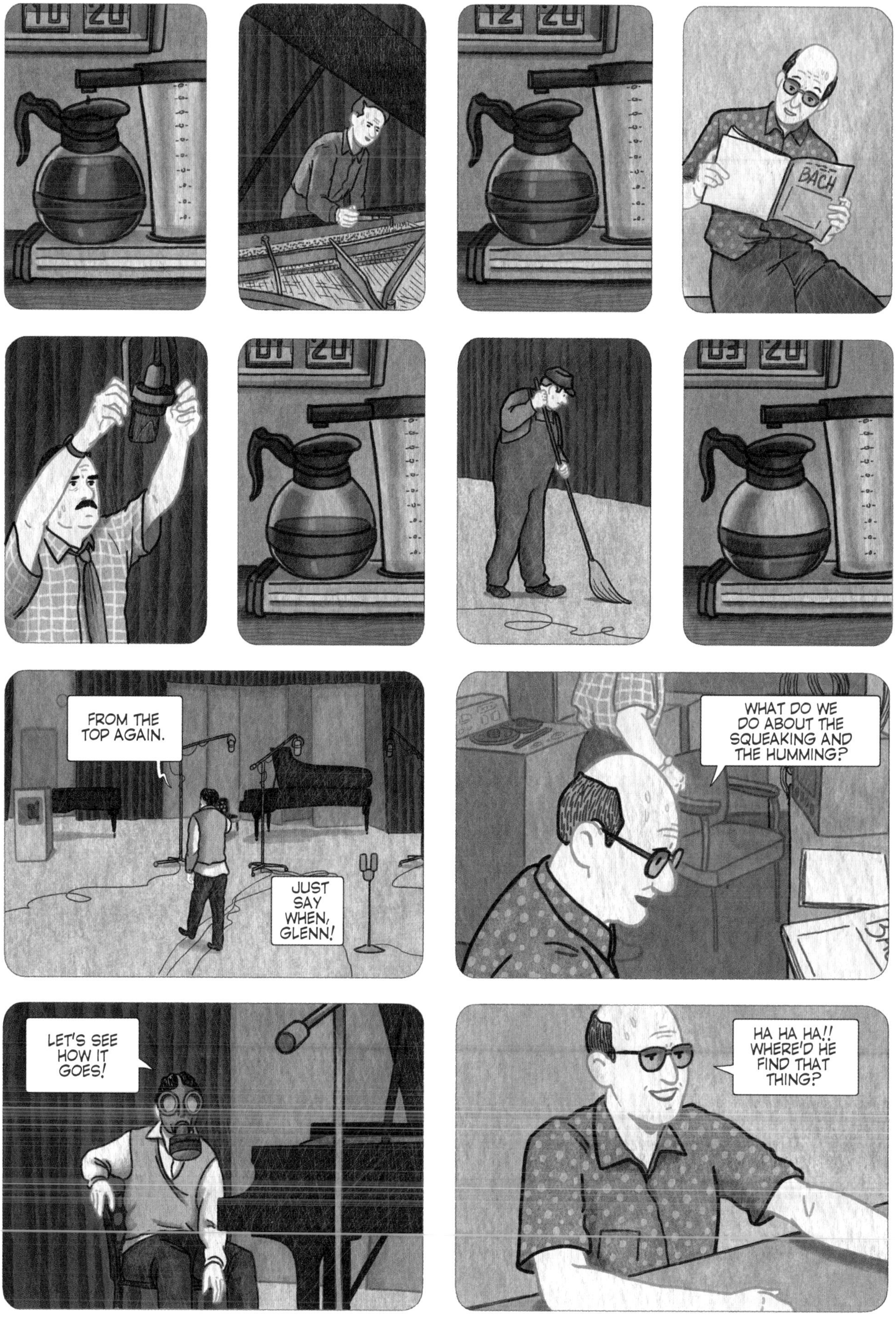
BACH
FROM THE TOP AGAIN.
JUST SAY WHEN, GLENN!
WHAT DO WE DO ABOUT THE SQUEAKING AND THE HUMMING?
LET'S SEE HOW IT GOES!
HA HA HA!! WHERE'D HE FIND THAT THING?

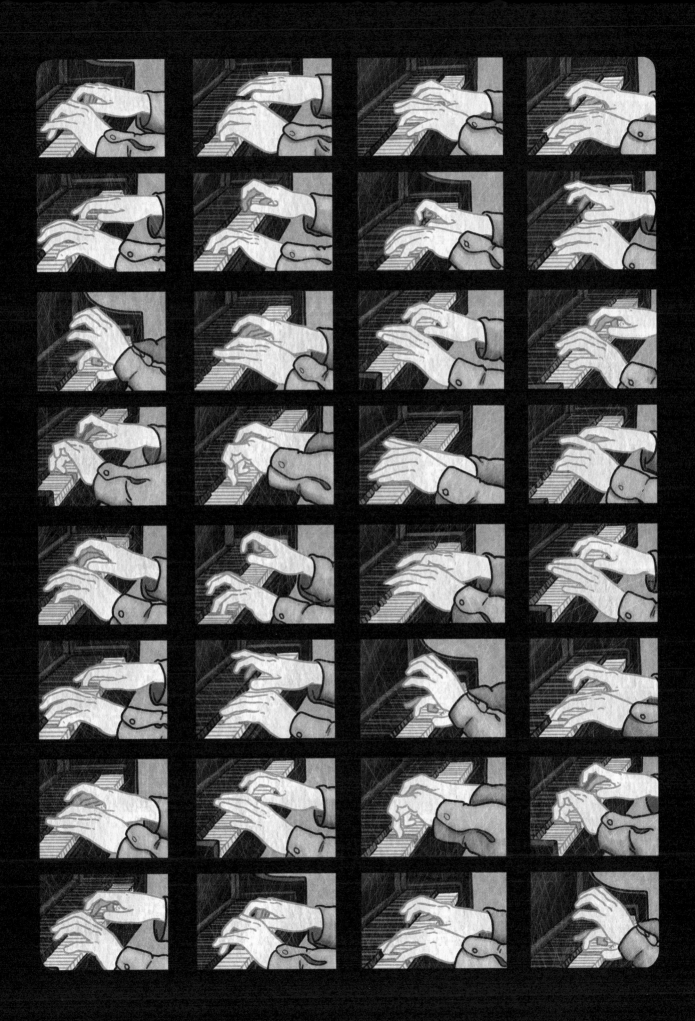

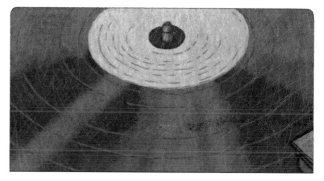

WHEN THE RECORDING OF THE GOLDBERG VARIATIONS CAME OUT, THE PRESS UNANIMOUSLY HAILED GLENN GOULD AS THE BEST PIANIST OF HIS GENERATION.

HIS MODERN AND ENERGETIC PLAYING CAUGHT PEOPLE OFF GUARD. AUDIENCES WERE STUNNED BY HIS UNIQUE APPROACH, WHICH MADE EACH NOTE STAND OUT.

HIS RECORDING OF THE GOLDBERG VARIATIONS WENT ON TO BECOME COLUMBIA'S TOP SELLING CLASSICAL ALBUM.

THE NOTORIETY THAT FIRST ALBUM BROUGHT, HOWEVER, DID NOT MAKE IT ACROSS THE IRON CURTAIN, UNFORTUNATELY. IN RUSSIA, GLENN GOULD REMAINED COMPLETELY UNKNOWN.

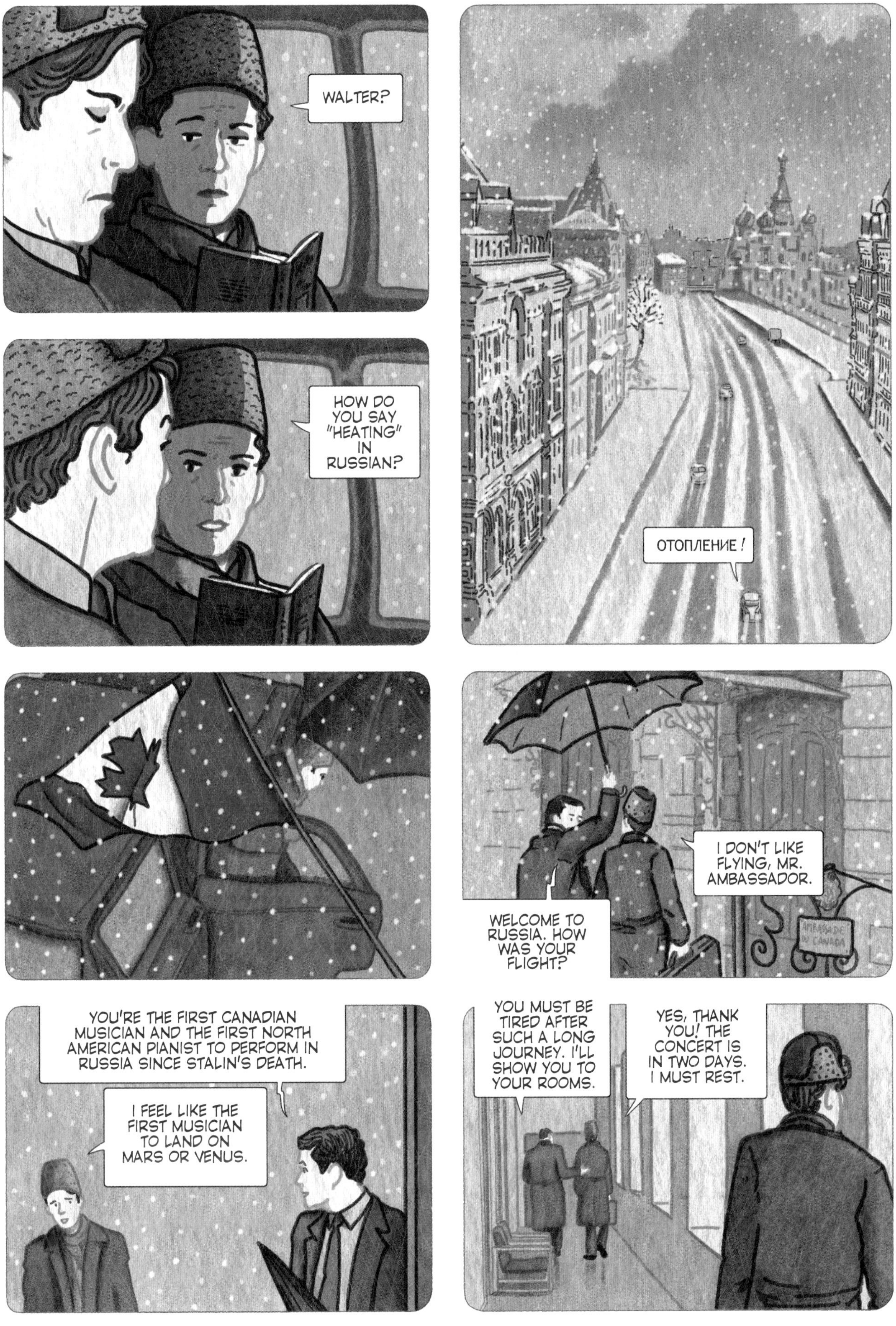
WALTER?
HOW DO YOU SAY "HEATING" IN RUSSIAN?
ОТОПЛЕНИЕ!
WELCOME TO RUSSIA. HOW WAS YOUR FLIGHT?
I DON'T LIKE FLYING, MR. AMBASSADOR.
AMBASSADE DU CANADA
YOU'RE THE FIRST CANADIAN MUSICIAN AND THE FIRST NORTH AMERICAN PIANIST TO PERFORM IN RUSSIA SINCE STALIN'S DEATH.
I FEEL LIKE THE FIRST MUSICIAN TO LAND ON MARS OR VENUS.
YOU MUST BE TIRED AFTER SUCH A LONG JOURNEY. I'LL SHOW YOU TO YOUR ROOMS.
YES, THANK YOU! THE CONCERT IS IN TWO DAYS. I MUST REST.

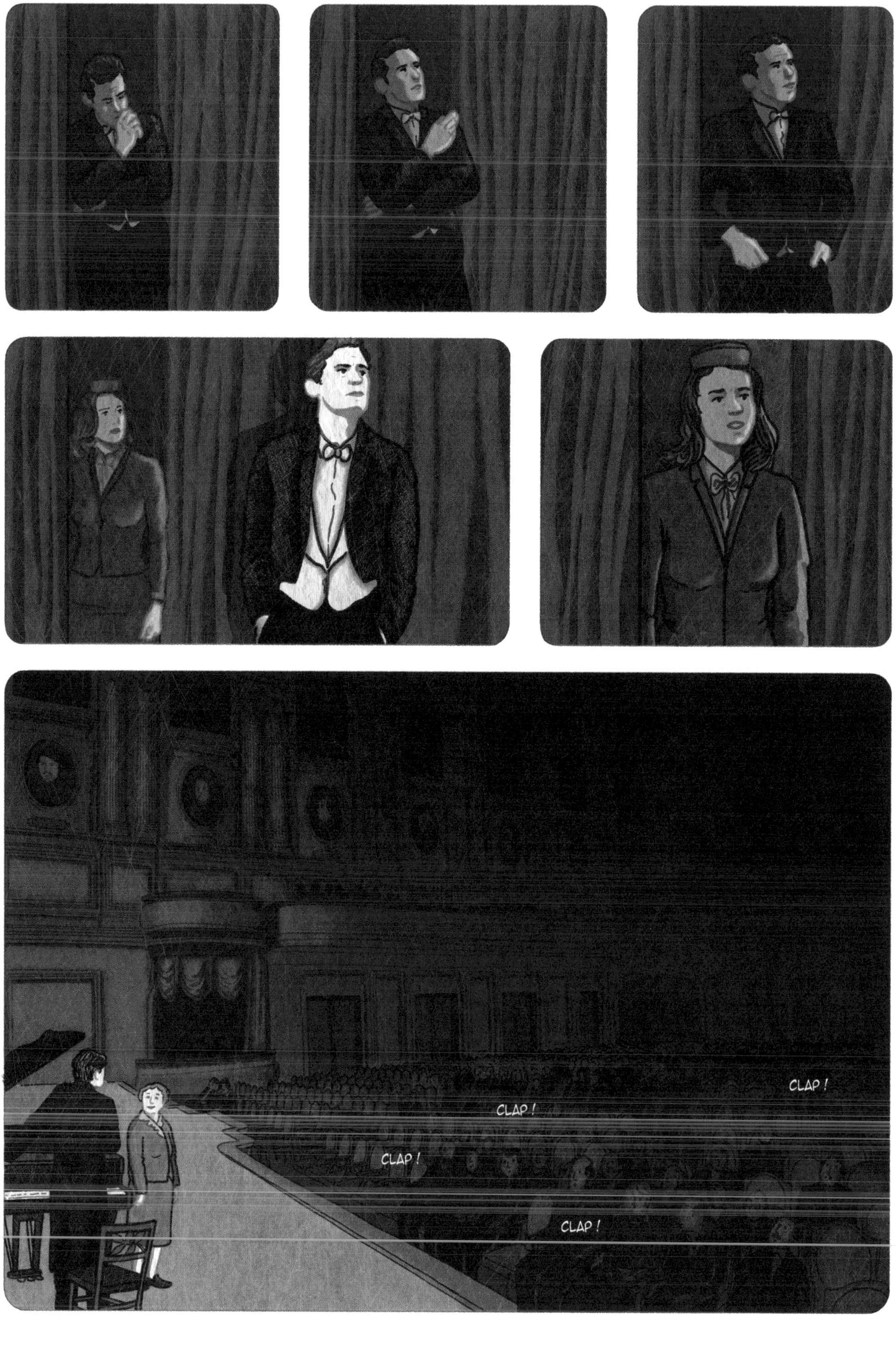
CLAP !
CLAP !
CLAP !
CLAP !

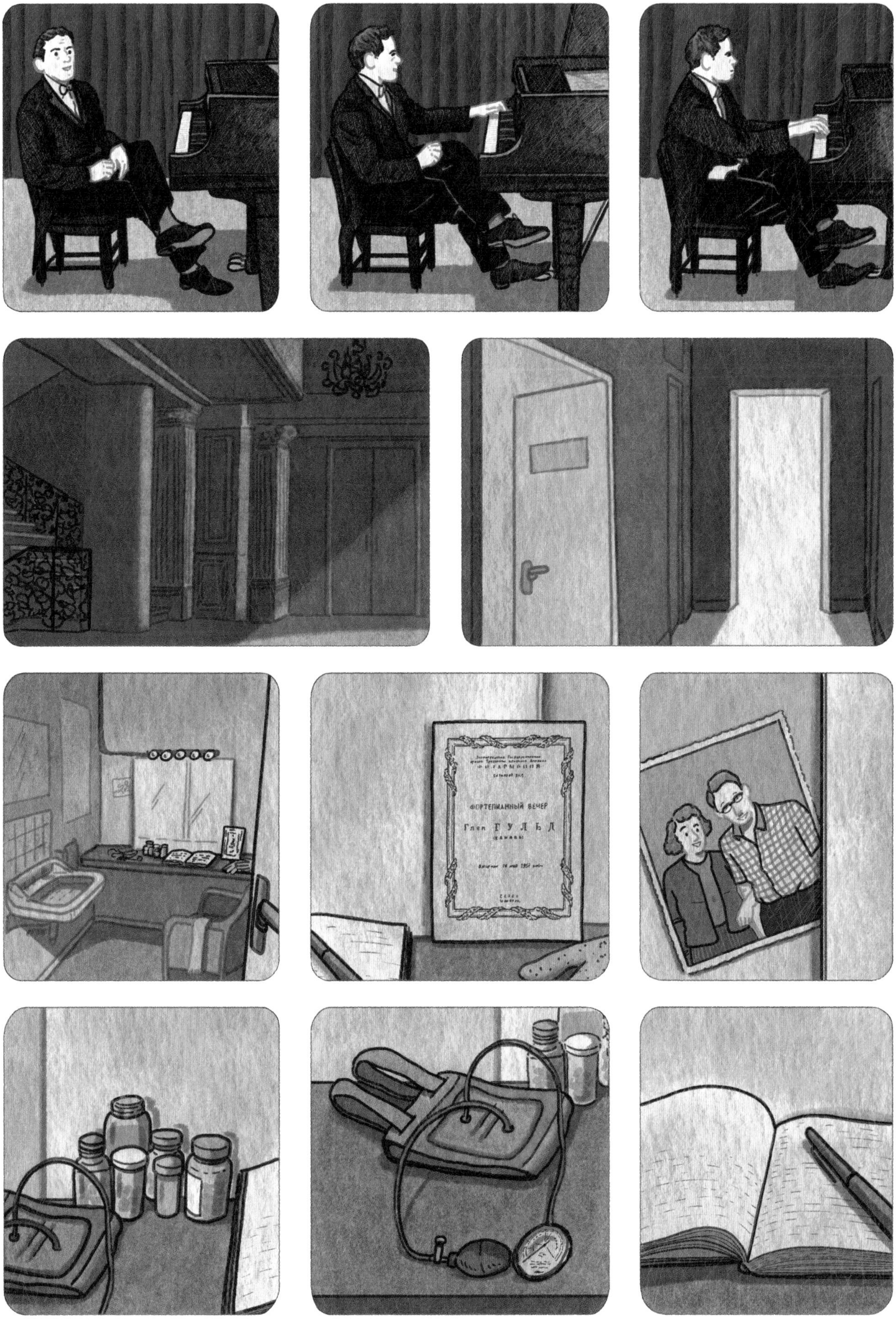
ФОРТЕПИАННЫЙ ВЕЧЕР
Глен ГУЛЬД

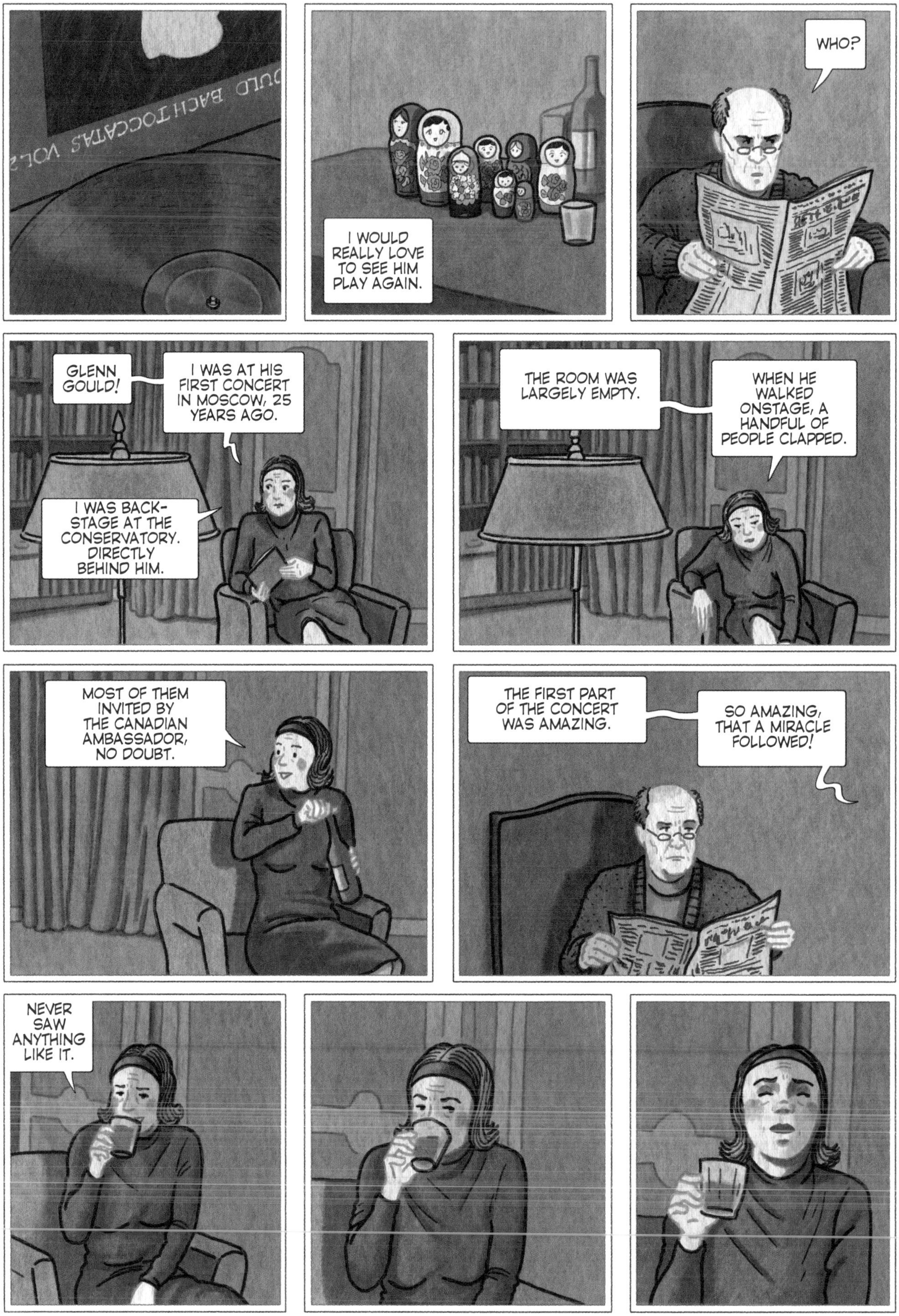
I WOULD REALLY LOVE TO SEE HIM PLAY AGAIN.
WHO?
GLENN GOULD!
I WAS AT HIS FIRST CONCERT IN MOSCOW, 25 YEARS AGO.
I WAS BACK-STAGE AT THE CONSERVATORY. DIRECTLY BEHIND HIM.
THE ROOM WAS LARGELY EMPTY.
WHEN HE WALKED ONSTAGE, A HANDFUL OF PEOPLE CLAPPED.
MOST OF THEM INVITED BY THE CANADIAN AMBASSADOR, NO DOUBT.
THE FIRST PART OF THE CONCERT WAS AMAZING.
SO AMAZING, THAT A MIRACLE FOLLOWED!
NEVER SAW ANYTHING LIKE IT.

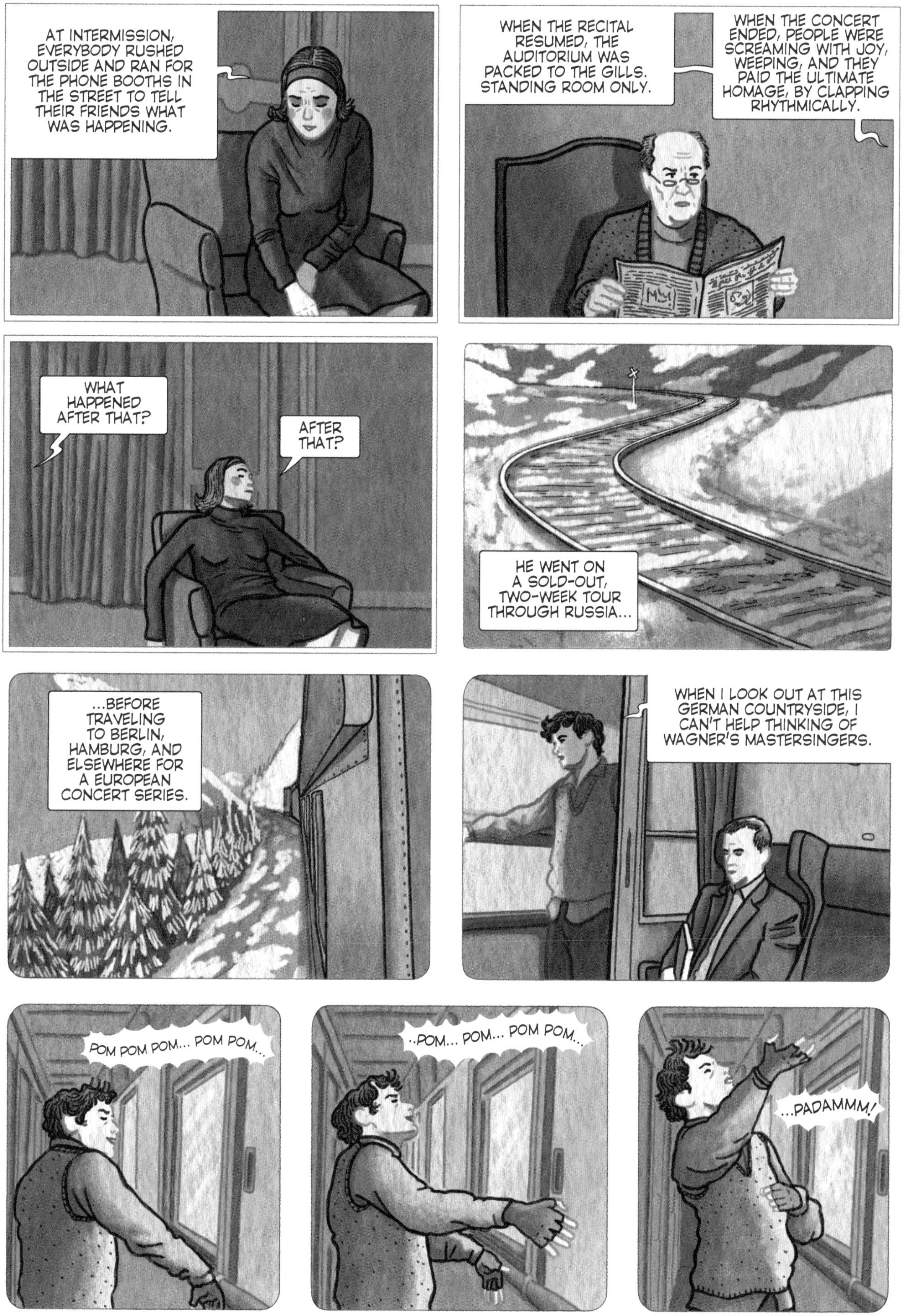
AT INTERMISSION, EVERYBODY RUSHED OUTSIDE AND RAN FOR THE PHONE BOOTHS IN THE STREET TO TELL THEIR FRIENDS WHAT WAS HAPPENING.
WHEN THE RECITAL RESUMED, THE AUDITORIUM WAS PACKED TO THE GILLS. STANDING ROOM ONLY.
WHEN THE CONCERT ENDED, PEOPLE WERE SCREAMING WITH JOY, WEEPING, AND THEY PAID THE ULTIMATE HOMAGE, BY CLAPPING RHYTHMICALLY.
WHAT HAPPENED AFTER THAT?
AFTER THAT?
HE WENT ON A SOLD-OUT, TWO-WEEK TOUR THROUGH RUSSIA...
...BEFORE TRAVELING TO BERLIN, HAMBURG, AND ELSEWHERE FOR A EUROPEAN CONCERT SERIES.
WHEN I LOOK OUT AT THIS GERMAN COUNTRYSIDE, I CAN'T HELP THINKING OF WAGNER'S MASTERSINGERS.
POM POM POM... POM POM...
..POM... POM... POM POM...
...PADAMMM!

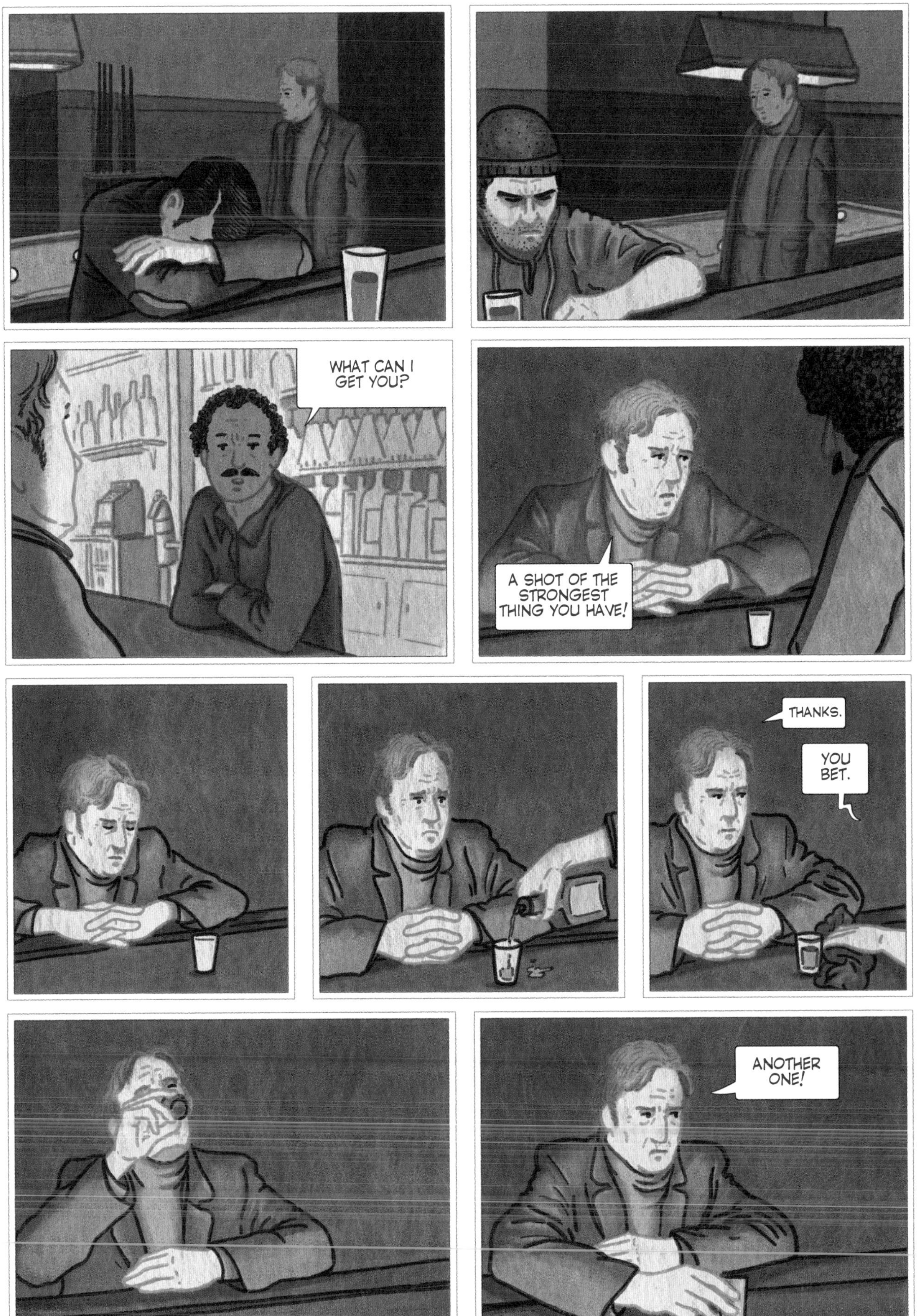
WHAT CAN I GET YOU?
A SHOT OF THE STRONGEST THING YOU HAVE!
THANKS.
YOU BET.
ANOTHER ONE!

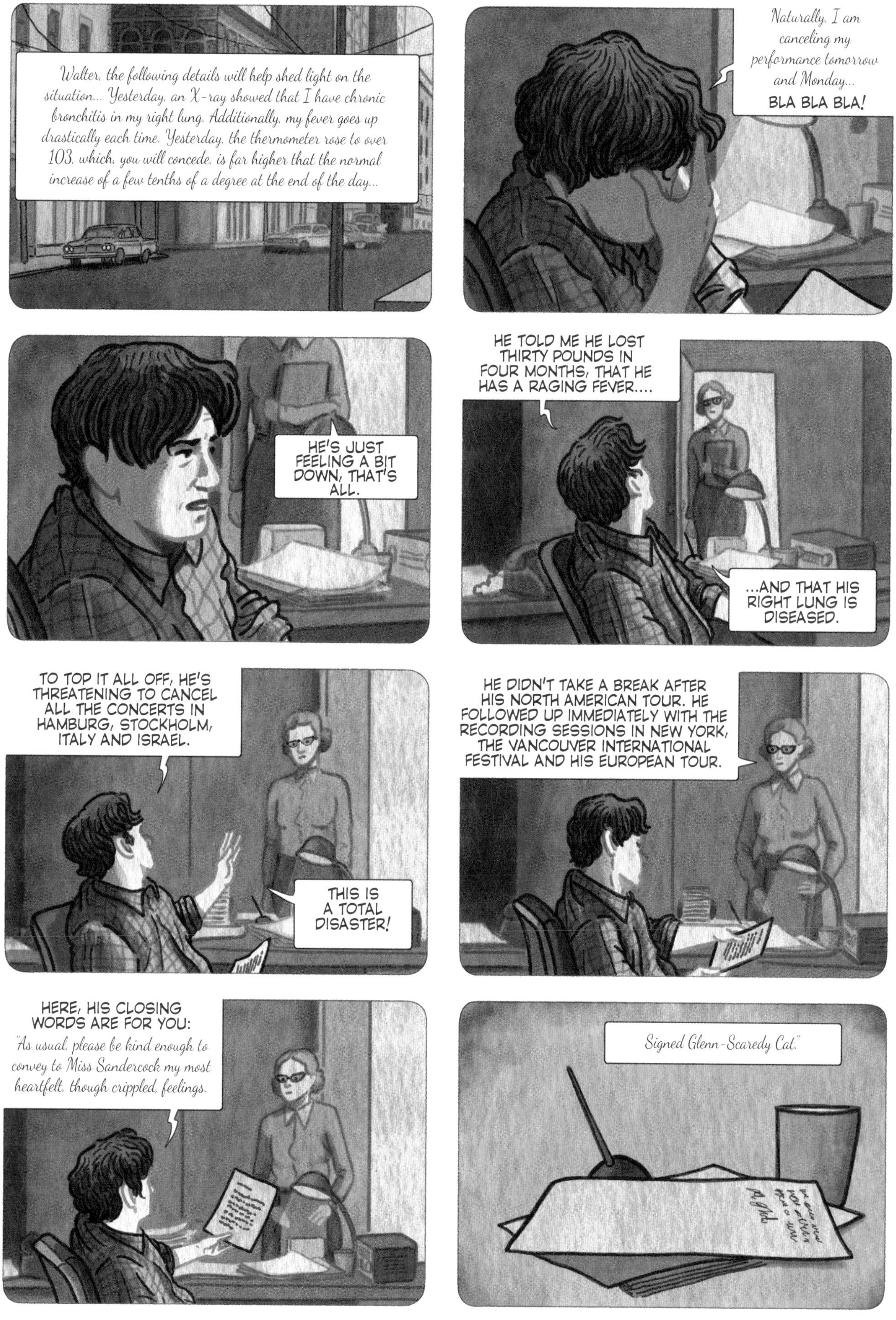
Walter, the following details will help shed light on the situation... Yesterday, an X-ray showed that I have chronic bronchitis in my right lung. Additionally, my fever goes up drastically each time. Yesterday, the thermometer rose to over 103, which, you will concede, is far higher that the normal increase of a few tenths of a degree at the end of the day...
Naturally, I am canceling my performance tomorrow and Monday... BLA BLA BLA!
HE'S JUST FEELING A BIT DOWN, THAT'S ALL.
HE TOLD ME HE LOST THIRTY POUNDS IN FOUR MONTHS, THAT HE HAS A RAGING FEVER....
...AND THAT HIS RIGHT LUNG IS DISEASED.
TO TOP IT ALL OFF, HE'S THREATENING TO CANCEL ALL THE CONCERTS IN HAMBURG, STOCKHOLM, ITALY AND ISRAEL.
THIS IS A TOTAL DISASTER!
HE DIDN'T TAKE A BREAK AFTER HIS NORTH AMERICAN TOUR. HE FOLLOWED UP IMMEDIATELY WITH THE RECORDING SESSIONS IN NEW YORK, THE VANCOUVER INTERNATIONAL FESTIVAL AND HIS EUROPEAN TOUR.
HERE, HIS CLOSING WORDS ARE FOR YOU:
"As usual, please be kind enough to convey to Miss Sandercock my most heartfelt, though crippled, feelings.
Signed Glenn-Scaredy Cat."

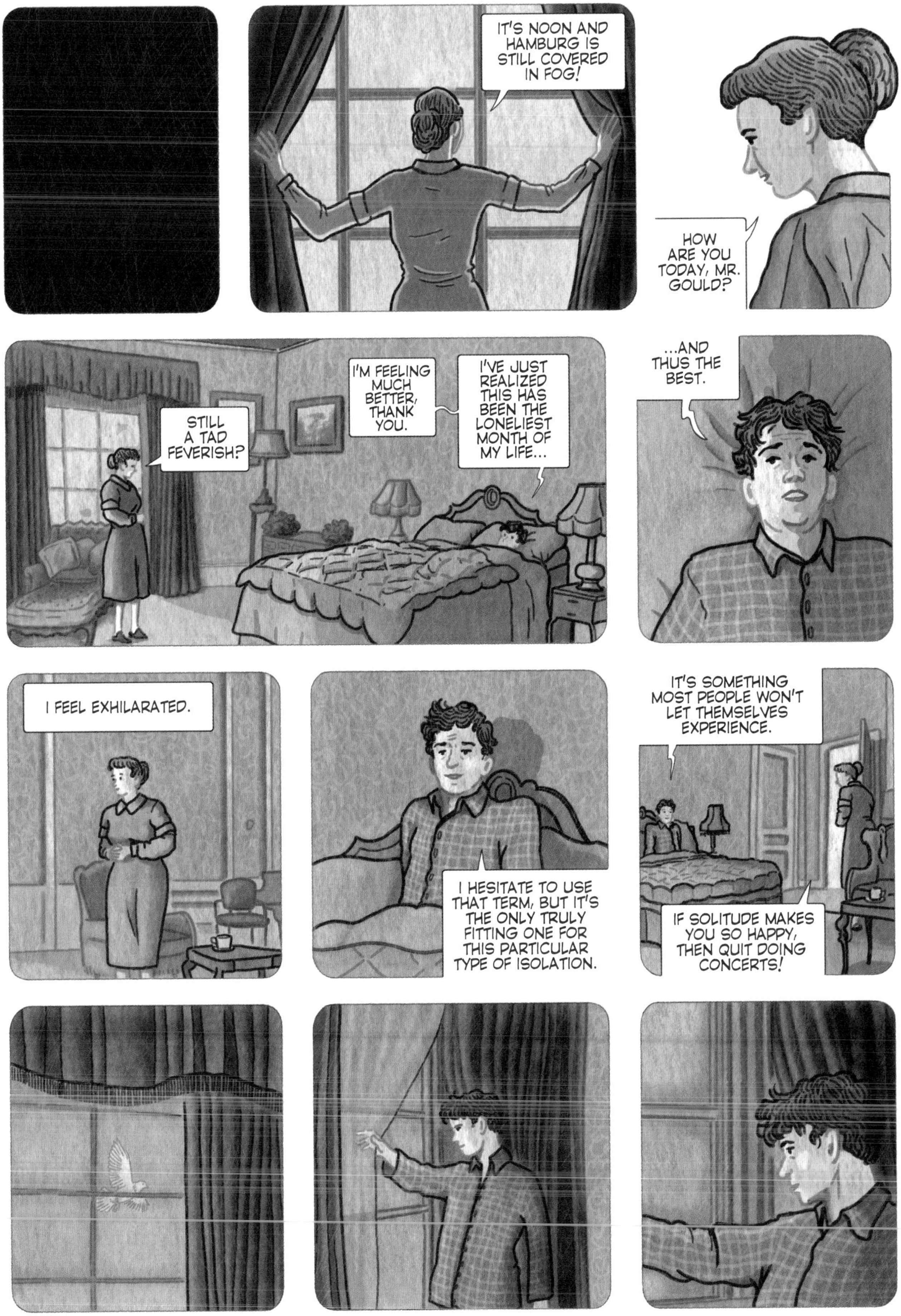
IT'S NOON AND HAMBURG IS STILL COVERED IN FOG!
HOW ARE YOU TODAY, MR. GOULD?
STILL A TAD FEVERISH?
I'M FEELING MUCH BETTER, THANK YOU.
I'VE JUST REALIZED THIS HAS BEEN THE LONELIEST MONTH OF MY LIFE...
...AND THUS THE BEST.
I FEEL EXHILARATED.
I HESITATE TO USE THAT TERM, BUT IT'S THE ONLY TRULY FITTING ONE FOR THIS PARTICULAR TYPE OF ISOLATION.
IT'S SOMETHING MOST PEOPLE WON'T LET THEMSELVES EXPERIENCE.
IF SOLITUDE MAKES YOU SO HAPPY, THEN QUIT DOING CONCERTS!

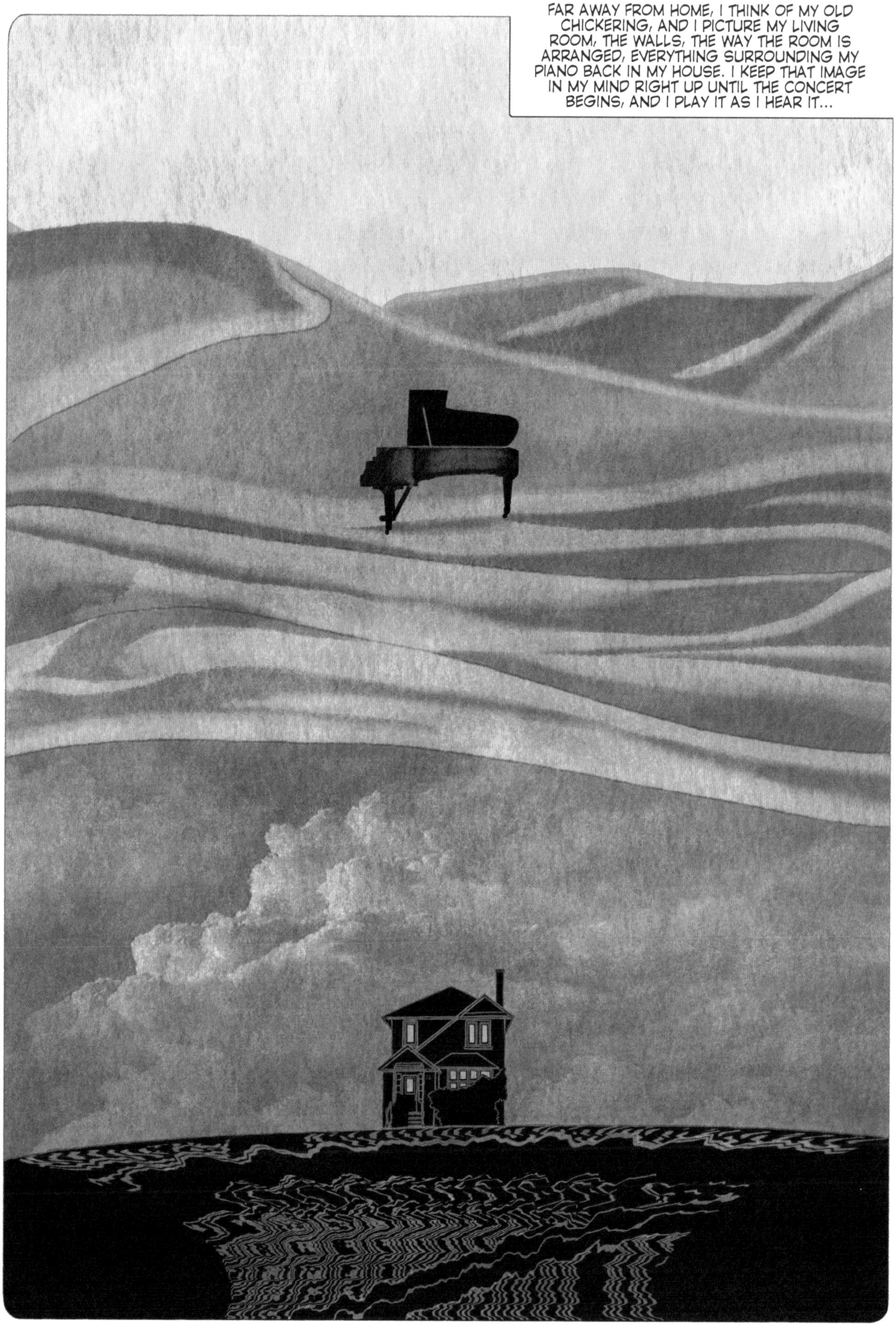
FAR AWAY FROM HOME, I THINK OF MY OLD CHICKERING, AND I PICTURE MY LIVING ROOM, THE WALLS, THE WAY THE ROOM IS ARRANGED, EVERYTHING SURROUNDING MY PIANO BACK IN MY HOUSE. I KEEP THAT IMAGE IN MY MIND RIGHT UP UNTIL THE CONCERT BEGINS, AND I PLAY IT AS I HEAR IT...

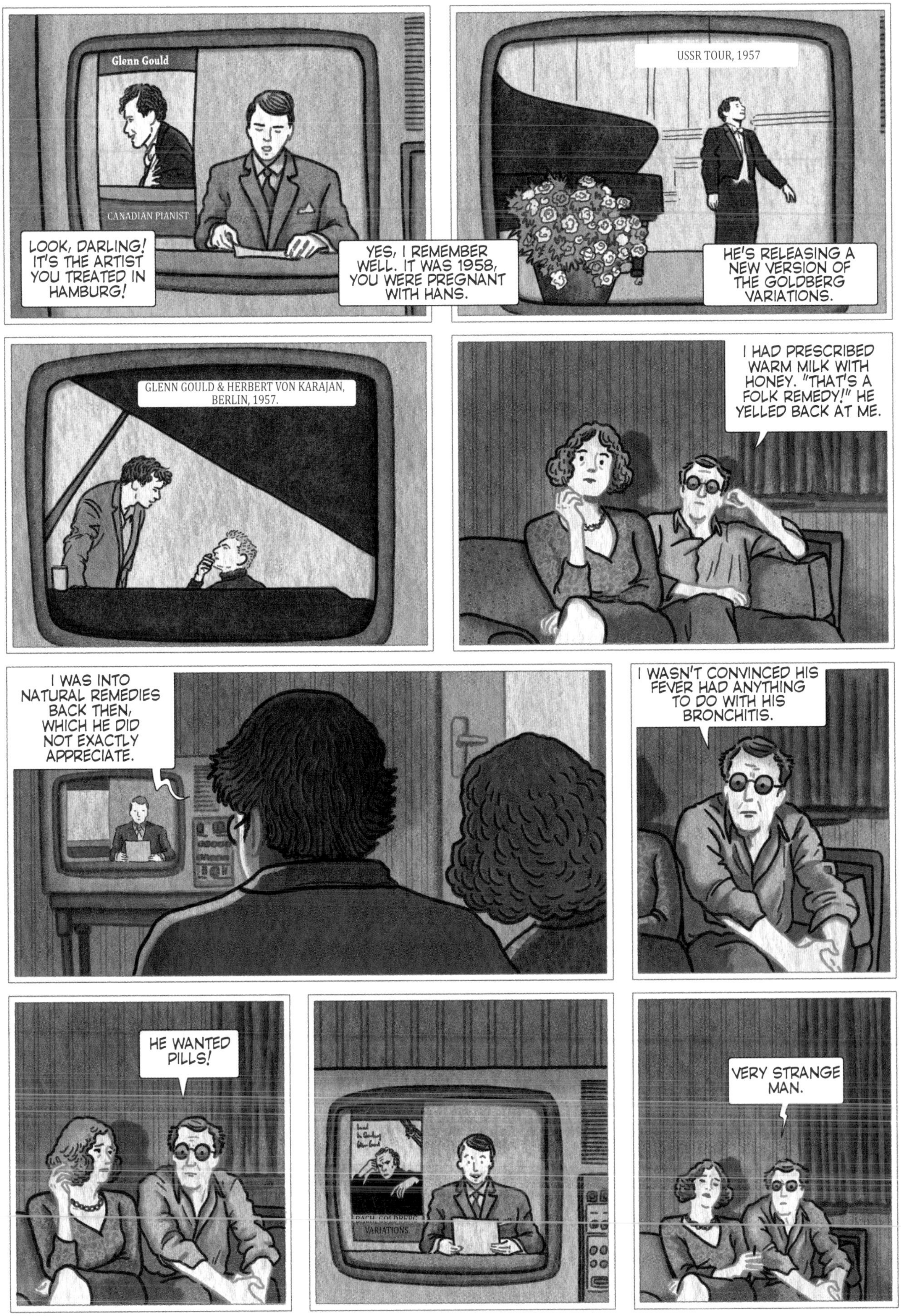
Glenn Gould
CANADIAN PIANIST
LOOK, DARLING! IT'S THE ARTIST YOU TREATED IN HAMBURG!
YES, I REMEMBER WELL. IT WAS 1958, YOU WERE PREGNANT WITH HANS.
USSR TOUR, 1957
HE'S RELEASING A NEW VERSION OF THE GOLDBERG VARIATIONS.
GLENN GOULD & HERBERT VON KARAJAN, BERLIN, 1957.
I HAD PRESCRIBED WARM MILK WITH HONEY. "THAT'S A FOLK REMEDY!" HE YELLED BACK AT ME.
I WAS INTO NATURAL REMEDIES BACK THEN, WHICH HE DID NOT EXACTLY APPRECIATE.
I WASN'T CONVINCED HIS FEVER HAD ANYTHING TO DO WITH HIS BRONCHITIS.
HE WANTED PILLS!
VARIATIONS
VERY STRANGE MAN.

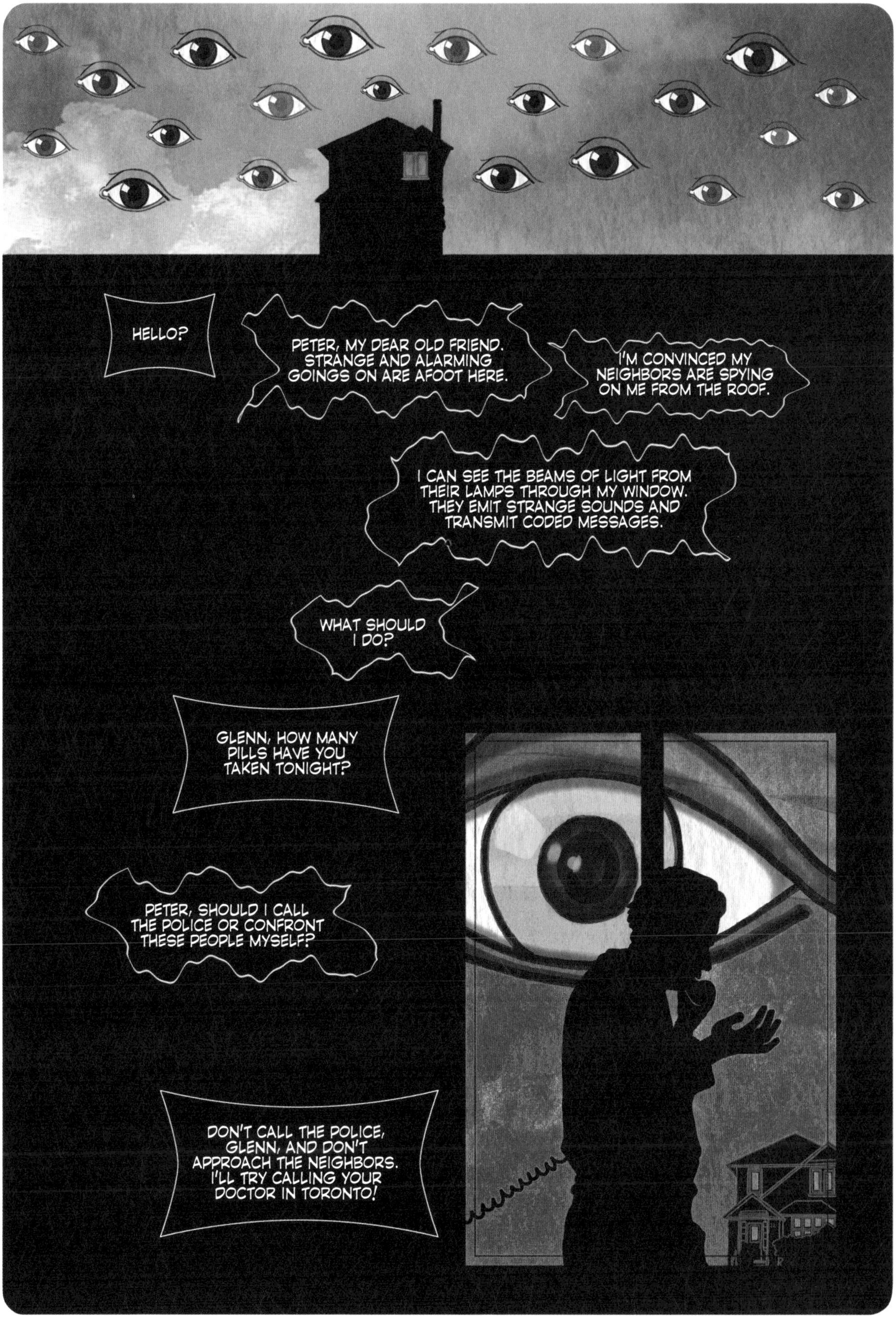

HELLO?
PETER, MY DEAR OLD FRIEND. STRANGE AND ALARMING GOINGS ON ARE AFOOT HERE.
I'M CONVINCED MY NEIGHBORS ARE SPYING ON ME FROM THE ROOF.
I CAN SEE THE BEAMS OF LIGHT FROM THEIR LAMPS THROUGH MY WINDOW. THEY EMIT STRANGE SOUNDS AND TRANSMIT CODED MESSAGES.
WHAT SHOULD I DO?
GLENN, HOW MANY PILLS HAVE YOU TAKEN TONIGHT?
PETER, SHOULD I CALL THE POLICE OR CONFRONT THESE PEOPLE MYSELF?
DON'T CALL THE POLICE, GLENN, AND DON'T APPROACH THE NEIGHBORS. I'LL TRY CALLING YOUR DOCTOR IN TORONTO!

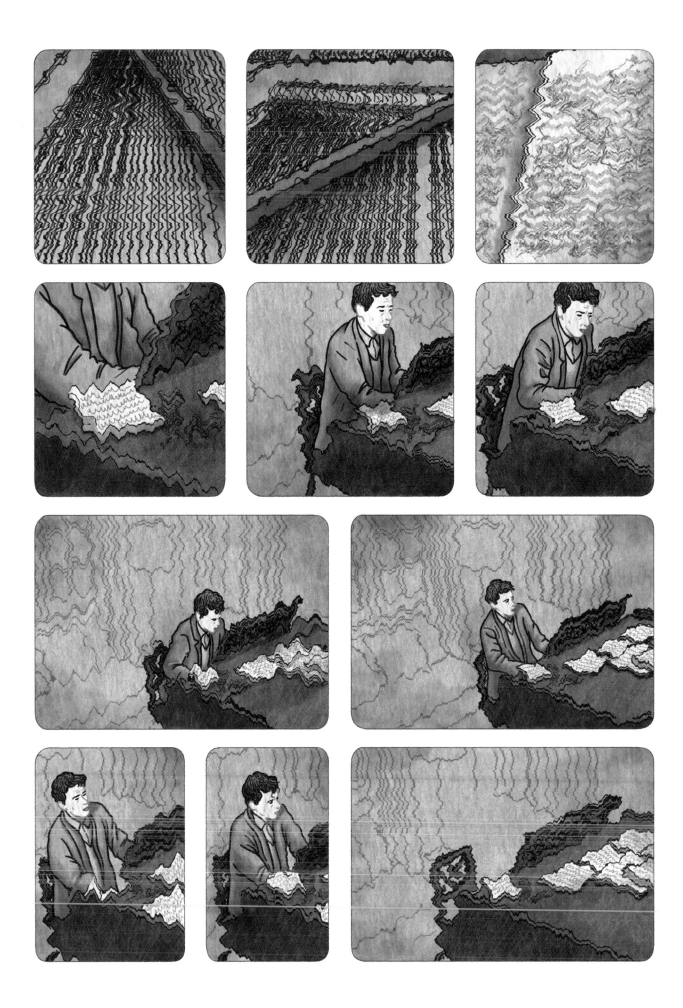

HE WAS THIRTEEN WHEN WE FIRST TEAMED UP.

HOW WAS HE, AS A KID?

HE WAS VERY EASY TO WORK WITH.

ALL GENIUSES HAVE THEIR QUIRKS, OR THEY WOULDN'T BE GENIUSES.

I GOT USED TO IT, AND WE BECAME GREAT FRIENDS.

IT PAINS ME TO HEAR HOW ILL HE IS. HE STILL HAS SO MUCH TO GIVE.

RUMOR HAS IT HE'S A PRIMA DONNA. IS THAT TRUE?

HE GETS VERY UNCOMFORTABLE, IN CERTAIN SITUATIONS, WHICH MAY EXPLAIN THE RUMOR. LIKE WHEN HE WAS LAID UP IN 1960.

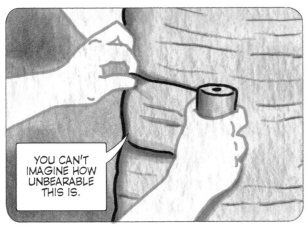

YOU CAN'T IMAGINE HOW UNBEARABLE THIS IS.

DOES THIS HURT?

NO. IT'S A LITTLE COLD.

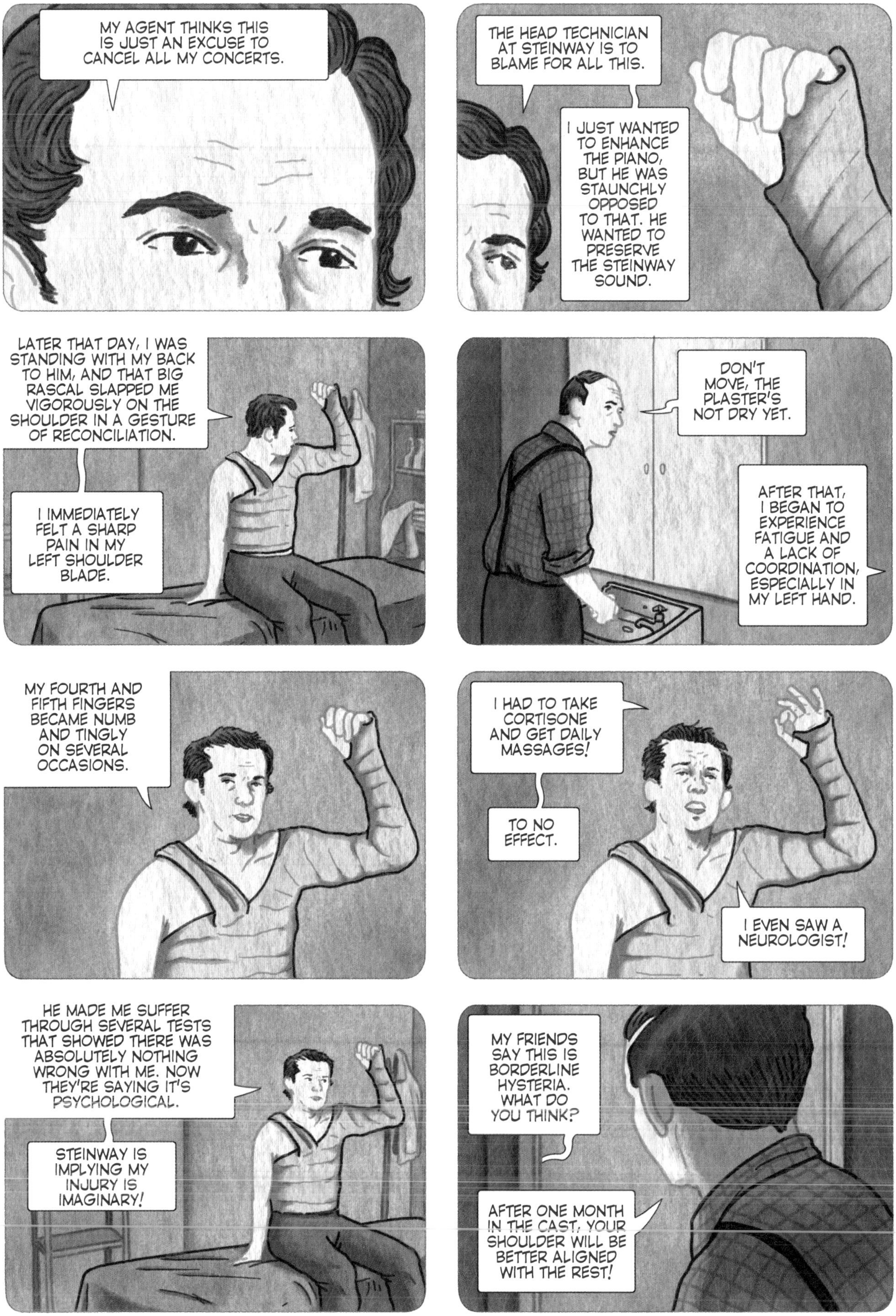
MY AGENT THINKS THIS IS JUST AN EXCUSE TO CANCEL ALL MY CONCERTS.
THE HEAD TECHNICIAN AT STEINWAY IS TO BLAME FOR ALL THIS.
I JUST WANTED TO ENHANCE THE PIANO, BUT HE WAS STAUNCHLY OPPOSED TO THAT. HE WANTED TO PRESERVE THE STEINWAY SOUND.
LATER THAT DAY, I WAS STANDING WITH MY BACK TO HIM, AND THAT BIG RASCAL SLAPPED ME VIGOROUSLY ON THE SHOULDER IN A GESTURE OF RECONCILIATION.
I IMMEDIATELY FELT A SHARP PAIN IN MY LEFT SHOULDER BLADE.
DON'T MOVE, THE PLASTER'S NOT DRY YET.
AFTER THAT, I BEGAN TO EXPERIENCE FATIGUE AND A LACK OF COORDINATION, ESPECIALLY IN MY LEFT HAND.
MY FOURTH AND FIFTH FINGERS BECAME NUMB AND TINGLY ON SEVERAL OCCASIONS.
I HAD TO TAKE CORTISONE AND GET DAILY MASSAGES!
TO NO EFFECT.
I EVEN SAW A NEUROLOGIST!
HE MADE ME SUFFER THROUGH SEVERAL TESTS THAT SHOWED THERE WAS ABSOLUTELY NOTHING WRONG WITH ME. NOW THEY'RE SAYING IT'S PSYCHOLOGICAL.
STEINWAY IS IMPLYING MY INJURY IS IMAGINARY!
MY FRIENDS SAY THIS IS BORDERLINE HYSTERIA. WHAT DO YOU THINK?
AFTER ONE MONTH IN THE CAST, YOUR SHOULDER WILL BE BETTER ALIGNED WITH THE REST!

HE WAS OBSESSED WITH MORE THAN JUST THE MECHANICS OF HIS BODY. HE WAS ALSO FIXATED ON HIS CHAIR AND ON HIS CD318.

GOULD DEFINED HIMSELF THROUGH HIS PIANO. HE WAS INCAPABLE OF PLAYING ON ANY OTHER ONE. IT WAS LIKE CO-DEPENDENCY.

IN MARCH OF '57, THE STEINWAY FELL OFF A TRUCK...

BOOM!

?...

!!!

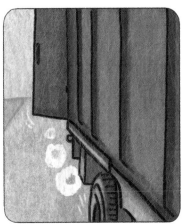

IT BROKE INTO PIECES ON THE WAY BACK FROM A CONCERT IN CLEVELAND.

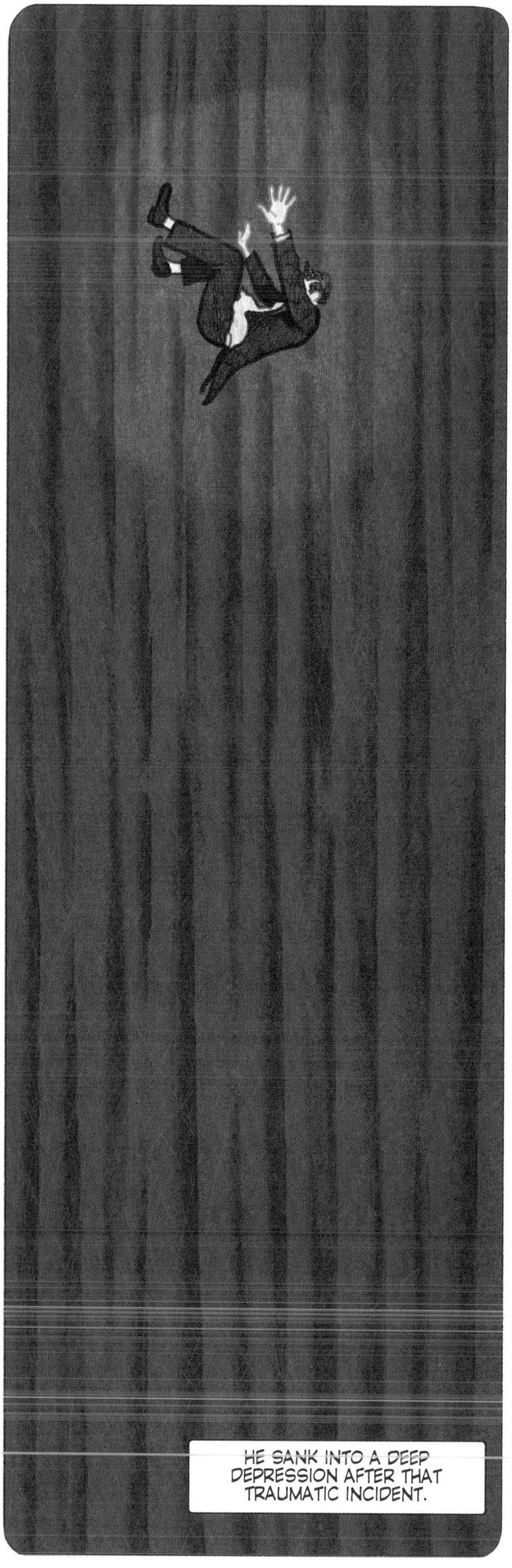
HE SANK INTO A DEEP DEPRESSION AFTER THAT TRAUMATIC INCIDENT.

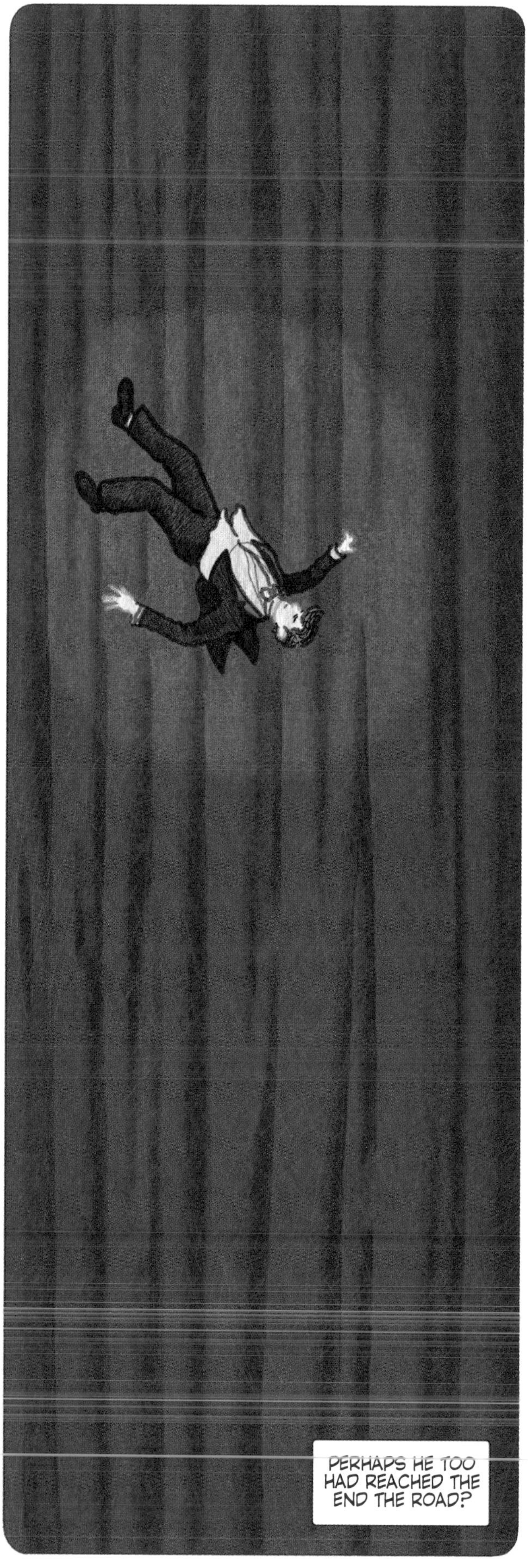
PERHAPS HE TOO HAD REACHED THE END THE ROAD?

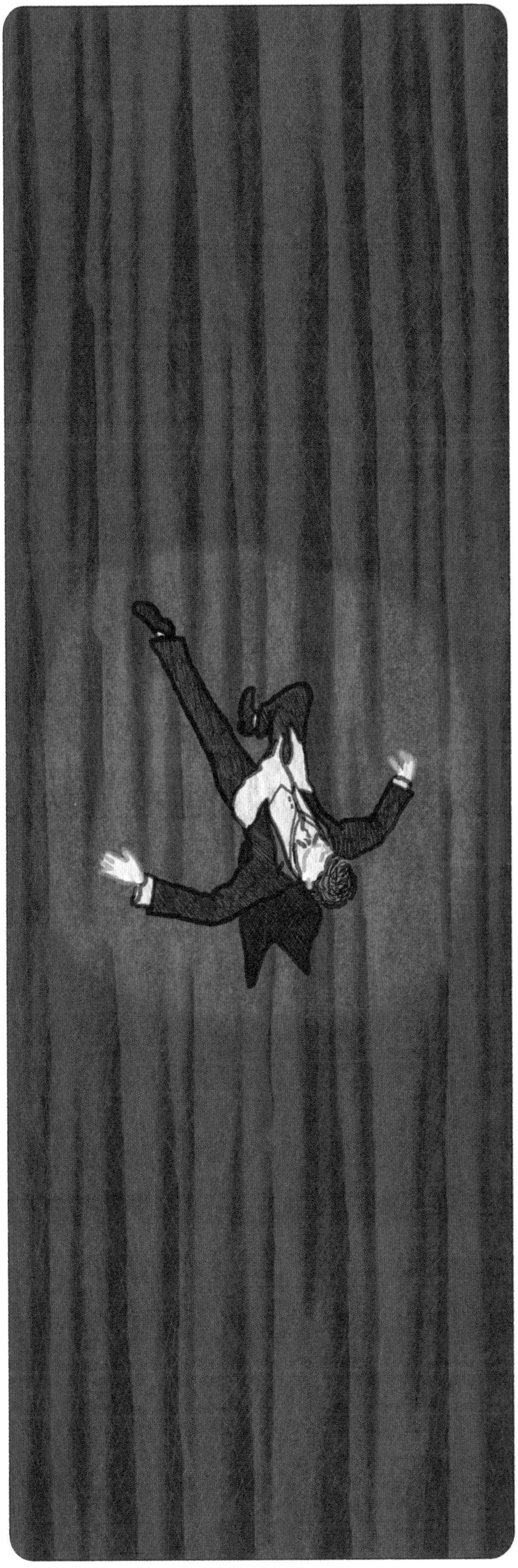
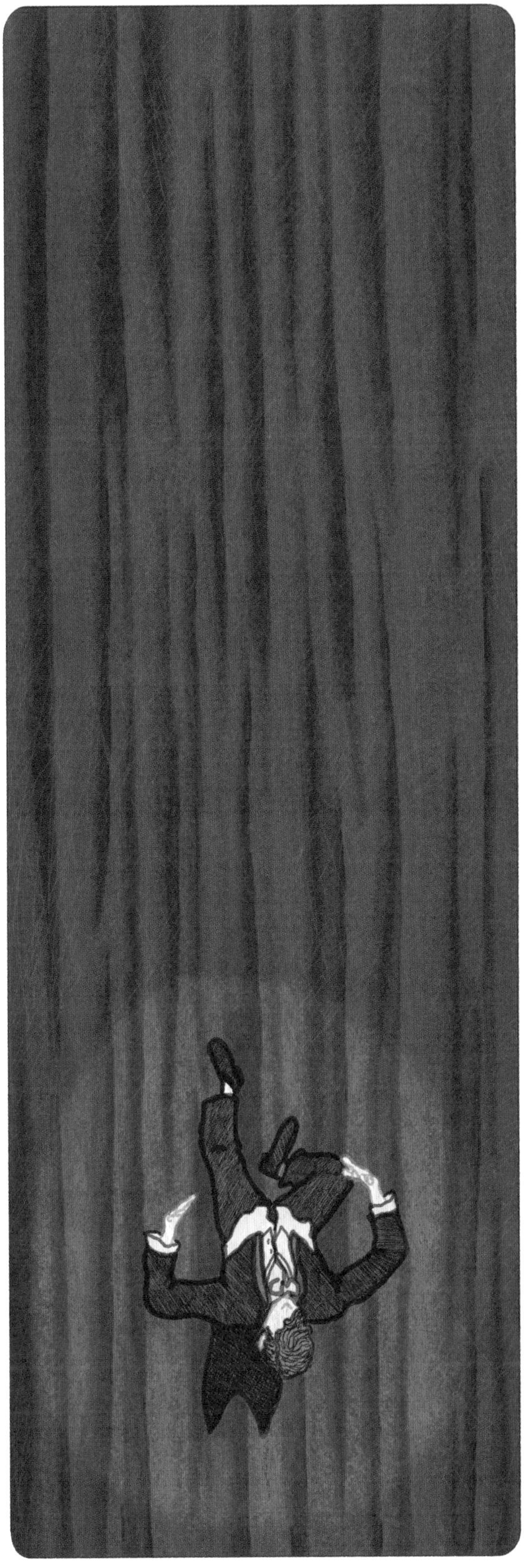

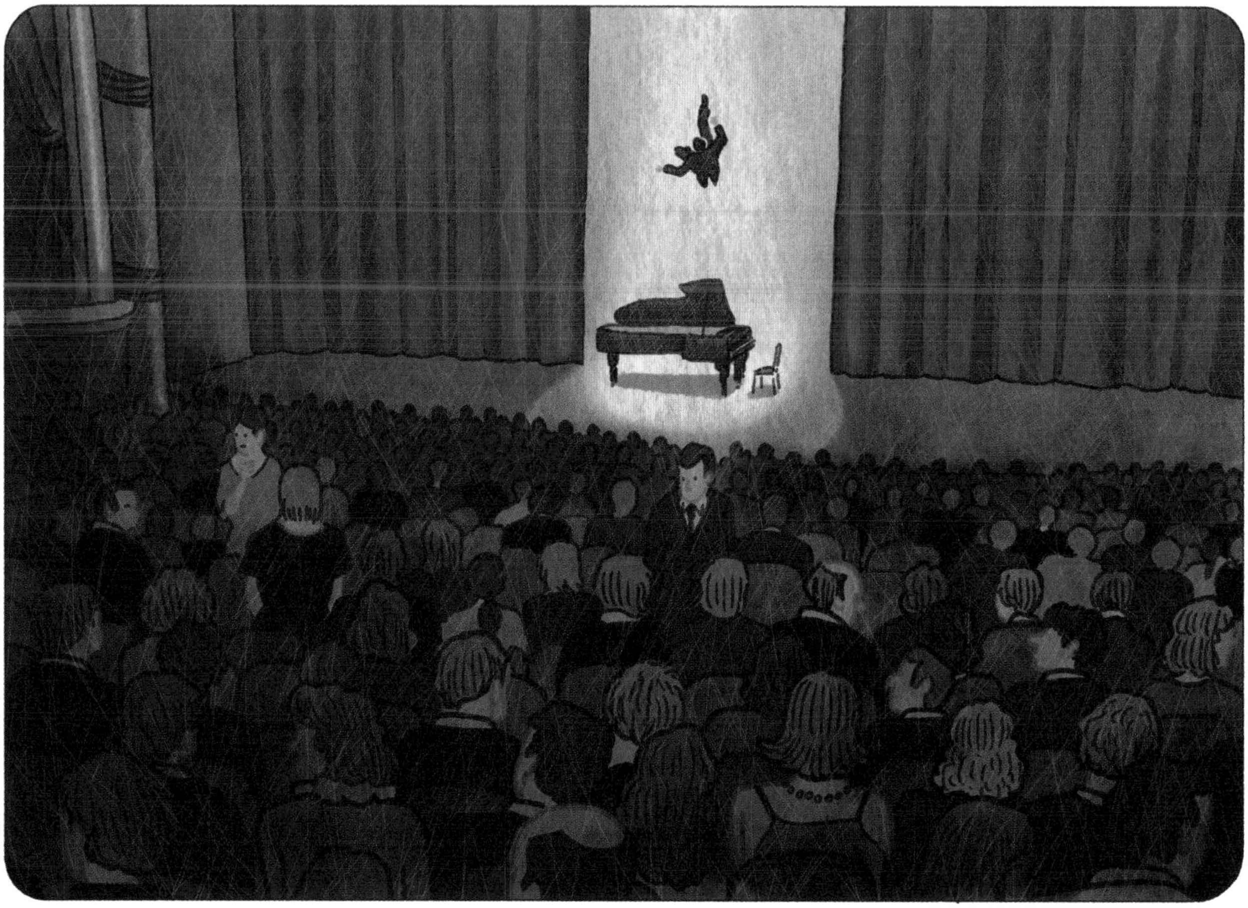
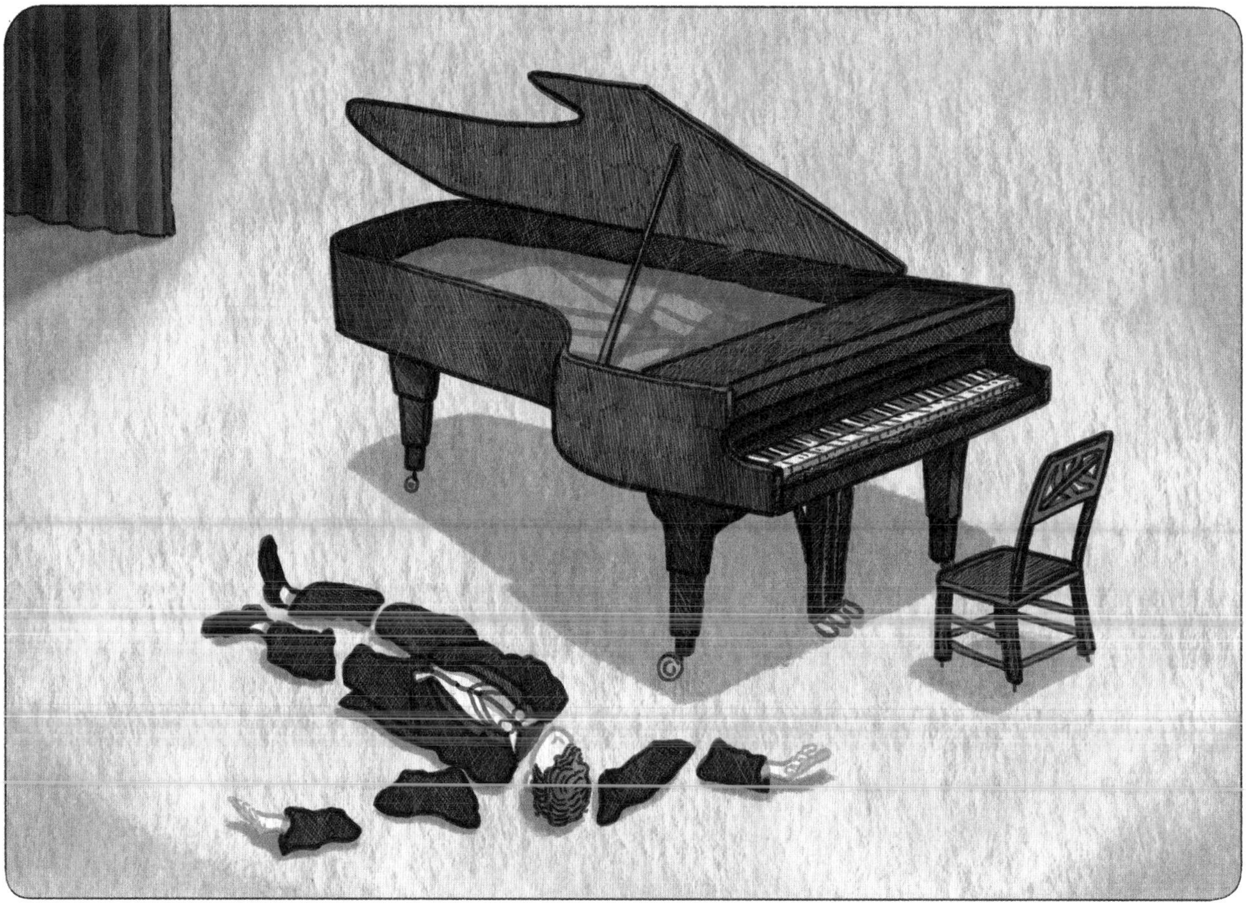

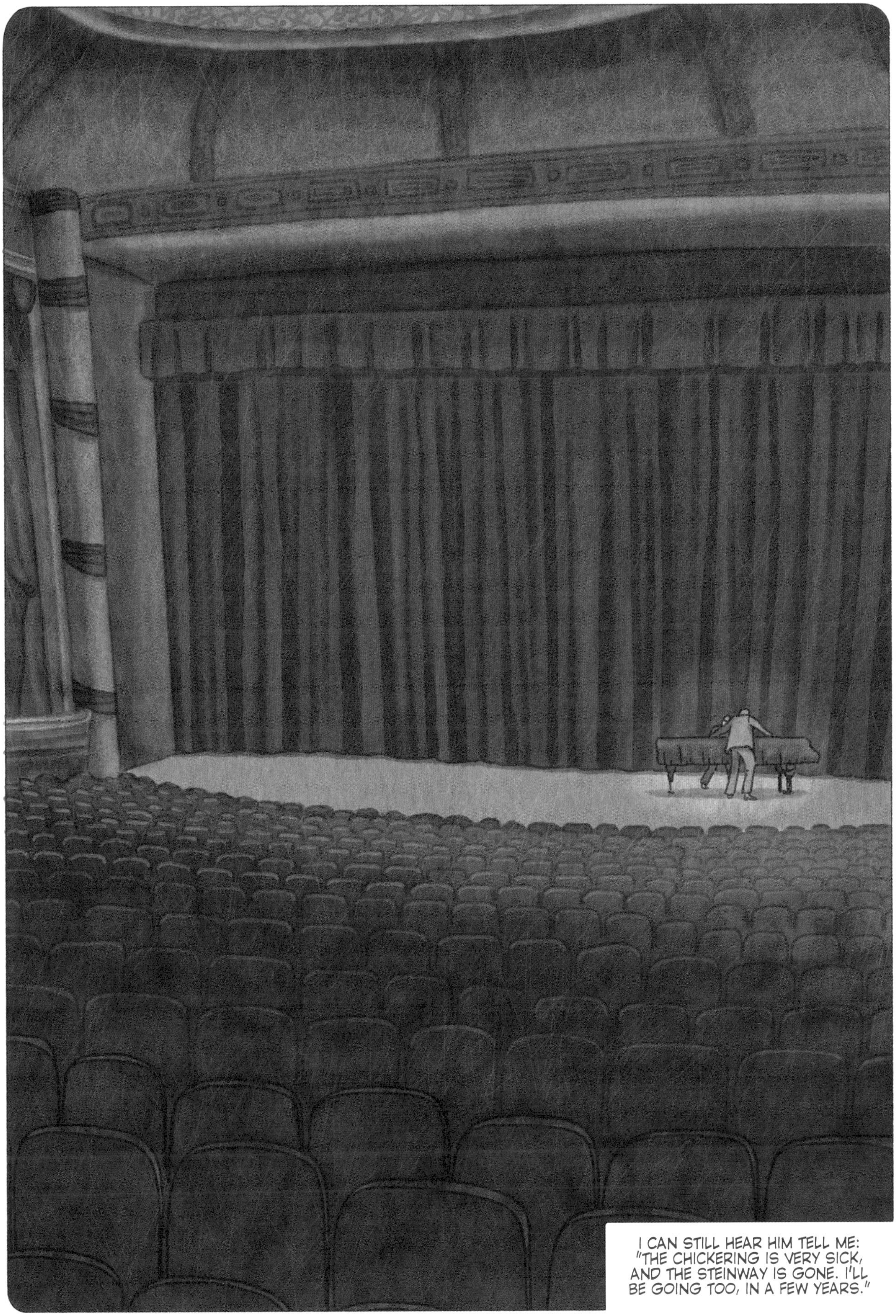
I CAN STILL HEAR HIM TELL ME: "THE CHICKERING IS VERY SICK, AND THE STEINWAY IS GONE. I'LL BE GOING TOO, IN A FEW YEARS."

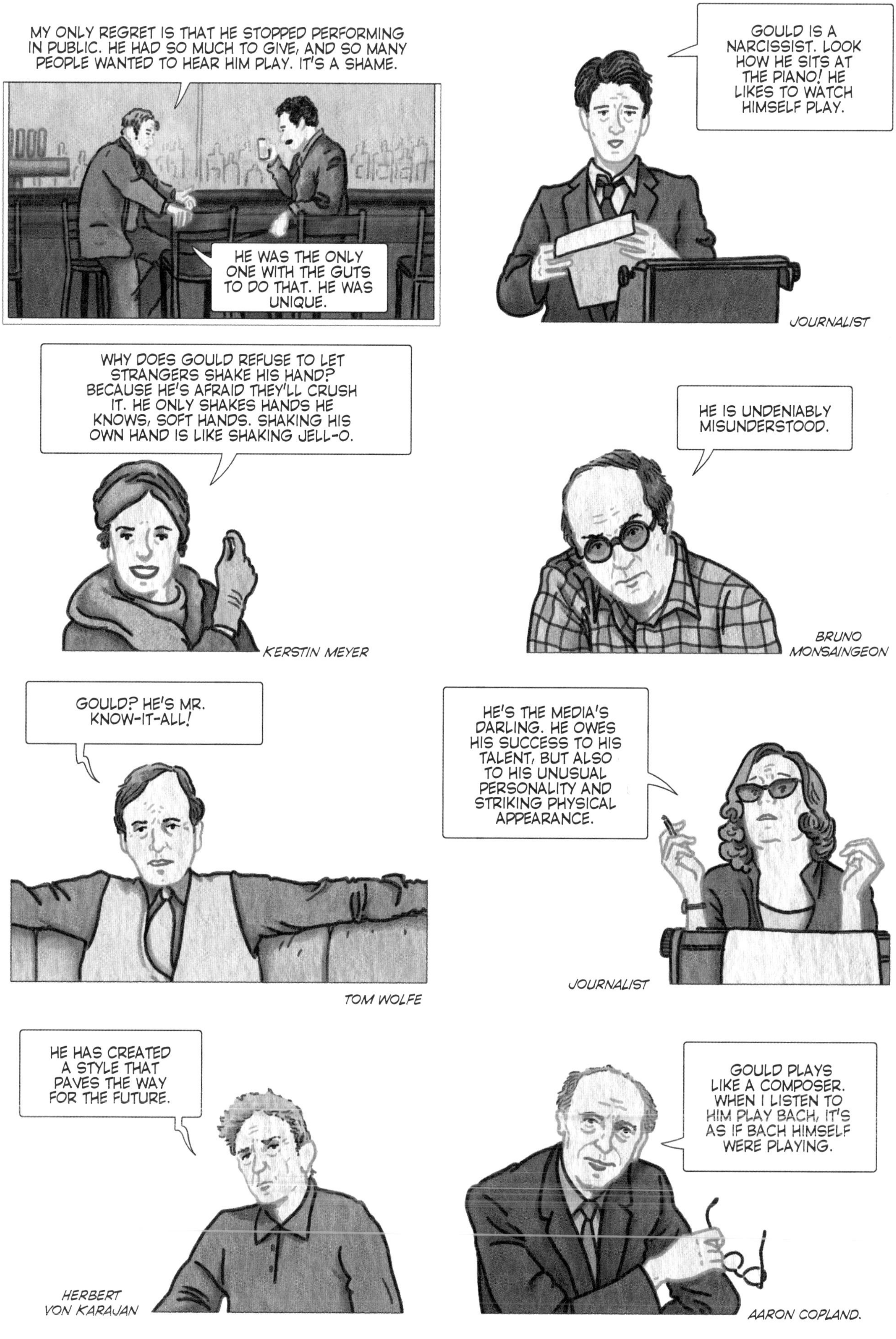
MY ONLY REGRET IS THAT HE STOPPED PERFORMING IN PUBLIC. HE HAD SO MUCH TO GIVE, AND SO MANY PEOPLE WANTED TO HEAR HIM PLAY. IT'S A SHAME.
HE WAS THE ONLY ONE WITH THE GUTS TO DO THAT. HE WAS UNIQUE.
GOULD IS A NARCISSIST. LOOK HOW HE SITS AT THE PIANO! HE LIKES TO WATCH HIMSELF PLAY.
JOURNALIST
WHY DOES GOULD REFUSE TO LET STRANGERS SHAKE HIS HAND? BECAUSE HE'S AFRAID THEY'LL CRUSH IT. HE ONLY SHAKES HANDS HE KNOWS, SOFT HANDS. SHAKING HIS OWN HAND IS LIKE SHAKING JELL-O.
KERSTIN MEYER
HE IS UNDENIABLY MISUNDERSTOOD.
BRUNO MONSAINGEON
GOULD? HE'S MR. KNOW-IT-ALL!
TOM WOLFE
HE'S THE MEDIA'S DARLING. HE OWES HIS SUCCESS TO HIS TALENT, BUT ALSO TO HIS UNUSUAL PERSONALITY AND STRIKING PHYSICAL APPEARANCE.
JOURNALIST
HE HAS CREATED A STYLE THAT PAVES THE WAY FOR THE FUTURE.
HERBERT VON KARAJAN
GOULD PLAYS LIKE A COMPOSER. WHEN I LISTEN TO HIM PLAY BACH, IT'S AS IF BACH HIMSELF WERE PLAYING.
AARON COPLAND.

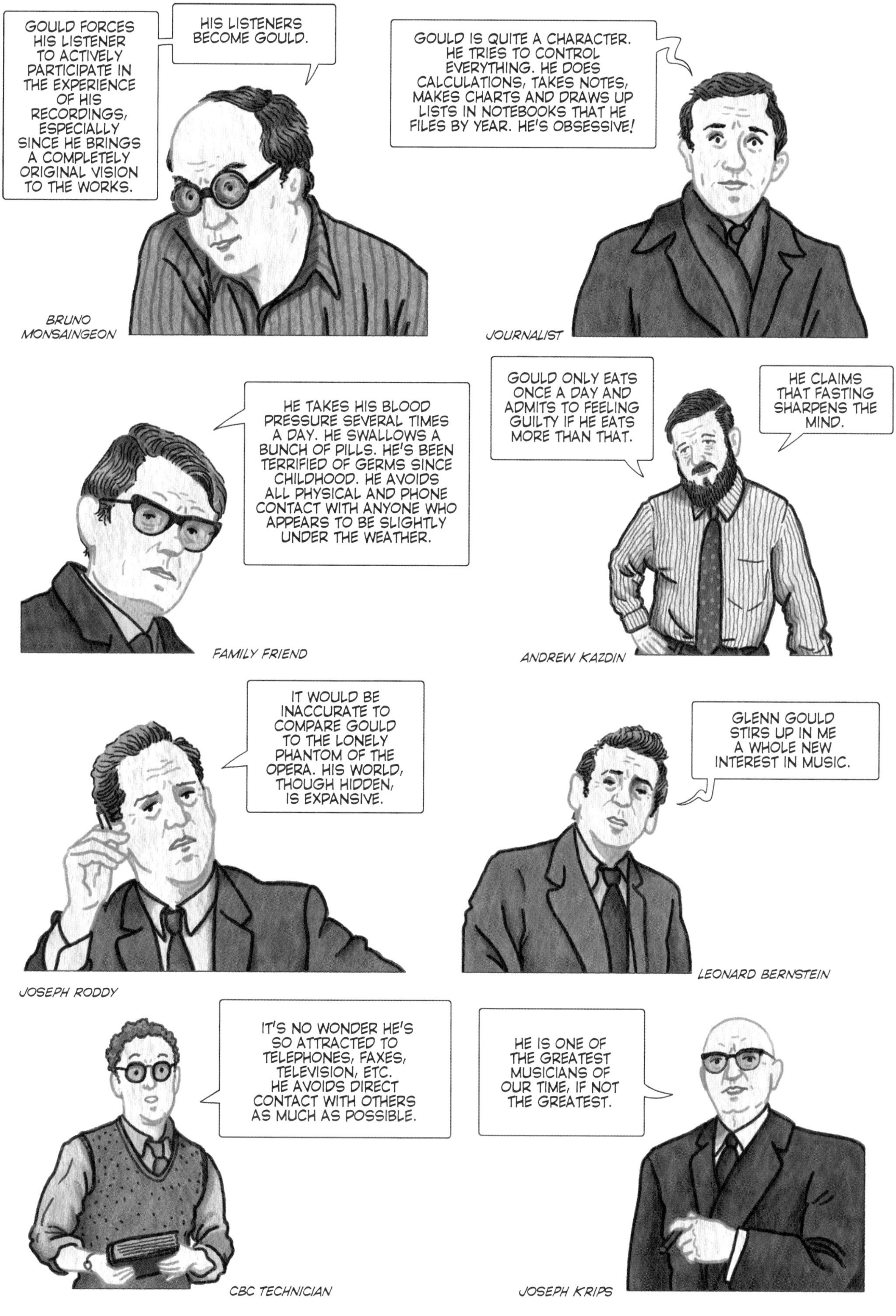
GOULD FORCES HIS LISTENER TO ACTIVELY PARTICIPATE IN THE EXPERIENCE OF HIS RECORDINGS, ESPECIALLY SINCE HE BRINGS A COMPLETELY ORIGINAL VISION TO THE WORKS.
HIS LISTENERS BECOME GOULD.
BRUNO MONSAINGEON
GOULD IS QUITE A CHARACTER. HE TRIES TO CONTROL EVERYTHING. HE DOES CALCULATIONS, TAKES NOTES, MAKES CHARTS AND DRAWS UP LISTS IN NOTEBOOKS THAT HE FILES BY YEAR. HE'S OBSESSIVE!
JOURNALIST
HE TAKES HIS BLOOD PRESSURE SEVERAL TIMES A DAY. HE SWALLOWS A BUNCH OF PILLS. HE'S BEEN TERRIFIED OF GERMS SINCE CHILDHOOD. HE AVOIDS ALL PHYSICAL AND PHONE CONTACT WITH ANYONE WHO APPEARS TO BE SLIGHTLY UNDER THE WEATHER.
FAMILY FRIEND
GOULD ONLY EATS ONCE A DAY AND ADMITS TO FEELING GUILTY IF HE EATS MORE THAN THAT.
HE CLAIMS THAT FASTING SHARPENS THE MIND.
ANDREW KAZDIN
IT WOULD BE INACCURATE TO COMPARE GOULD TO THE LONELY PHANTOM OF THE OPERA. HIS WORLD, THOUGH HIDDEN, IS EXPANSIVE.
JOSEPH RODDY
GLENN GOULD STIRS UP IN ME A WHOLE NEW INTEREST IN MUSIC.
LEONARD BERNSTEIN
IT'S NO WONDER HE'S SO ATTRACTED TO TELEPHONES, FAXES, TELEVISION, ETC. HE AVOIDS DIRECT CONTACT WITH OTHERS AS MUCH AS POSSIBLE.
CBC TECHNICIAN
HE IS ONE OF THE GREATEST MUSICIANS OF OUR TIME, IF NOT THE GREATEST.
JOSEPH KRIPS

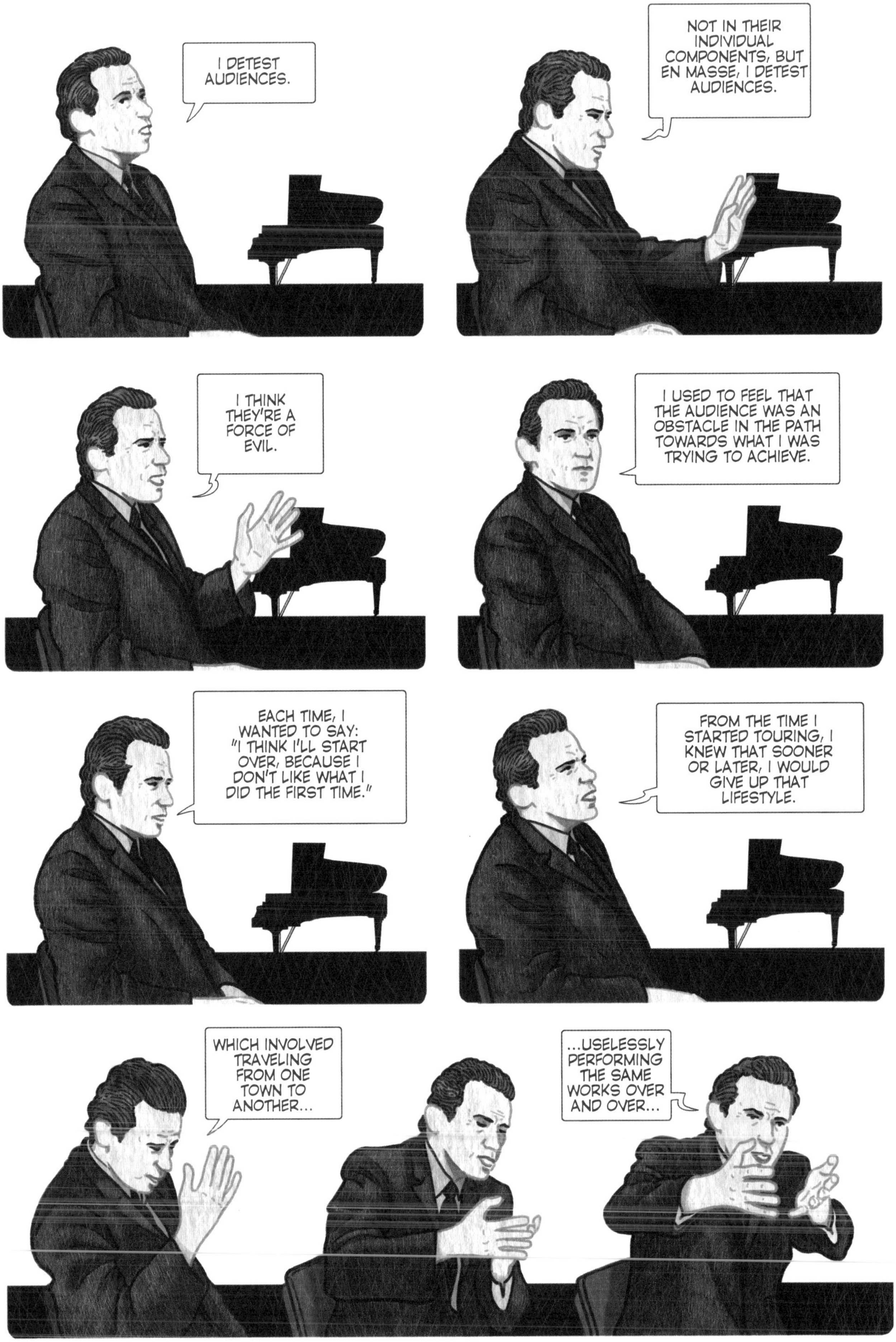
I DETEST AUDIENCES.
NOT IN THEIR INDIVIDUAL COMPONENTS, BUT EN MASSE, I DETEST AUDIENCES.
I THINK THEY'RE A FORCE OF EVIL.
I USED TO FEEL THAT THE AUDIENCE WAS AN OBSTACLE IN THE PATH TOWARDS WHAT I WAS TRYING TO ACHIEVE.
EACH TIME, I WANTED TO SAY: "I THINK I'LL START OVER, BECAUSE I DON'T LIKE WHAT I DID THE FIRST TIME."
FROM THE TIME I STARTED TOURING, I KNEW THAT SOONER OR LATER, I WOULD GIVE UP THAT LIFESTYLE.
WHICH INVOLVED TRAVELING FROM ONE TOWN TO ANOTHER...
...USELESSLY PERFORMING THE SAME WORKS OVER AND OVER...

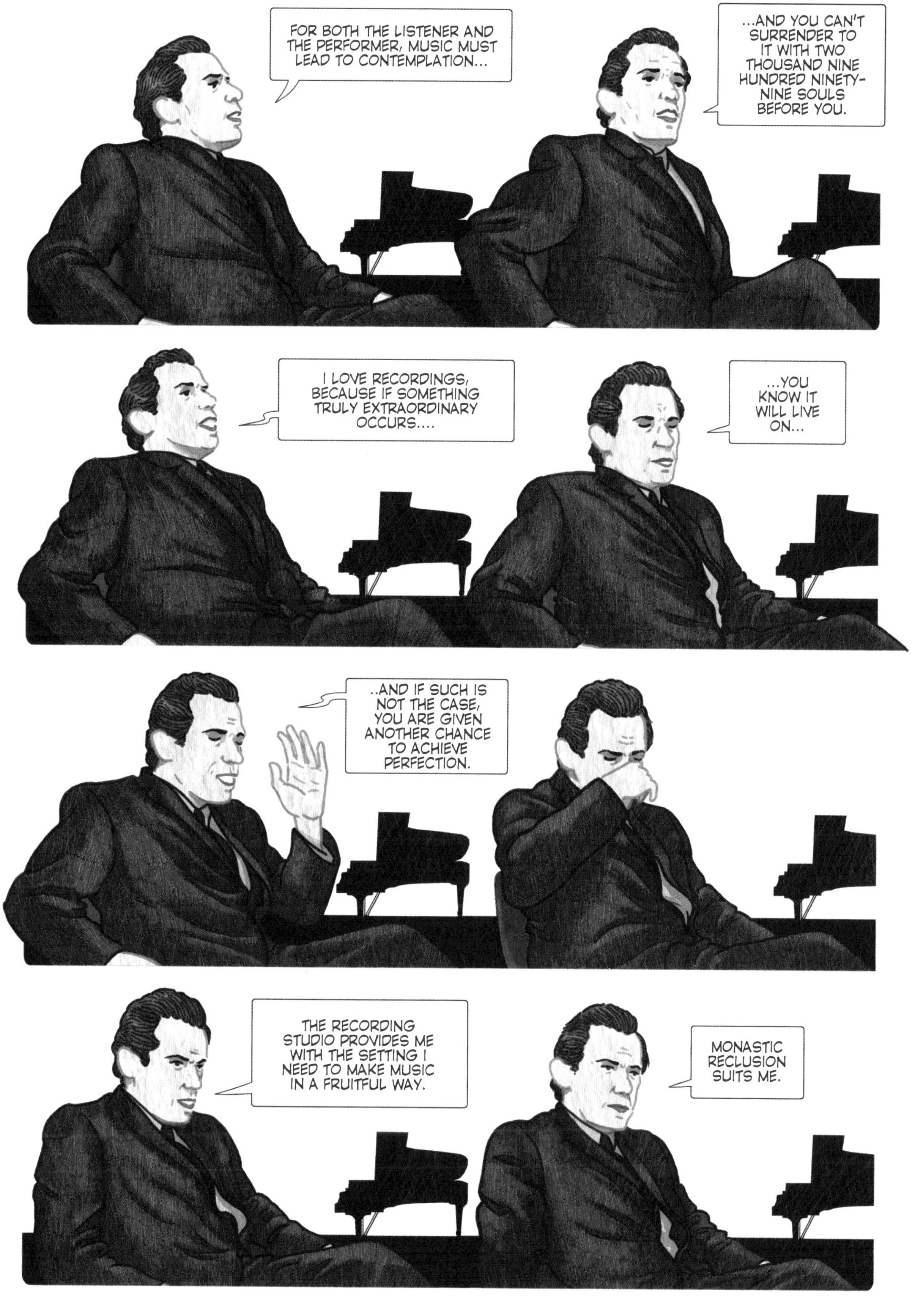
FOR BOTH THE LISTENER AND THE PERFORMER, MUSIC MUST LEAD TO CONTEMPLATION...
...AND YOU CAN'T SURRENDER TO IT WITH TWO THOUSAND NINE HUNDRED NINETY-NINE SOULS BEFORE YOU.
I LOVE RECORDINGS, BECAUSE IF SOMETHING TRULY EXTRAORDINARY OCCURS....
...YOU KNOW IT WILL LIVE ON...
..AND IF SUCH IS NOT THE CASE, YOU ARE GIVEN ANOTHER CHANCE TO ACHIEVE PERFECTION.
THE RECORDING STUDIO PROVIDES ME WITH THE SETTING I NEED TO MAKE MUSIC IN A FRUITFUL WAY.
MONASTIC RECLUSION SUITS ME.

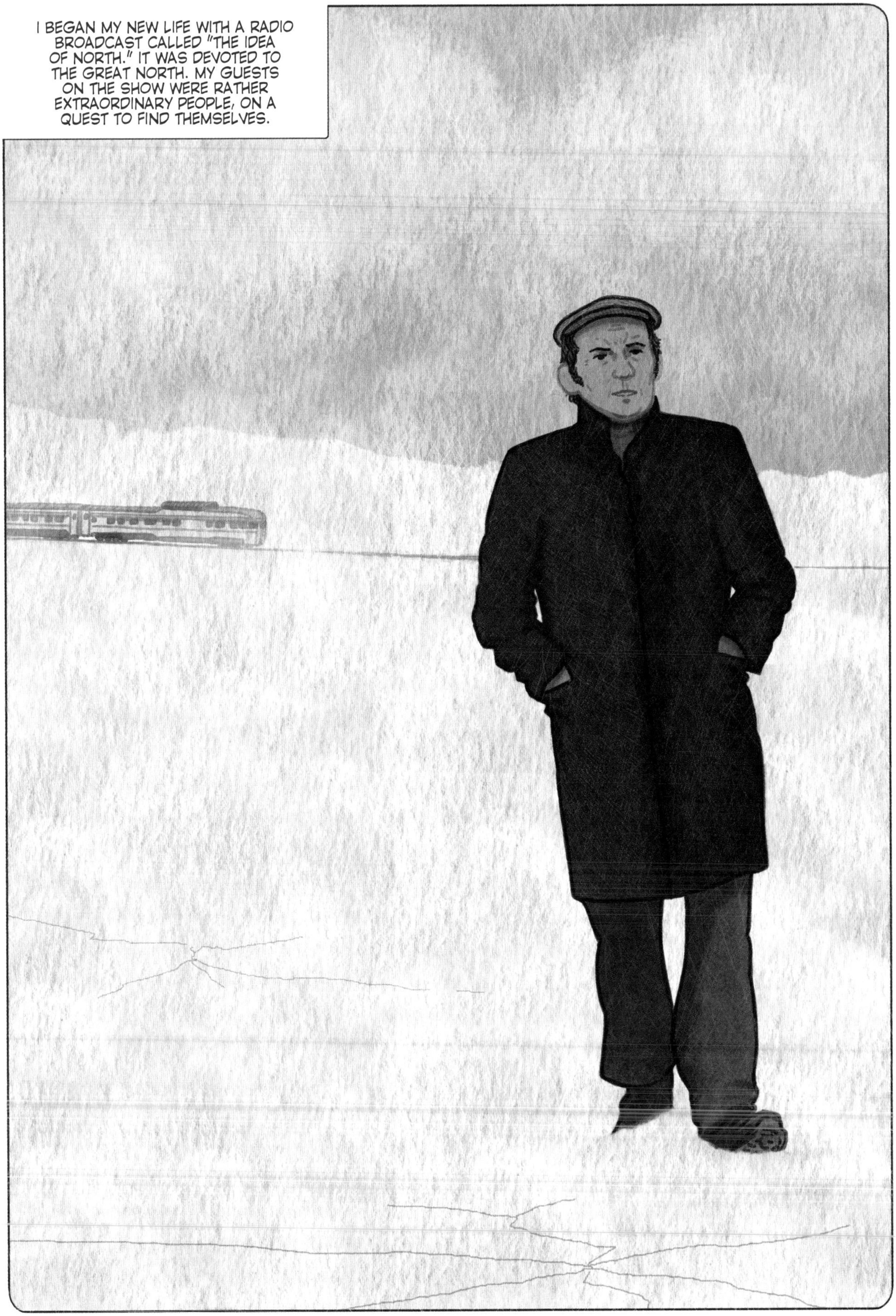
I BEGAN MY NEW LIFE WITH A RADIO BROADCAST CALLED "THE IDEA OF NORTH." IT WAS DEVOTED TO THE GREAT NORTH. MY GUESTS ON THE SHOW WERE RATHER EXTRAORDINARY PEOPLE, ON A QUEST TO FIND THEMSELVES.

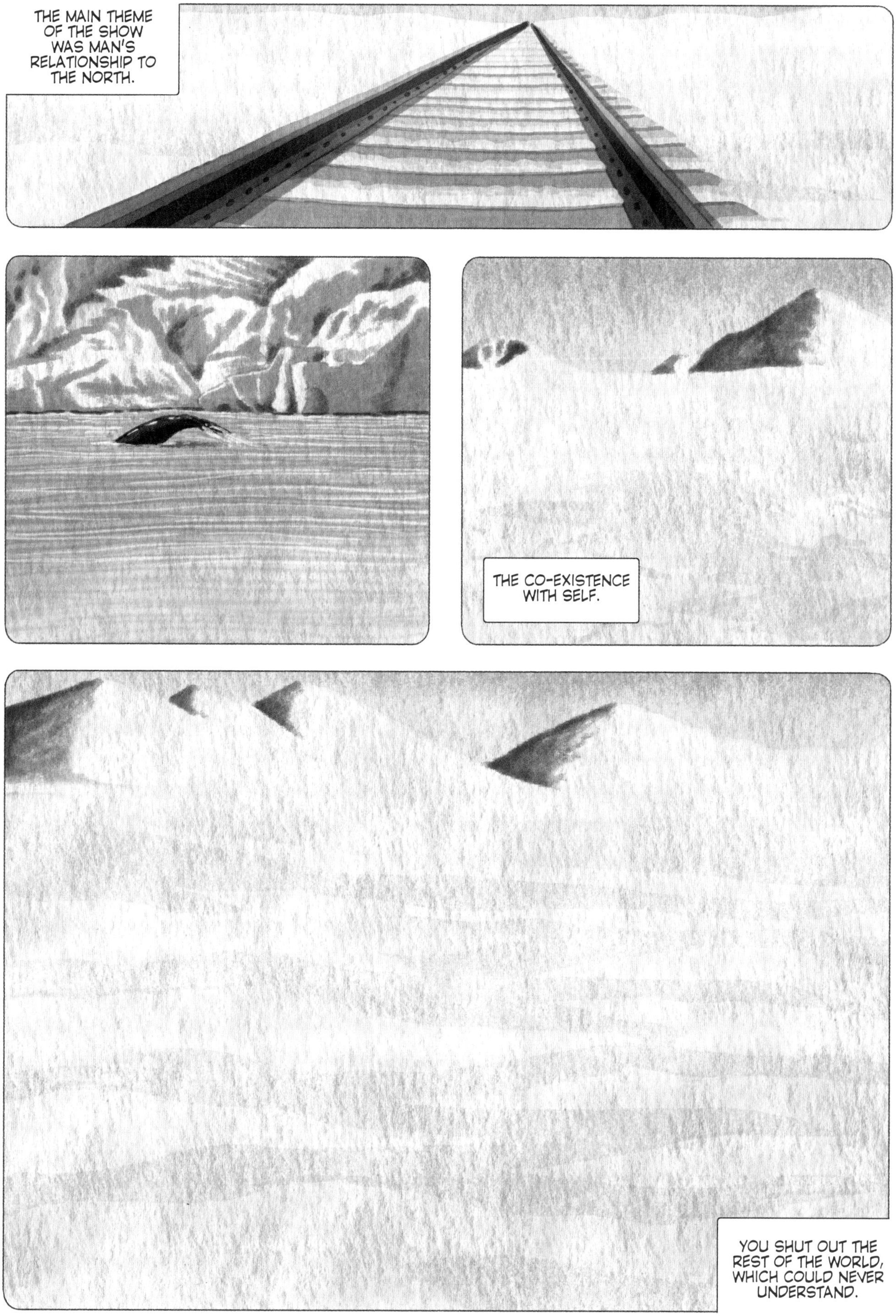
THE MAIN THEME OF THE SHOW WAS MAN'S RELATIONSHIP TO THE NORTH.
THE CO-EXISTENCE WITH SELF.
YOU SHUT OUT THE REST OF THE WORLD, WHICH COULD NEVER UNDERSTAND.

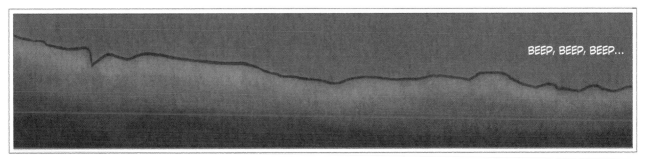

BEEP, BEEP, BEEP...

BEEP, BEEP, BEEP...

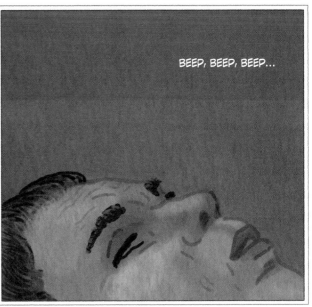

BEEP, BEEP, BEEP...

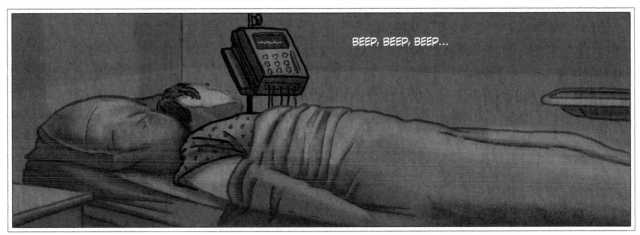

BEEP, BEEP, BEEP...

BEEP, BEEP, BEEP...

BEEP, BEEP, BEEP...

WHAT IS IT, LORN?

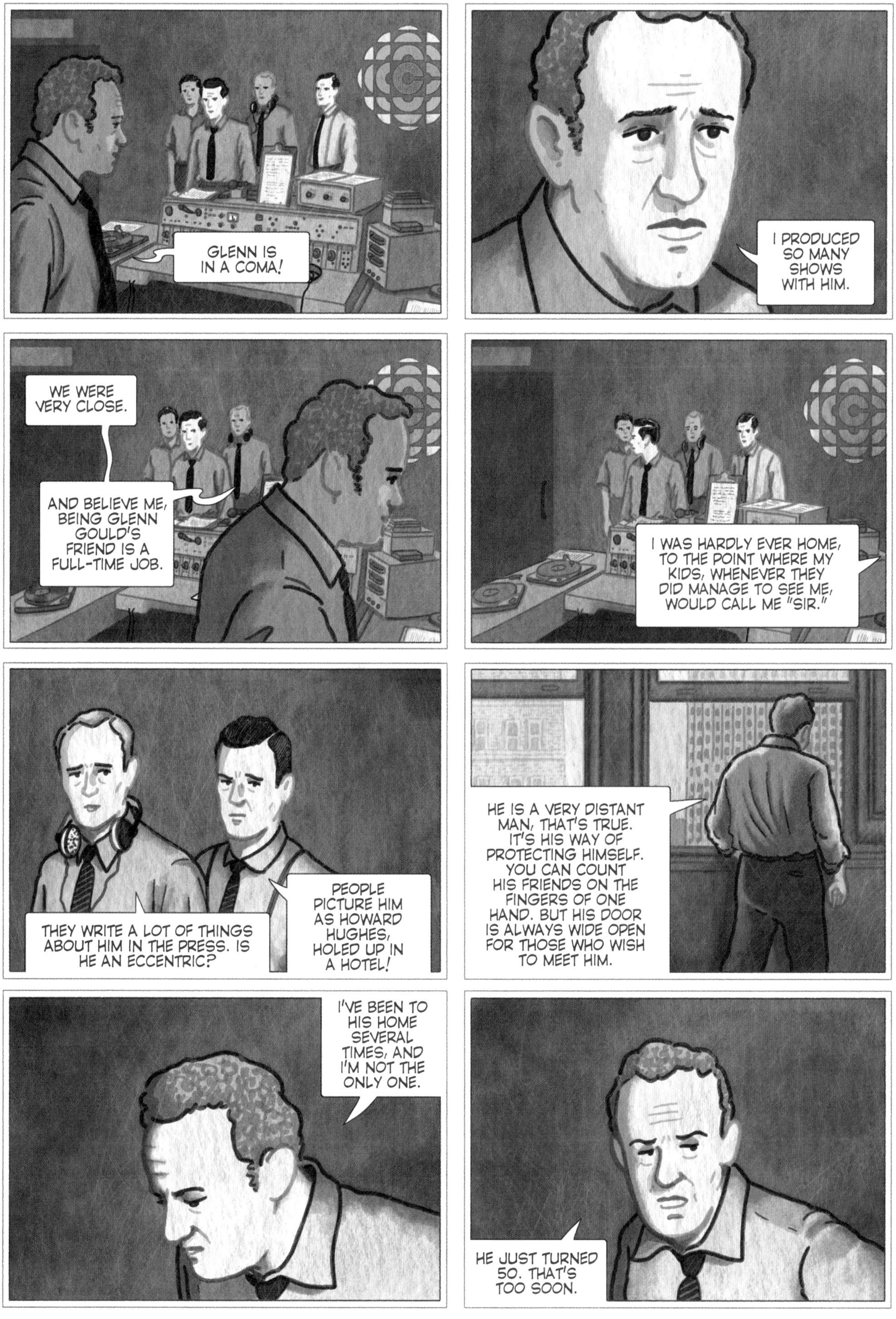
GLENN IS IN A COMA!
I PRODUCED SO MANY SHOWS WITH HIM.
WE WERE VERY CLOSE.
AND BELIEVE ME, BEING GLENN GOULD'S FRIEND IS A FULL-TIME JOB.
I WAS HARDLY EVER HOME, TO THE POINT WHERE MY KIDS, WHENEVER THEY DID MANAGE TO SEE ME, WOULD CALL ME "SIR."
THEY WRITE A LOT OF THINGS ABOUT HIM IN THE PRESS. IS HE AN ECCENTRIC?
PEOPLE PICTURE HIM AS HOWARD HUGHES, HOLED UP IN A HOTEL!
HE IS A VERY DISTANT MAN, THAT'S TRUE. IT'S HIS WAY OF PROTECTING HIMSELF. YOU CAN COUNT HIS FRIENDS ON THE FINGERS OF ONE HAND. BUT HIS DOOR IS ALWAYS WIDE OPEN FOR THOSE WHO WISH TO MEET HIM.
I'VE BEEN TO HIS HOME SEVERAL TIMES, AND I'M NOT THE ONLY ONE.
HE JUST TURNED 50. THAT'S TOO SOON.

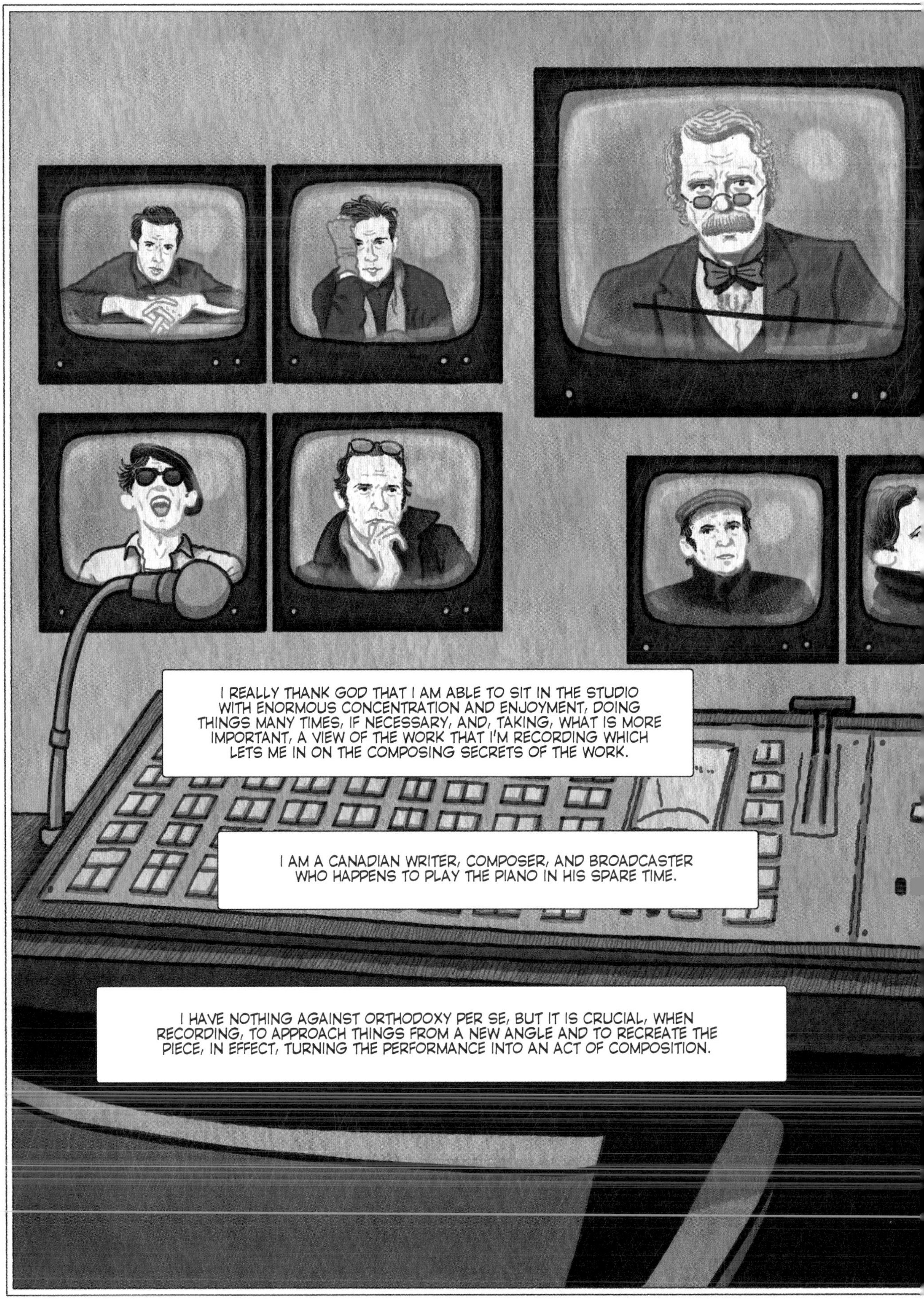
I REALLY THANK GOD THAT I AM ABLE TO SIT IN THE STUDIO WITH ENORMOUS CONCENTRATION AND ENJOYMENT, DOING THINGS MANY TIMES, IF NECESSARY, AND, TAKING, WHAT IS MORE IMPORTANT, A VIEW OF THE WORK THAT I'M RECORDING WHICH LETS ME IN ON THE COMPOSING SECRETS OF THE WORK.
I AM A CANADIAN WRITER, COMPOSER, AND BROADCASTER WHO HAPPENS TO PLAY THE PIANO IN HIS SPARE TIME.
I HAVE NOTHING AGAINST ORTHODOXY PER SE, BUT IT IS CRUCIAL, WHEN RECORDING, TO APPROACH THINGS FROM A NEW ANGLE AND TO RECREATE THE PIECE, IN EFFECT, TURNING THE PERFORMANCE INTO AN ACT OF COMPOSITION.

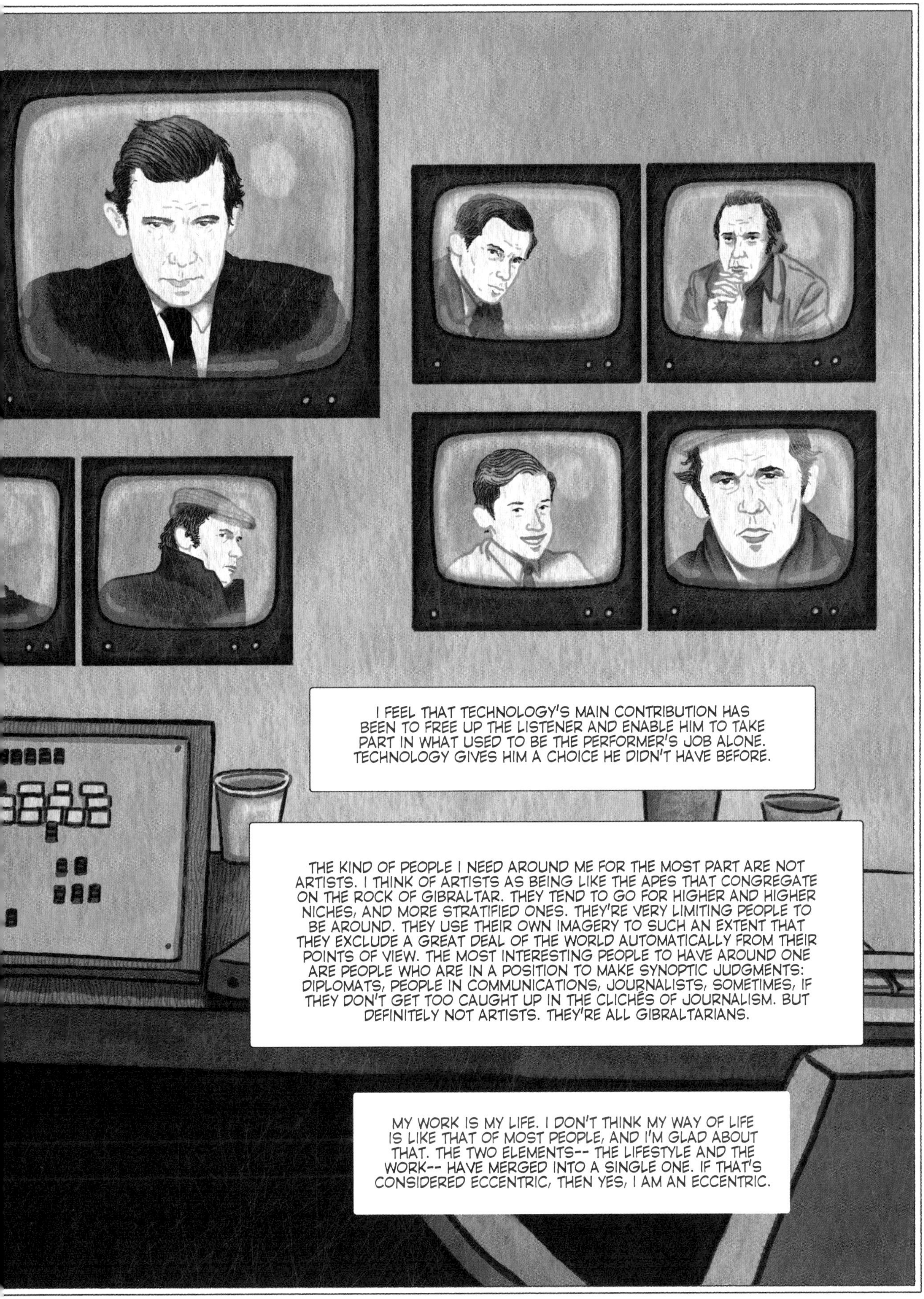
I FEEL THAT TECHNOLOGY'S MAIN CONTRIBUTION HAS BEEN TO FREE UP THE LISTENER AND ENABLE HIM TO TAKE PART IN WHAT USED TO BE THE PERFORMER'S JOB ALONE. TECHNOLOGY GIVES HIM A CHOICE HE DIDN'T HAVE BEFORE.
THE KIND OF PEOPLE I NEED AROUND ME FOR THE MOST PART ARE NOT ARTISTS. I THINK OF ARTISTS AS BEING LIKE THE APES THAT CONGREGATE ON THE ROCK OF GIBRALTAR. THEY TEND TO GO FOR HIGHER AND HIGHER NICHES, AND MORE STRATIFIED ONES. THEY'RE VERY LIMITING PEOPLE TO BE AROUND. THEY USE THEIR OWN IMAGERY TO SUCH AN EXTENT THAT THEY EXCLUDE A GREAT DEAL OF THE WORLD AUTOMATICALLY FROM THEIR POINTS OF VIEW. THE MOST INTERESTING PEOPLE TO HAVE AROUND ONE ARE PEOPLE WHO ARE IN A POSITION TO MAKE SYNOPTIC JUDGMENTS: DIPLOMATS, PEOPLE IN COMMUNICATIONS, JOURNALISTS, SOMETIMES, IF THEY DON'T GET TOO CAUGHT UP IN THE CLICHÉS OF JOURNALISM. BUT DEFINITELY NOT ARTISTS. THEY'RE ALL GIBRALTARIANS.
MY WORK IS MY LIFE. I DON'T THINK MY WAY OF LIFE IS LIKE THAT OF MOST PEOPLE, AND I'M GLAD ABOUT THAT. THE TWO ELEMENTS-- THE LIFESTYLE AND THE WORK-- HAVE MERGED INTO A SINGLE ONE. IF THAT'S CONSIDERED ECCENTRIC, THEN YES, I AM AN ECCENTRIC.

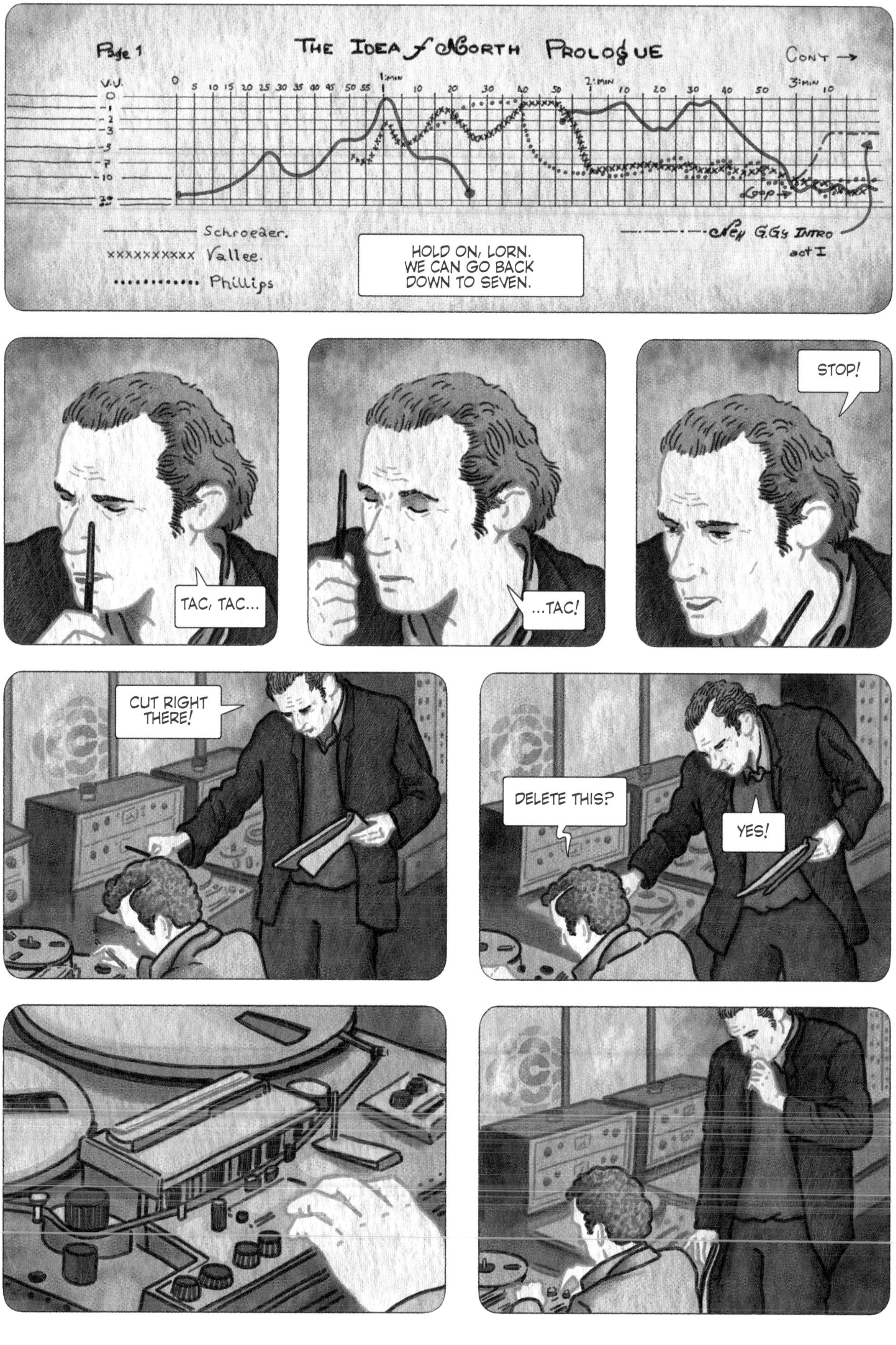
Page 1
THE IDEA of NORTH PROLOGUE
CONT →
V.U.
1:MIN
2:MIN
3:MIN
Loop
Schroeder.
Vallee.
Phillips
New G.G's INTRO
act I
HOLD ON, LORN. WE CAN GO BACK DOWN TO SEVEN.
TAC, TAC...
...TAC!
STOP!
CUT RIGHT THERE!
DELETE THIS?
YES!

WE WERE DOING GOOD WORK. I LOVED WORKING WITH HIM.

ONE DAY, I RODE IN HIS LINCOLN, WHICH IS PRACTICALLY HIS SECOND HOME.

HE KEEPS THE HEAT ON FULL BLAST, ALL THE WINDOWS UP, AND HE OBSERVES OTHERS FROM A SAFE DISTANCE.

HE'S A PUBLIC MENACE AT THE WHEEL. HE DRIVES REALLY FAST, WITH HIS LEGS CROSSED, HOLDING THE WHEEL WITH ONE FINGER AND READING ONE OF THE MANY SCORES THAT LITTER HIS CAR AT THE SAME TIME.

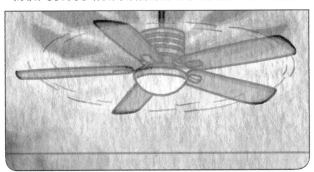

HE LIKES PULLING OVER AT TRUCK STOPS.

HE LISTENS TO PEOPLE'S MUNDANE CONVERSATIONS FOR HOURS.

HE TAKES A MENTAL PICTURE OF THEM.

HE LOVES BEING SURROUNDED BY A RICHLY VARIED TAPESTRY OF SOUND. IT'S LIKE SHELTER, LIKE PROTECTION. IT SETS HIM APART.

HE REFUSES TO BE LIKE OTHERS.

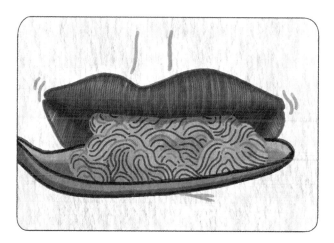

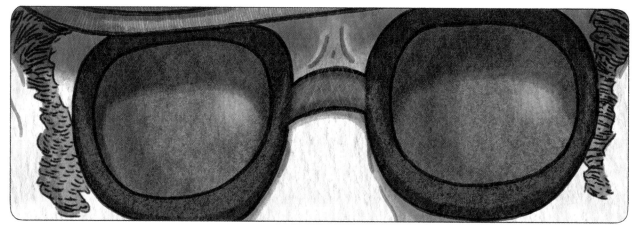

JUST LISTEN TO THE MUSIC OF THE TRAFFIC IN THE CITY... ...LINGER ON THE SIDEWALK WHERE THE NEON SIGNS ARE PRETTY HOW CAN YOU LOSE?

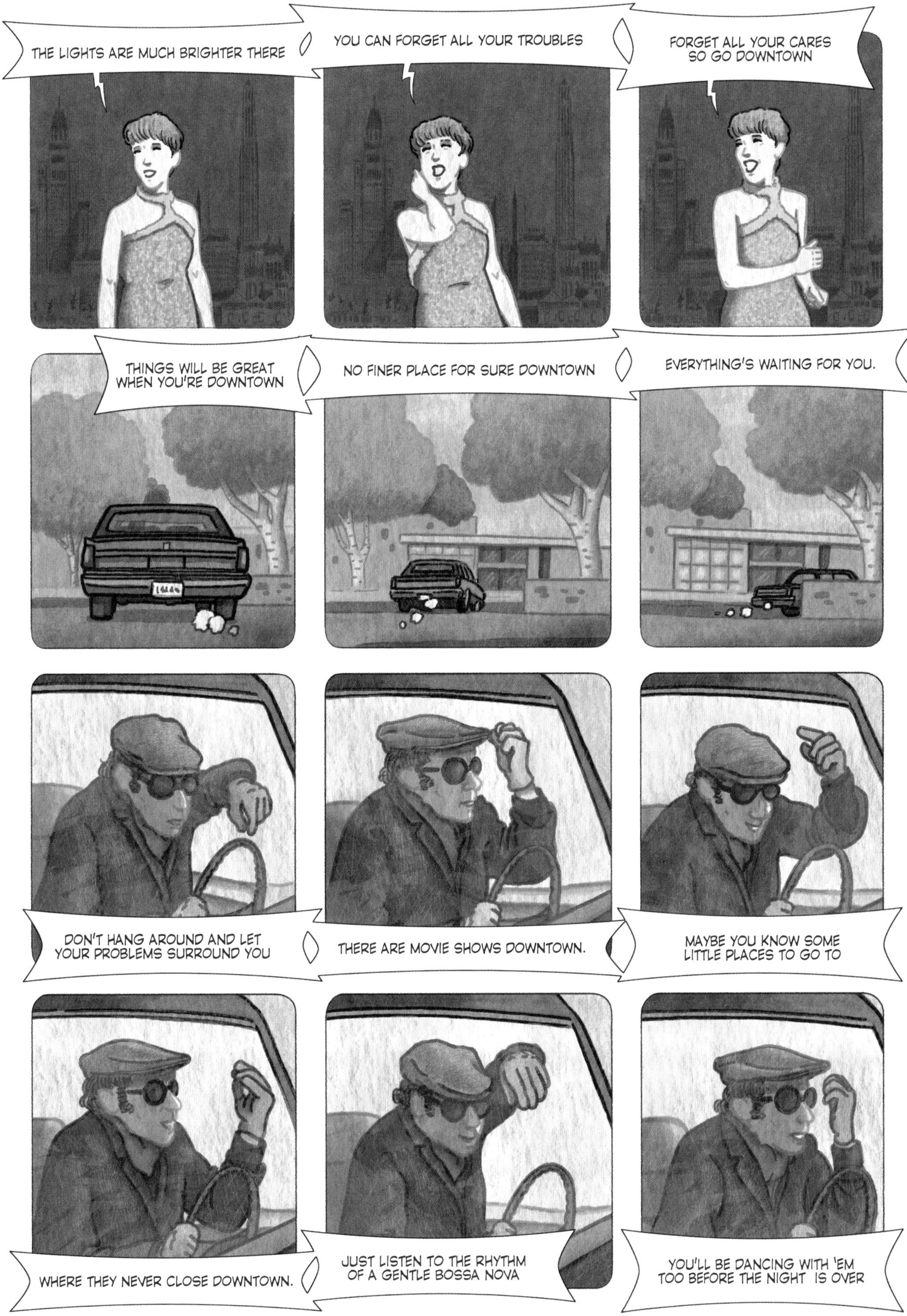
THE LIGHTS ARE MUCH BRIGHTER THERE
YOU CAN FORGET ALL YOUR TROUBLES
FORGET ALL YOUR CARES
SO GO DOWNTOWN
THINGS WILL BE GREAT
WHEN YOU'RE DOWNTOWN
NO FINER PLACE FOR SURE DOWNTOWN
EVERYTHING'S WAITING FOR YOU.
DON'T HANG AROUND AND LET
YOUR PROBLEMS SURROUND YOU
THERE ARE MOVIE SHOWS DOWNTOWN.
MAYBE YOU KNOW SOME
LITTLE PLACES TO GO TO
WHERE THEY NEVER CLOSE DOWNTOWN.
JUST LISTEN TO THE RHYTHM
OF A GENTLE BOSSA NOVA
YOU'LL BE DANCING WITH 'EM
TOO BEFORE THE NIGHT IS OVER

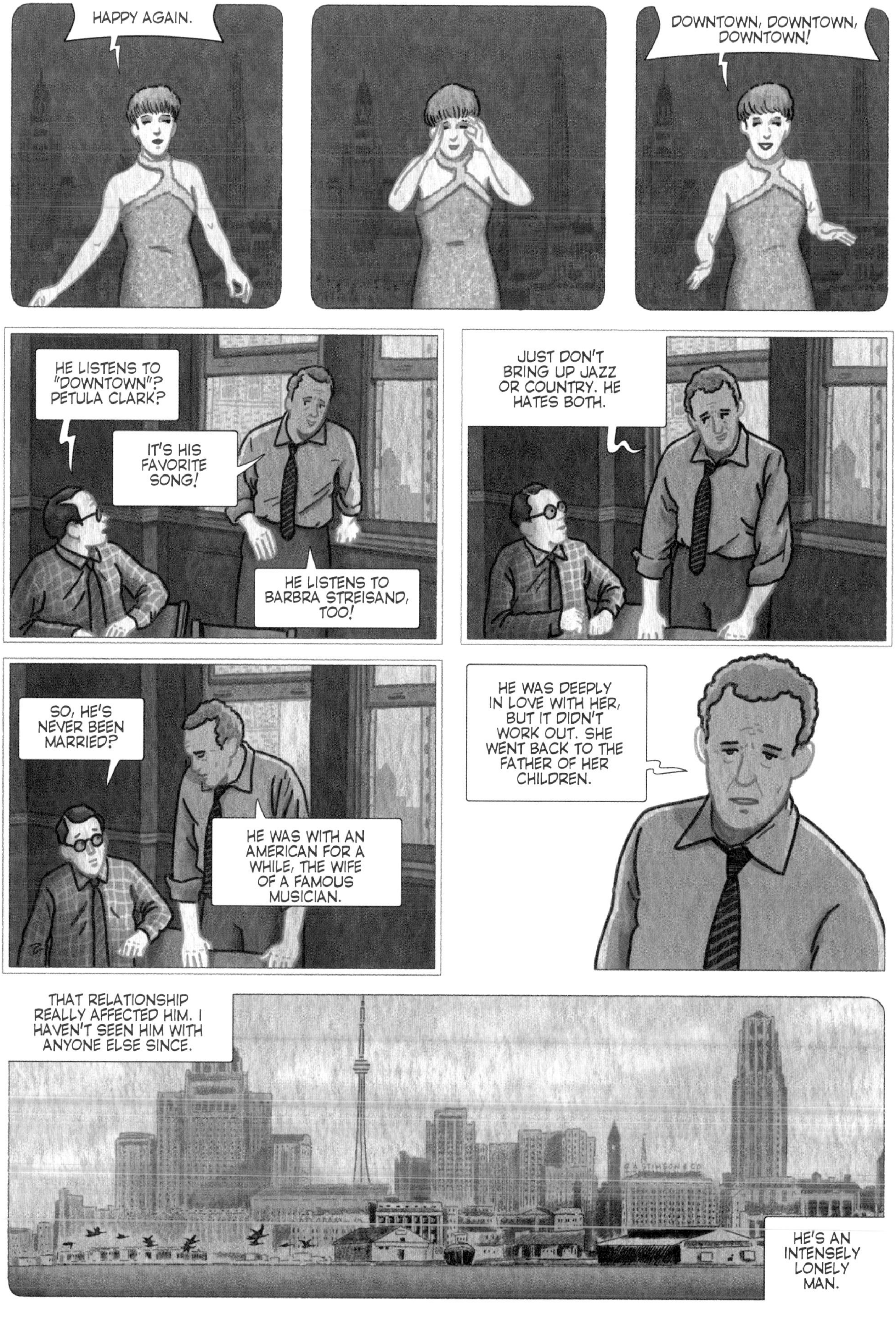
HAPPY AGAIN.
DOWNTOWN, DOWNTOWN, DOWNTOWN!
HE LISTENS TO "DOWNTOWN"? PETULA CLARK?
IT'S HIS FAVORITE SONG!
HE LISTENS TO BARBRA STREISAND, TOO!
JUST DON'T BRING UP JAZZ OR COUNTRY. HE HATES BOTH.
SO, HE'S NEVER BEEN MARRIED?
HE WAS WITH AN AMERICAN FOR A WHILE, THE WIFE OF A FAMOUS MUSICIAN.
HE WAS DEEPLY IN LOVE WITH HER, BUT IT DIDN'T WORK OUT. SHE WENT BACK TO THE FATHER OF HER CHILDREN.
THAT RELATIONSHIP REALLY AFFECTED HIM. I HAVEN'T SEEN HIM WITH ANYONE ELSE SINCE.
HE'S AN INTENSELY LONELY MAN.

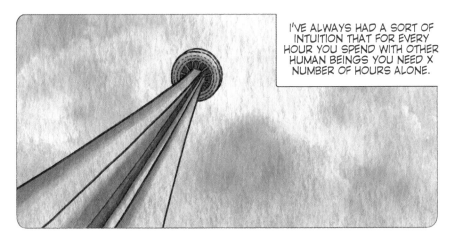

I'VE ALWAYS HAD A SORT OF INTUITION THAT FOR EVERY HOUR YOU SPEND WITH OTHER HUMAN BEINGS YOU NEED X NUMBER OF HOURS ALONE.

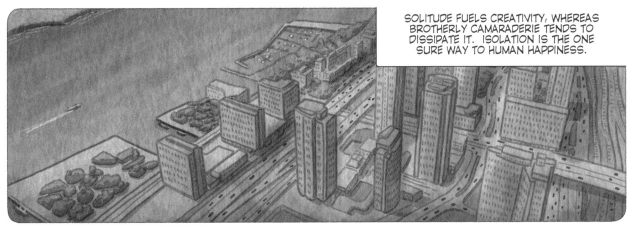

SOLITUDE FUELS CREATIVITY, WHEREAS BROTHERLY CAMARADERIE TENDS TO DISSIPATE IT. ISOLATION IS THE ONE SURE WAY TO HUMAN HAPPINESS.

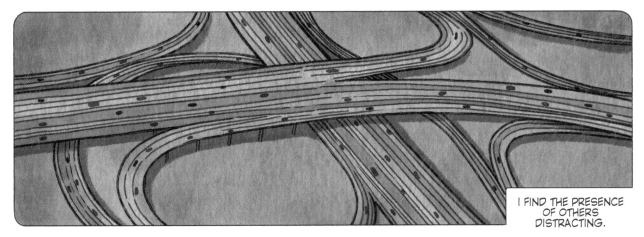

I FIND THE PRESENCE OF OTHERS DISTRACTING.

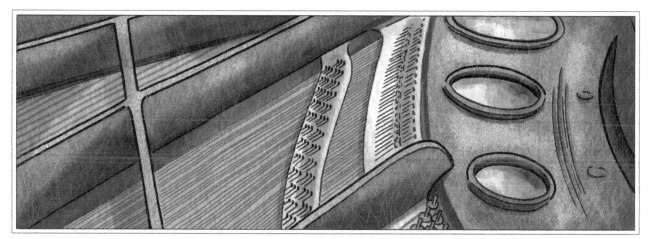

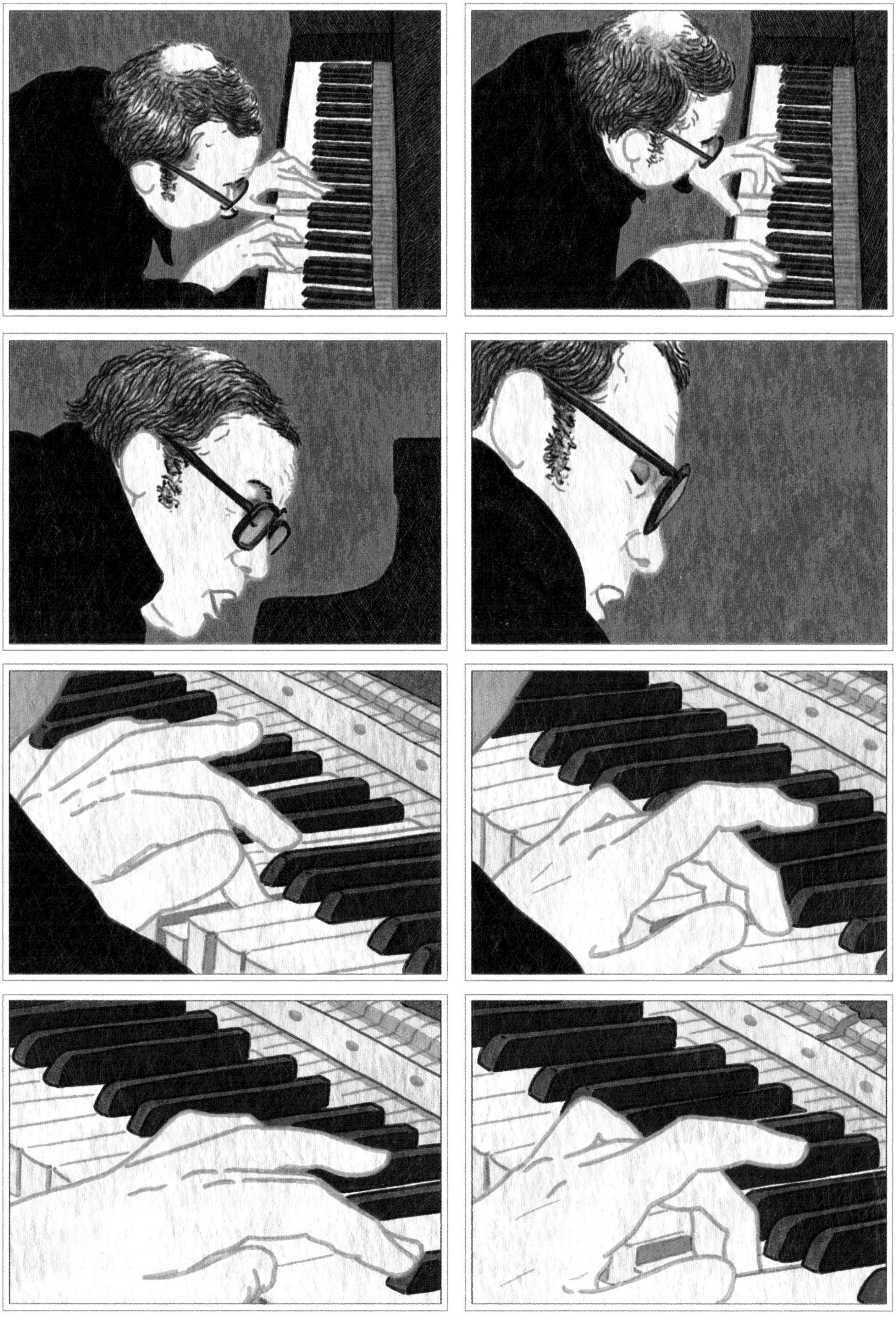

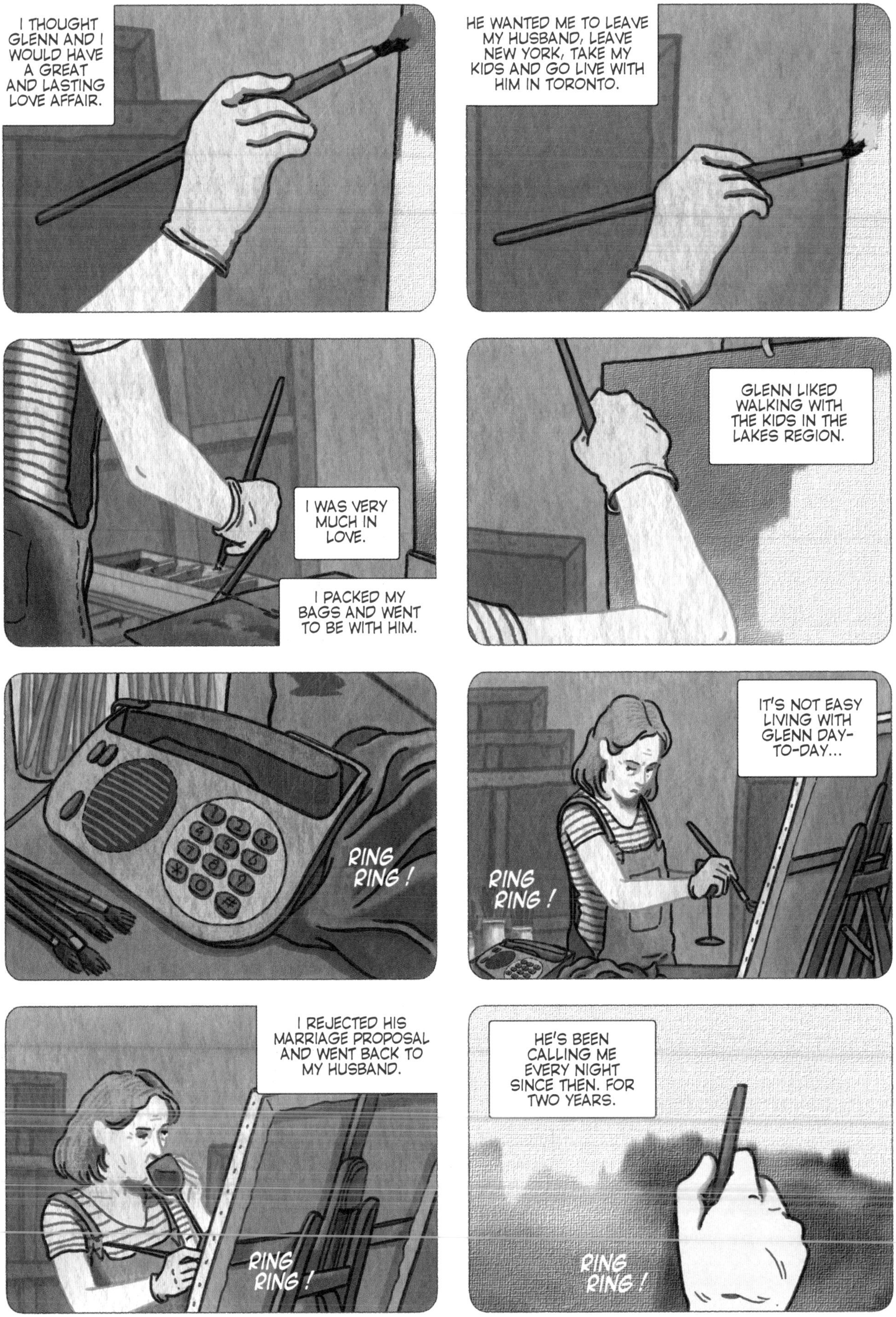
I THOUGHT GLENN AND I WOULD HAVE A GREAT AND LASTING LOVE AFFAIR.
HE WANTED ME TO LEAVE MY HUSBAND, LEAVE NEW YORK, TAKE MY KIDS AND GO LIVE WITH HIM IN TORONTO.
I WAS VERY MUCH IN LOVE.
I PACKED MY BAGS AND WENT TO BE WITH HIM.
GLENN LIKED WALKING WITH THE KIDS IN THE LAKES REGION.
RING RING !
IT'S NOT EASY LIVING WITH GLENN DAY-TO-DAY...
RING RING !
I REJECTED HIS MARRIAGE PROPOSAL AND WENT BACK TO MY HUSBAND.
RING RING !
HE'S BEEN CALLING ME EVERY NIGHT SINCE THEN. FOR TWO YEARS.
RING RING !

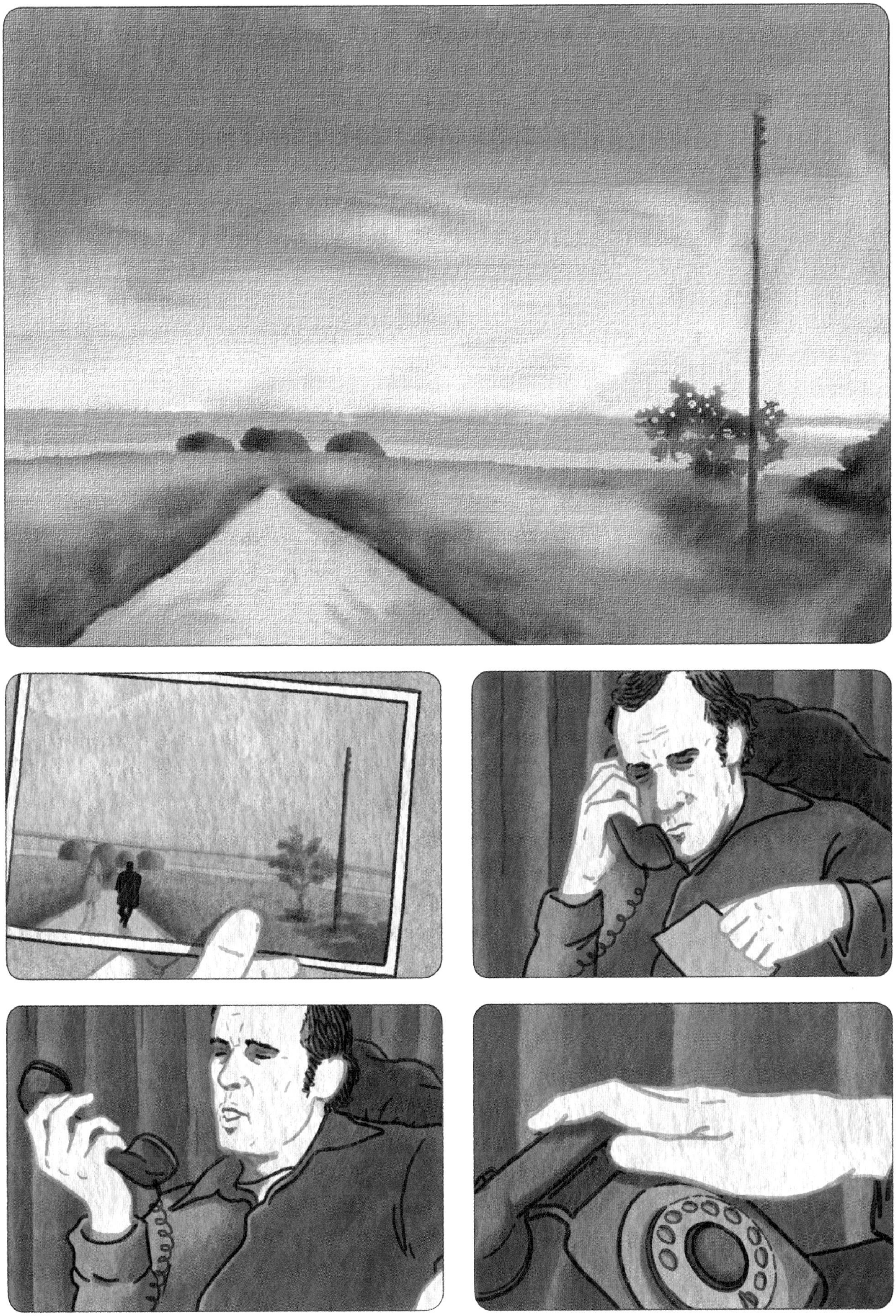

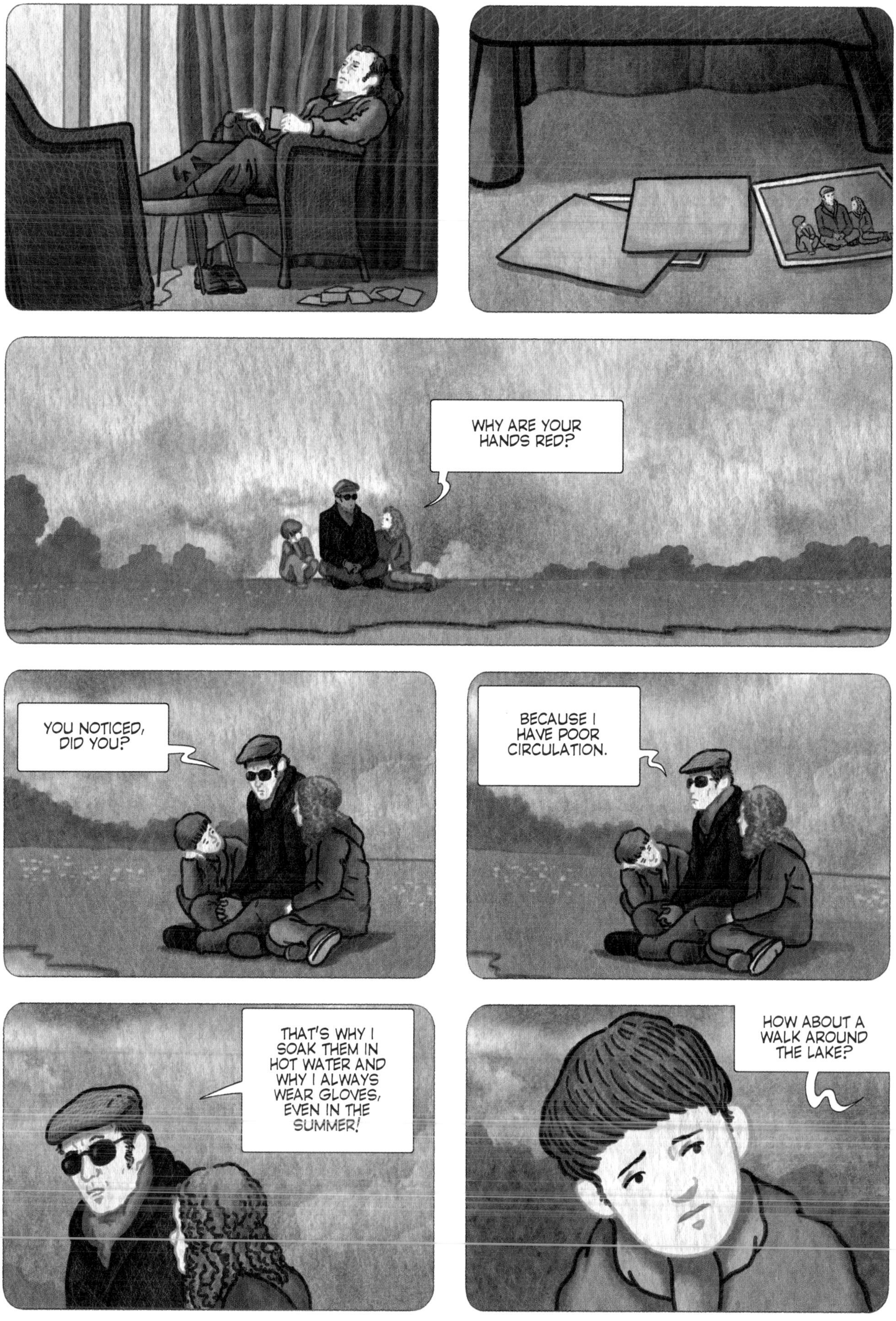
WHY ARE YOUR HANDS RED?
YOU NOTICED, DID YOU?
BECAUSE I HAVE POOR CIRCULATION.
THAT'S WHY I SOAK THEM IN HOT WATER AND WHY I ALWAYS WEAR GLOVES, EVEN IN THE SUMMER!
HOW ABOUT A WALK AROUND THE LAKE?

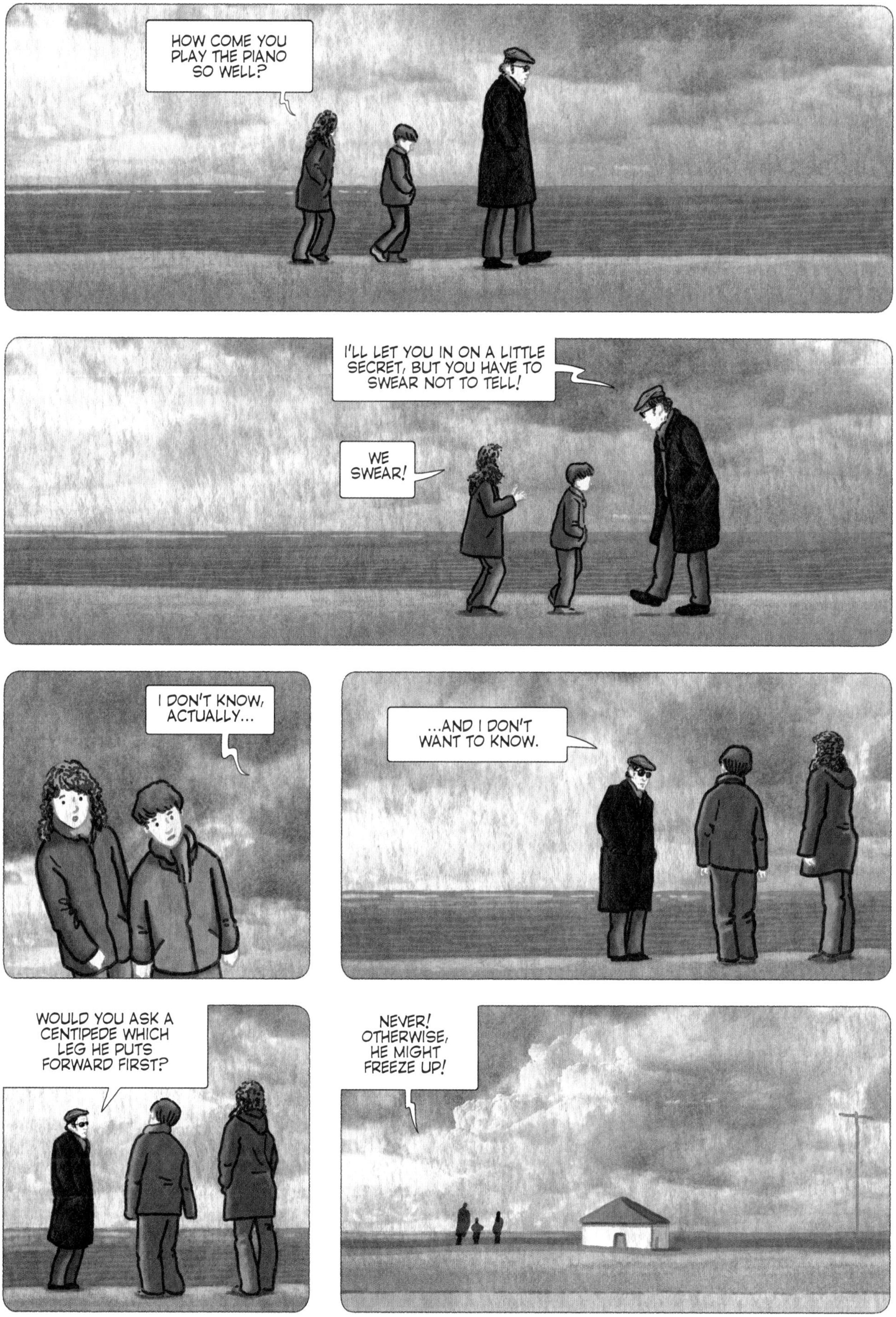
HOW COME YOU PLAY THE PIANO SO WELL?
I'LL LET YOU IN ON A LITTLE SECRET, BUT YOU HAVE TO SWEAR NOT TO TELL!
WE SWEAR!
I DON'T KNOW, ACTUALLY...
...AND I DON'T WANT TO KNOW.
WOULD YOU ASK A CENTIPEDE WHICH LEG HE PUTS FORWARD FIRST?
NEVER! OTHERWISE, HE MIGHT FREEZE UP!

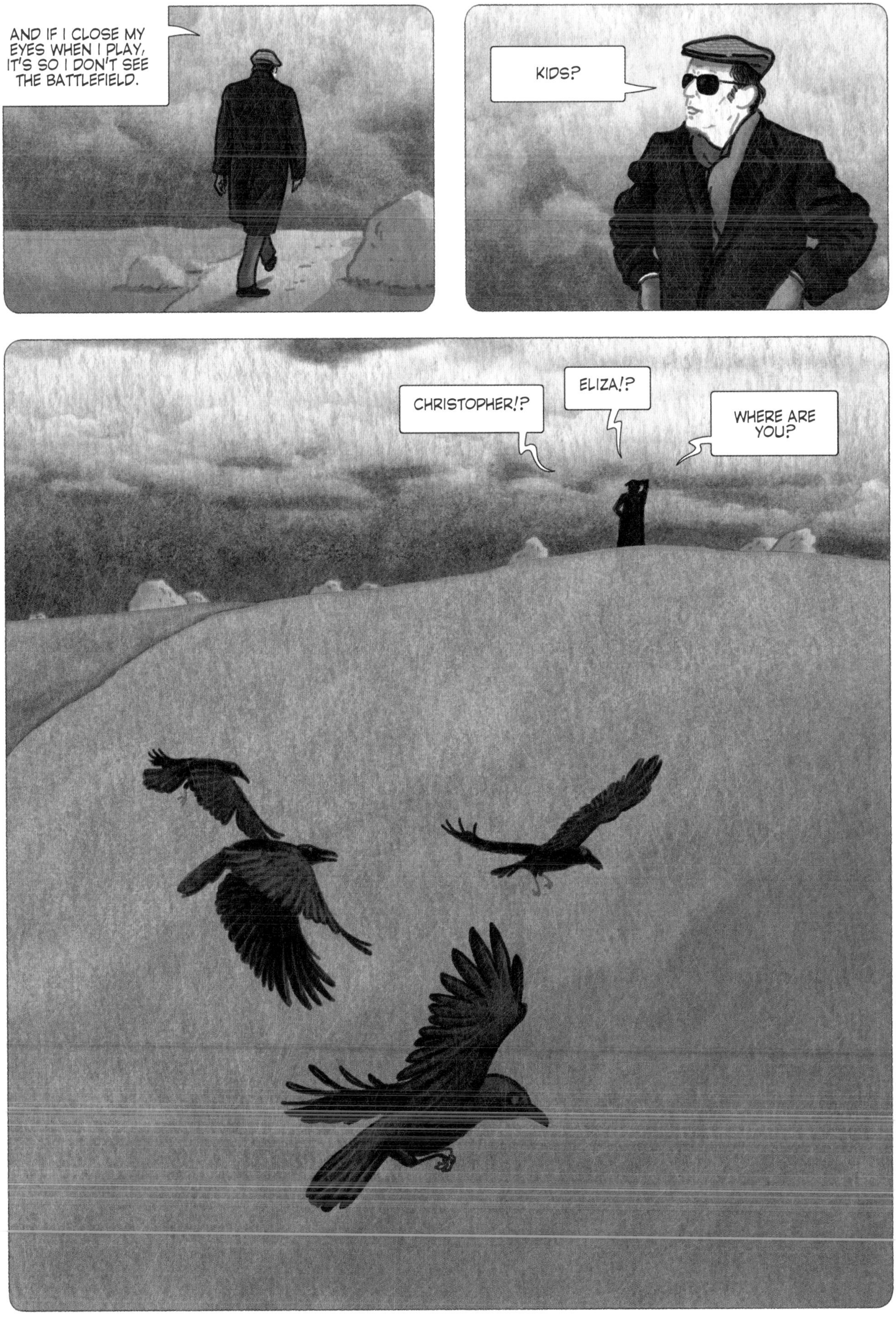
AND IF I CLOSE MY EYES WHEN I PLAY, IT'S SO I DON'T SEE THE BATTLEFIELD.
KIDS?
CHRISTOPHER!?
ELIZA!?
WHERE ARE YOU?

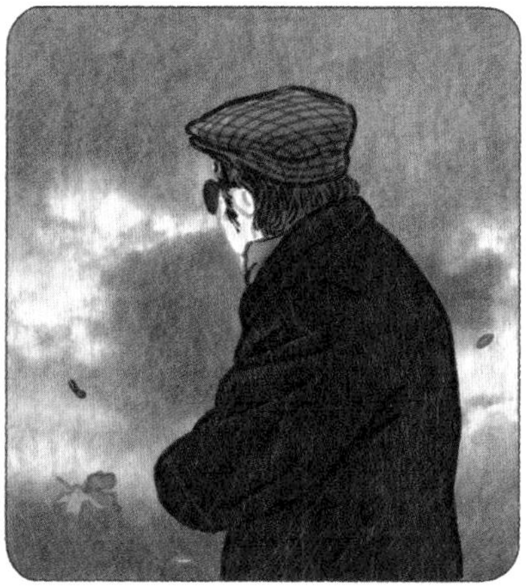

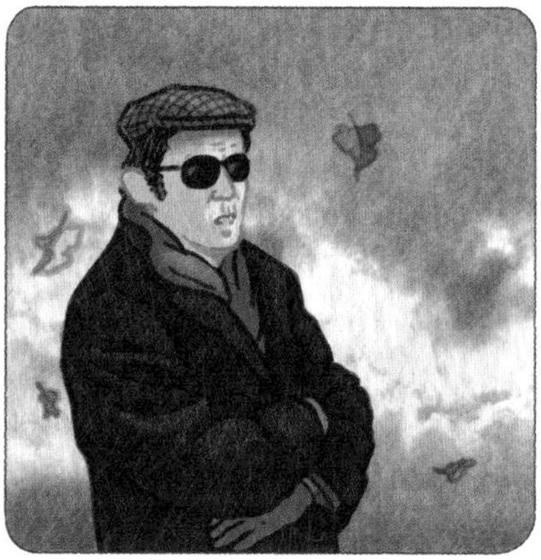

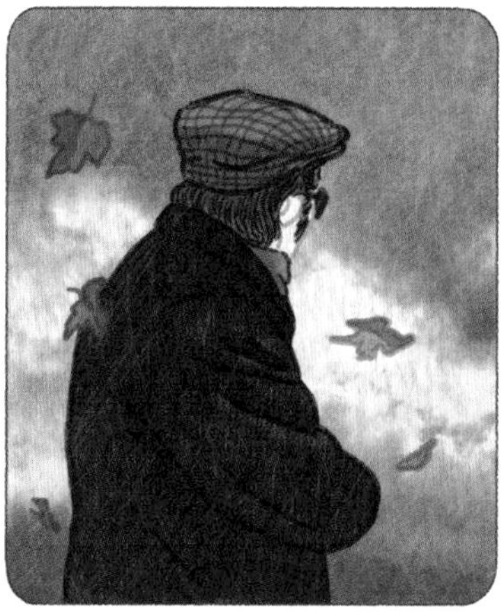

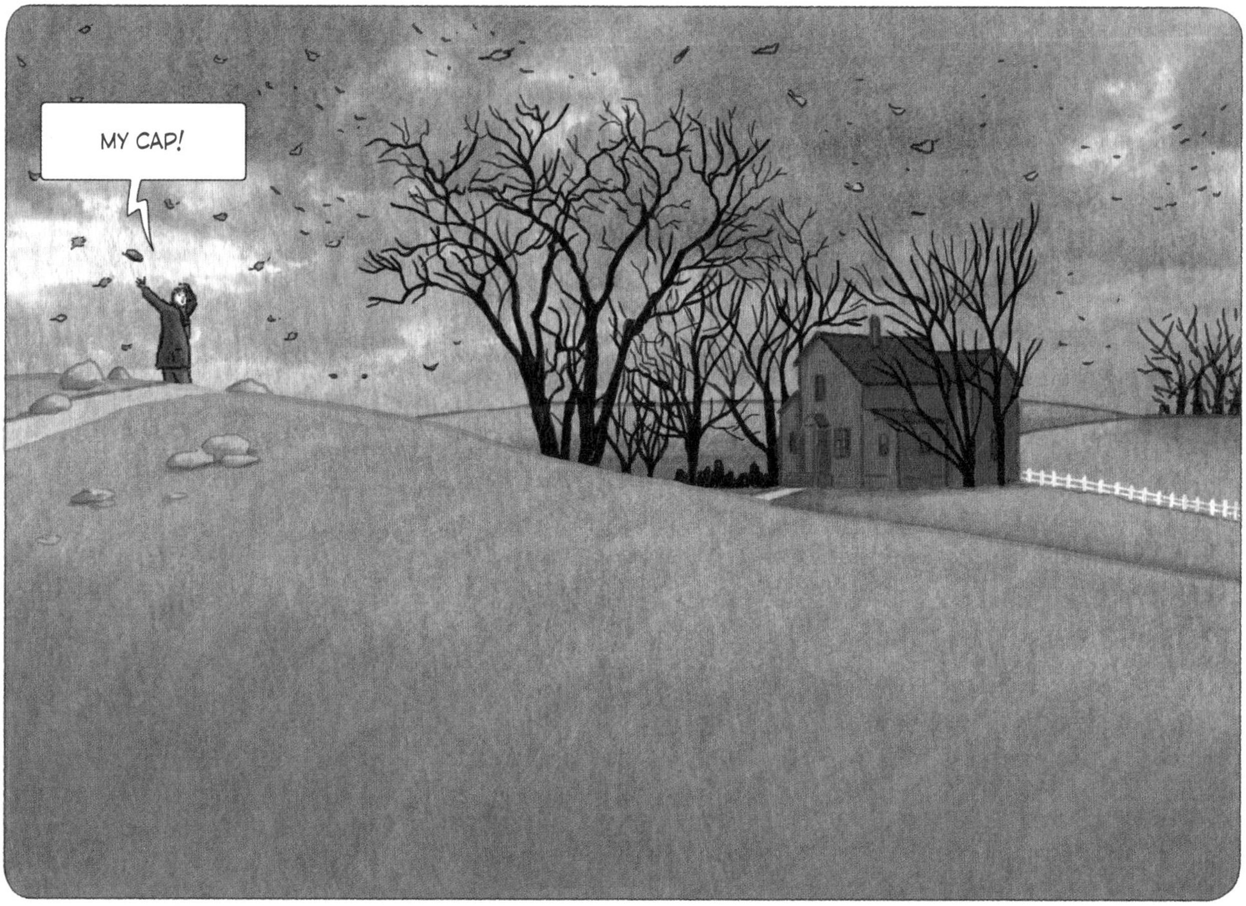
MY CAP!

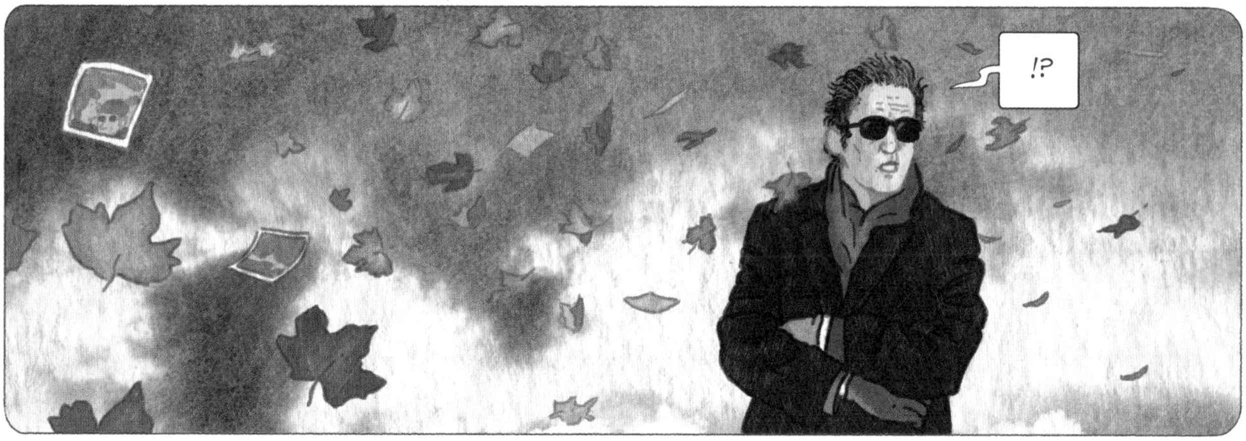
!?

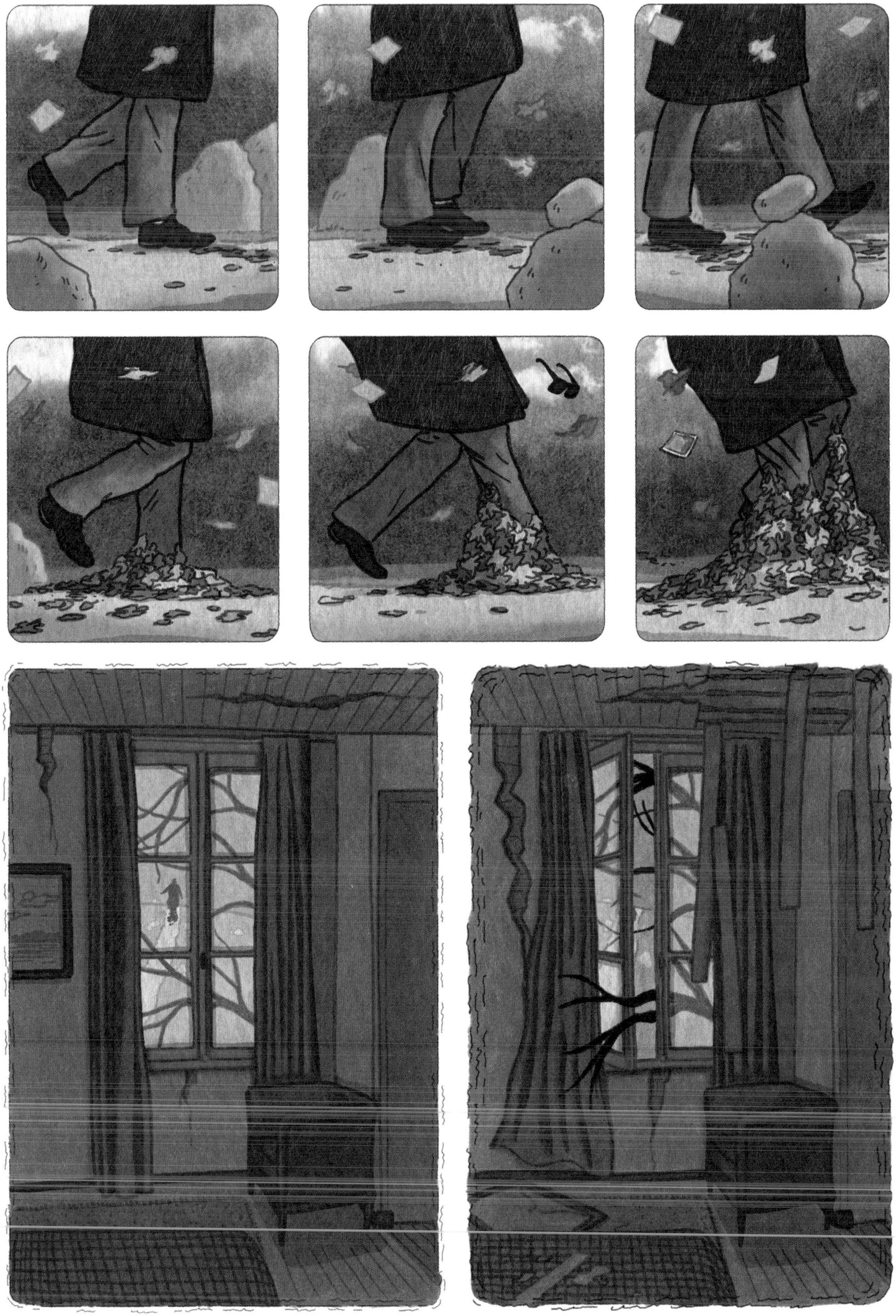

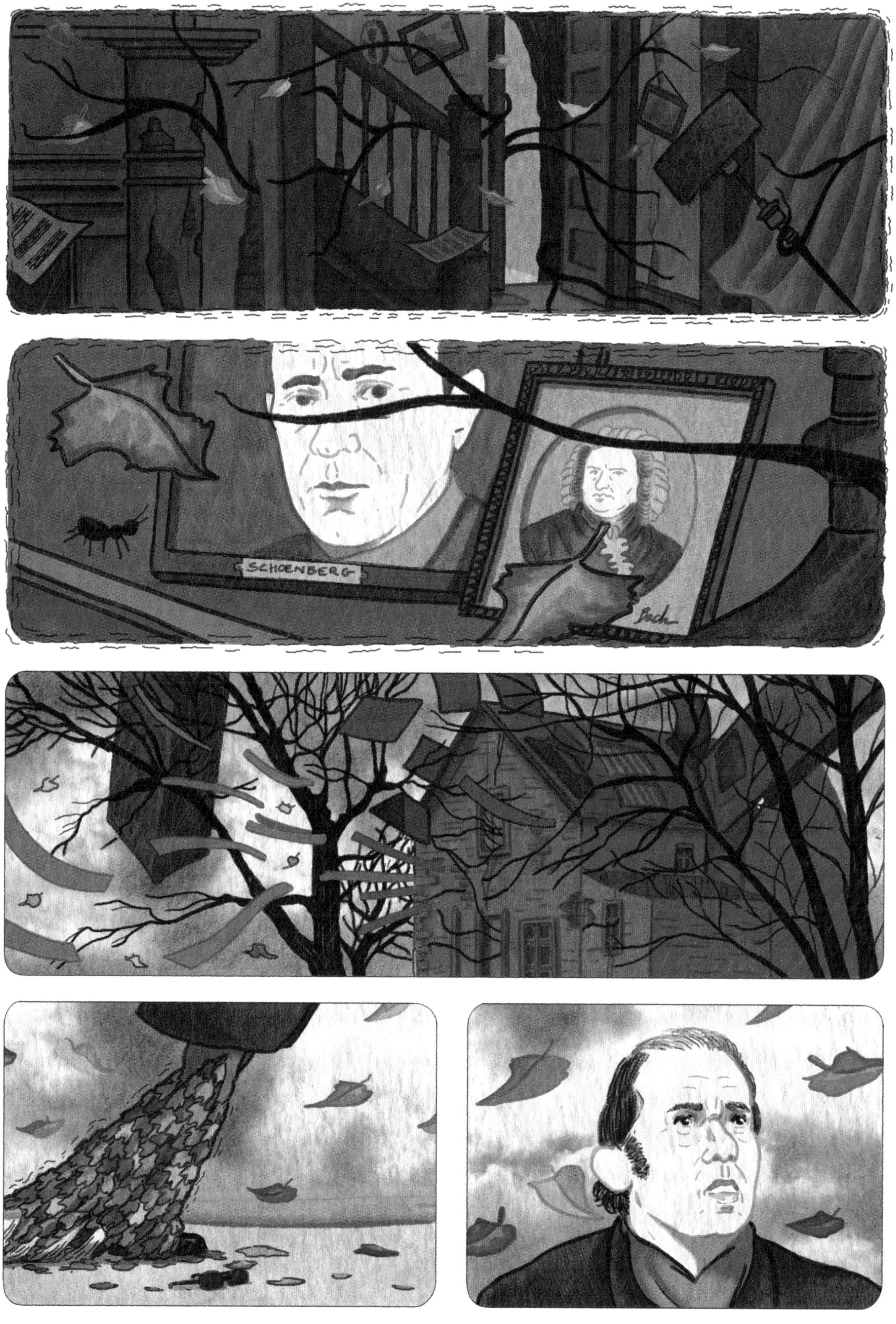
SCHOENBERG
Bach

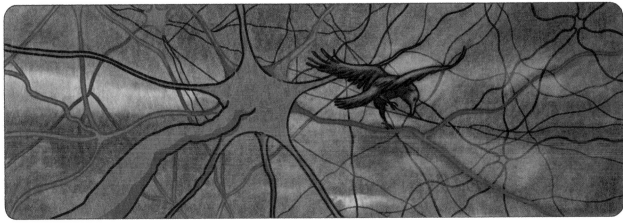

AAARRH...
MY HEAD'S
ABOUT TO
EXPLODE!

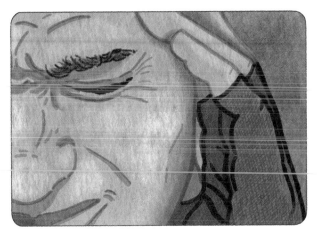

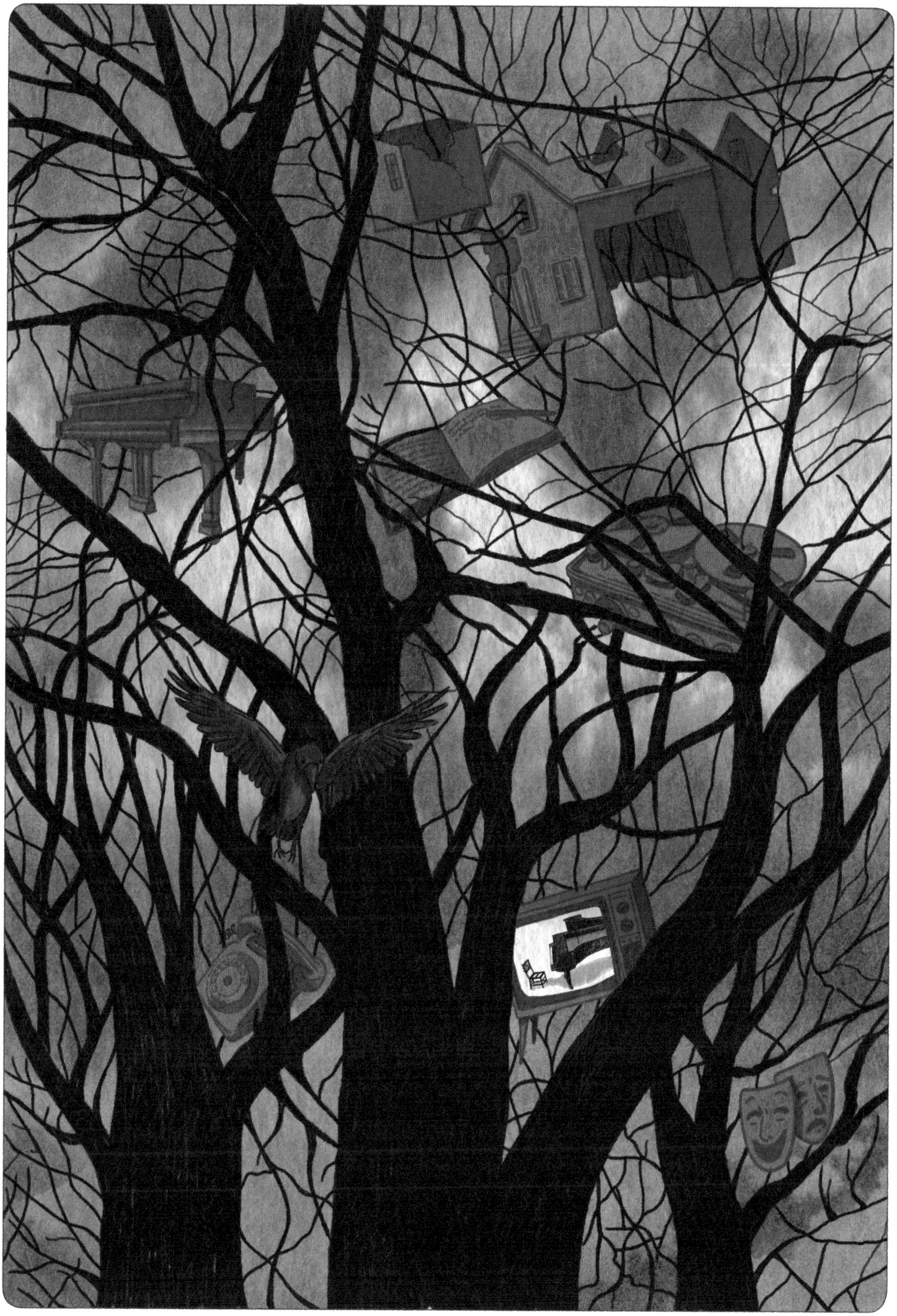

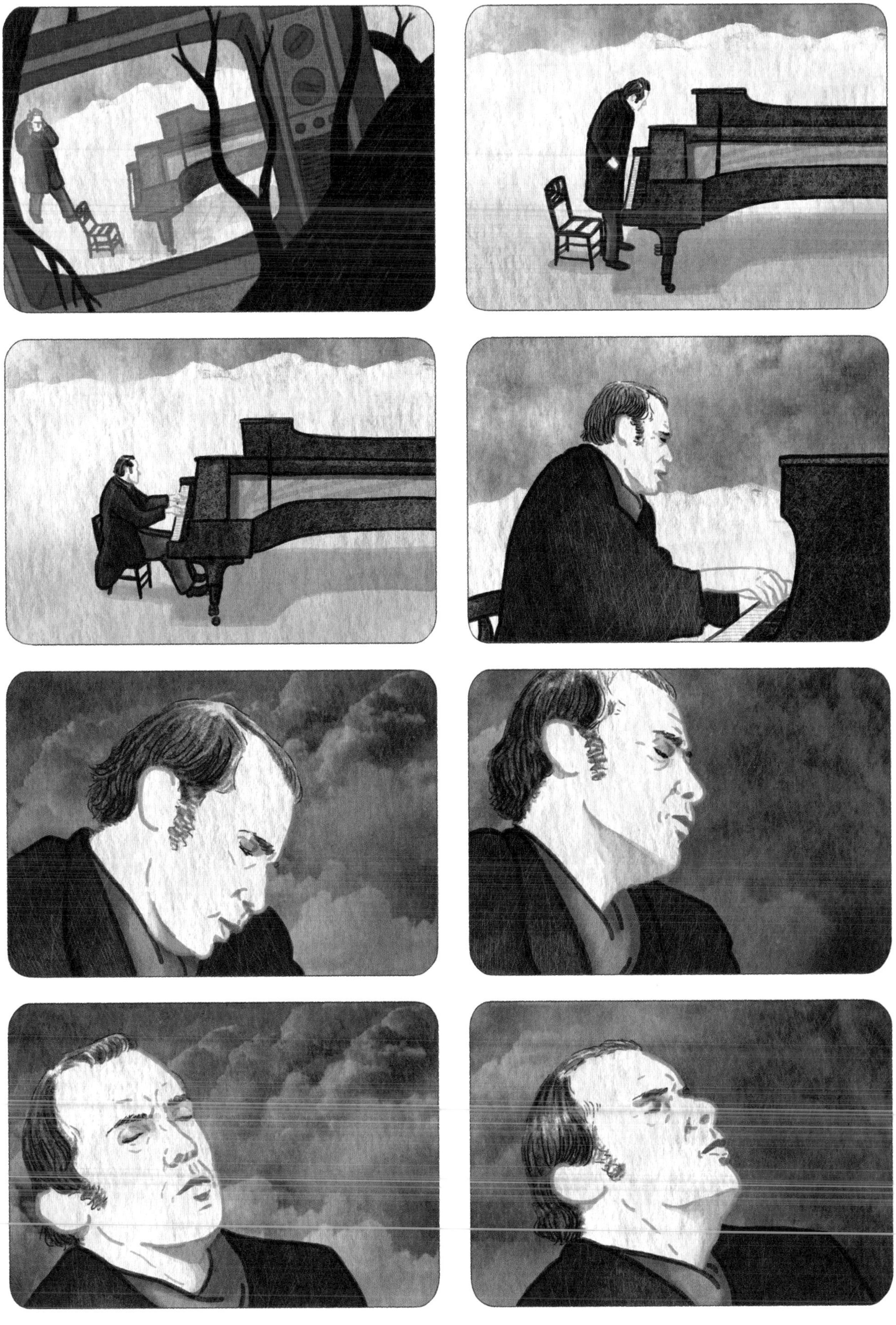

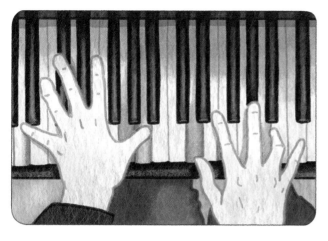
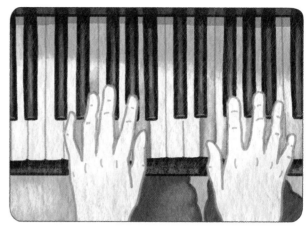
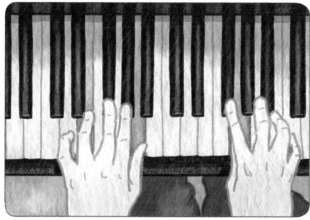
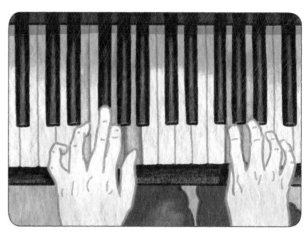
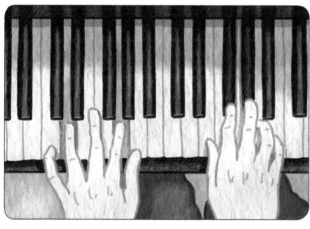
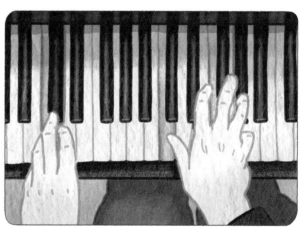
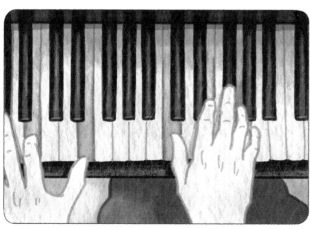

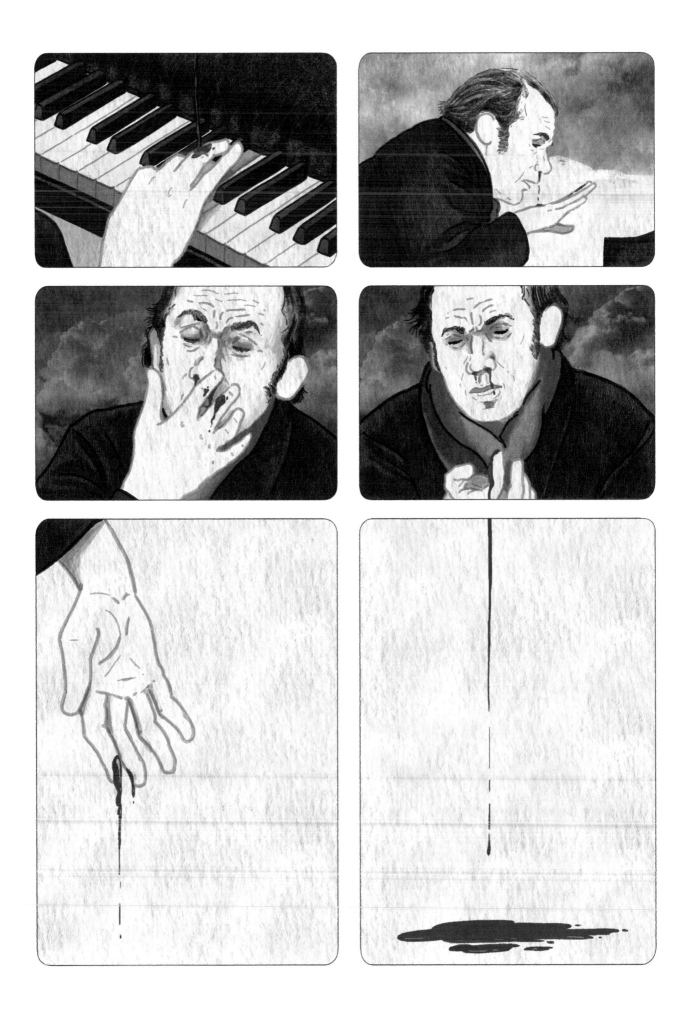

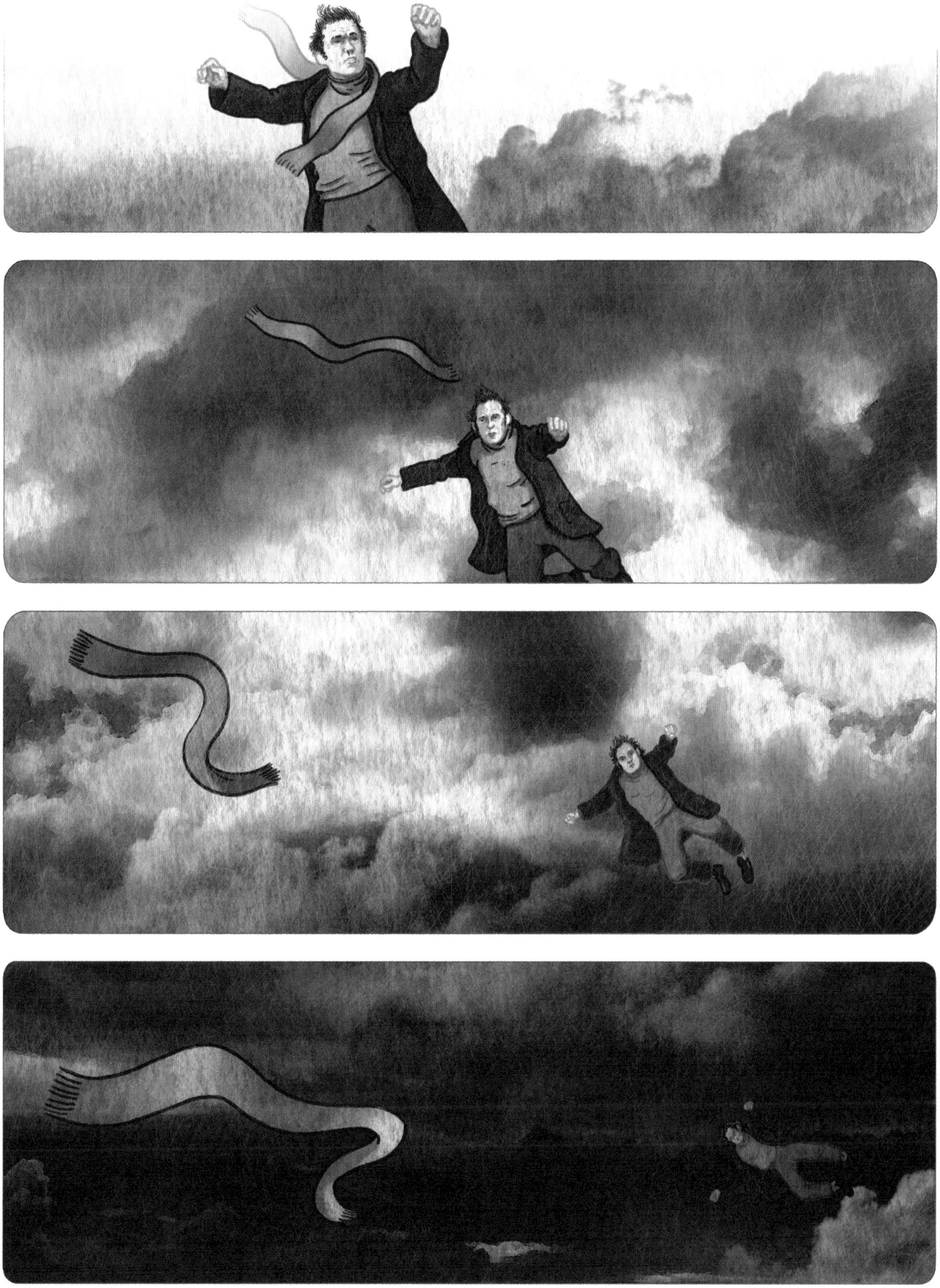

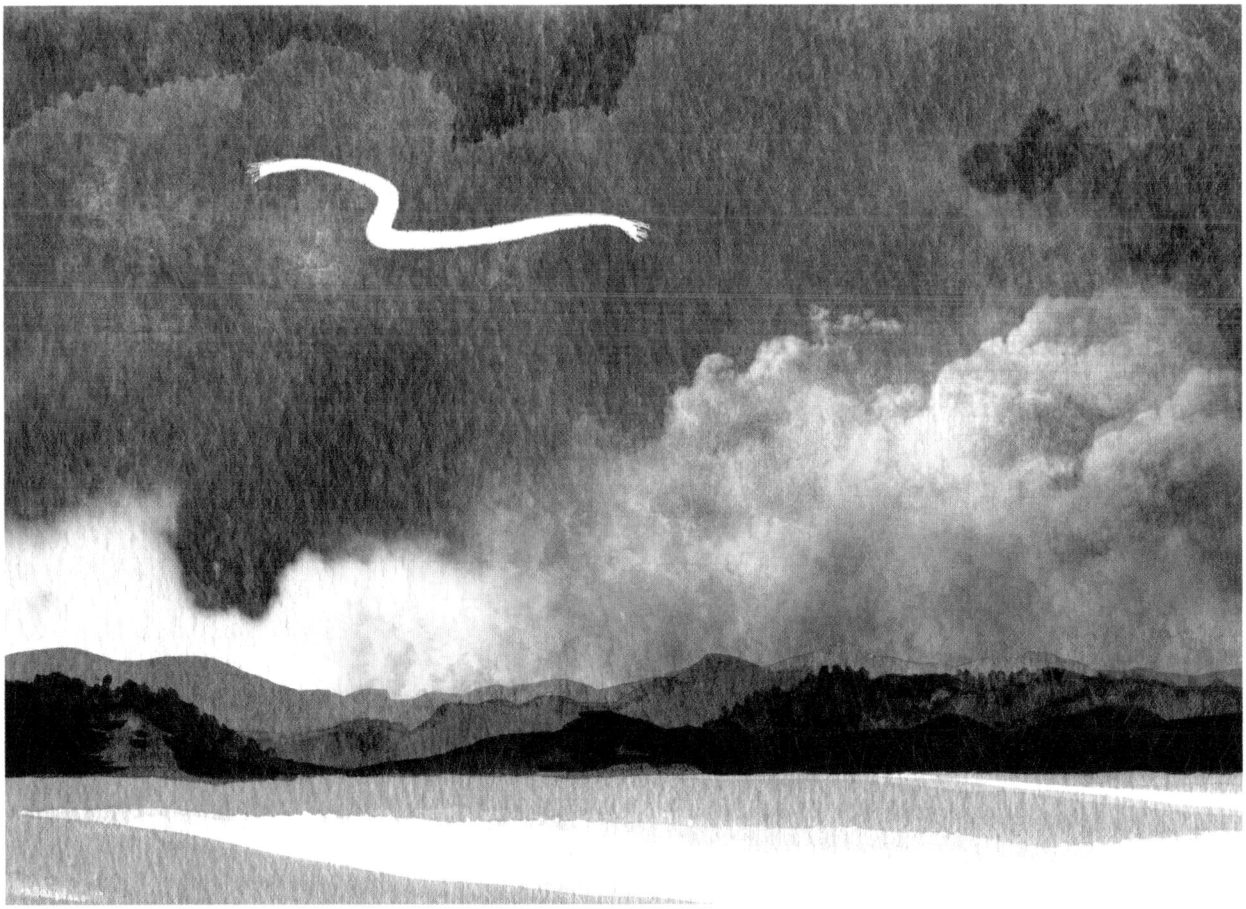

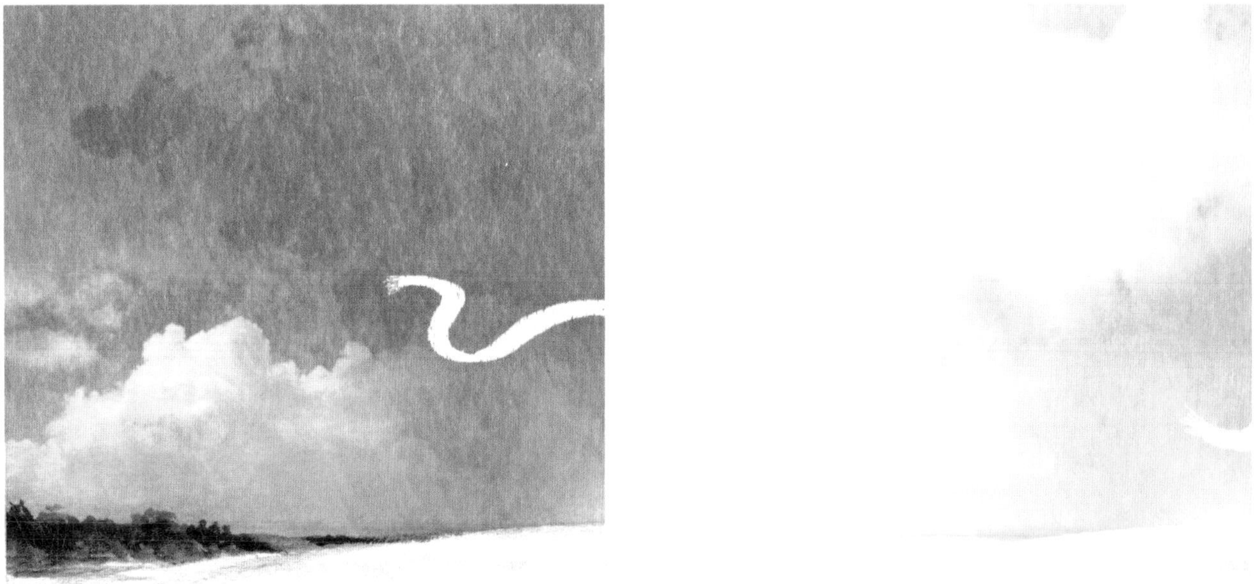

«I always assumed everybody shared my love
for overcast skies. It came as a shock to find
out that some people prefer sunshine.»

Glenn Gould

Glenn Gould was pronounced dead at 11:00 a.m. on October 4, 1982.

APPENDICES

The author listened to the following pieces while working on this book:

Glenn Gould, Bach: Goldberg Variations, BWV 988. 1955 and 1981 versions.
Glenn Gould, Bach: The Well Tempered Clavier, books 1 and 2
Glenn Gould, Bach: Partitas 1, 2, 5 and 6; Italian Concerto
Glenn Gould, Bach: Cantata BWV 54 «Widerstehe och der Sünde»
Glenn Gould, Schoenberg: Three pieces for piano, Op. 11: II. Mässig
Glenn Gould, Brahms: 10 Intermezzi for piano
Glenn Gould, Silver Jubilee Album: So You Want to Write a Fugue? For Four Voices and String Quartet
Leonard Bernstein, Glenn Gould, Brahms: Concerto for piano no. 1

SELECTED ANNOTATED DISCOGRAPHY OF GLENN GOULD:
(ALL ALBUMS AVAILABLE AT SONY)

Johann Sebastian Bach (1685-1750)
Goldberg Variations, BWV 988
1955 Recording

The Birth of a Legend: Gould's first recording for Columbia, playing Bach as if someone had parted the curtains and thrown open the windows in a dark, stuffy room. The critics were ecstatic; the release broke all records and is still considered one of the ten most significant and successful classical recordings of all time.

LP release date: March 1st, 1956. Total running time: 38:23; Recorded at Columbia 30th Street Studio, New York, NY. USA, June 10, and 14-16, 1955; produced by Howard H. Scott.

Johann Sebastian Bach
Italian Concerto in F Major, BWV 971
Partita No. 1 in B-flat Major, BWV 825
Partita No. 2 in C minor, BWV 826

Gould's tenth recording for Columbia was accompanied by a two-part film portrait entitled Off the Record / On the Record – a sure indication of the star status he had by now attained. He was considered "music's most successful hipster" and "the object of a sort of James Dean cult" – perhaps classical music's first pop star. For the time being he still played along with the media hype …

LP release date: June 6, 1960. Total running time: 40:05; Recorded at Columbia 30th Street Studio, New York, NY. USA, June 22-26, 1959 (tracks 1-3); May 1st and 8 and September 22, 1959 (tracks 4-9); June 22-23, 1959 (tracks 10-15); produced by Howard H. Scott.

Johann Sebastian Bach
The Well-Tempered Clavier, Book I, BWV 846-853,
Preludes and Fugues 1-8

Gould launched his complete recording of the "Pianists' Old Testament" on 10 January 1962. It would eventually occupy him for more than nine years. "We recorded ten or even fifteen different versions of some of the preludes and fugues. Nearly every one was perfect, note for note, yet still completely different. It was an amazing experience to witness how each version became something completely new in Gould's hands."

LP release date: January 14, 1963. Total running time: 37:18; Recorded at Columbia 30th Street Studio, New York, NY. USA, June 7 and September 21, 1962 (tracks 1-2); June 7, 1962 (tracks 3-4); June 7 and September 20, 1962 (track 5-6); September 21, 1962 (tracks 7-8); September 20, 1962 (tracks 9-10 and 13-16); June 14, 1962 (track 11-12); produced by Paul Myers (tracks 1-2, 5-10, and 13-16) and Joseph Scianni (tracks 3-4 and 11-12).

Johann Sebastian Bach
Two and Three Part Inventions and Sinfonias,
BWV 772-801

Gould's first release after becoming a "concert drop-out." For years he had put his Steinway CD 318 through myriad "operations" in order "to try to design an instrument […] which can add to the undeniable resource of the modern piano something of the clarity and tactile facility of the harpsichord." The result was "a slight nervous tic in the middle register which in the slower passages can be heard emitting a sort of hiccup." Indeed it can!

LP release date: August 10, 1964. Total running time: 50:02; Recorded at Columbia 30th Street Studio, New York, NY. USA, March 18-19, 1964; produced by Paul Myers.

Ludwig van Beethoven (1770-1827)
Concerto No. 5 in E-Flat Major for Piano and Orchestra,
Op. 73, "Emperor"

Gould's sole collaboration with Leopold Stokowski, to whom he devoted a large radio portrait for the CBC in 1971. This musical "summit meeting" between the thirty-four-year-old Canadian and a maestro nearly half a century his senior caused yet another dream to come true: Gould's first encounter with his revered Barbra Streisand, who was recording her latest album next door …

LP release date: May 16, 1966. Total running time: 42:34; Recorded at Manhattan Center, New York, NY. USA, March 1st and 4, 1966; produced by Andrew Kazdin; Leopold Stokowski conductor; Glenn Gould piano; America Symphony Orchestra.

Johann Sebastian Bach
Three Keyboard Concertos, BWV 1054, 1056 & 1058
(Vol. I)

Ten years after the release of D-minor Concerto under Leonard Bernstein, Gould now issued Volume 1 of the Bach concertos under Vladimir Golschmann. "I want to tell you how much I enjoyed the recording. Please keep in mind always that if no other conductor will go into the studio with you, I will go!"

LP release date: July 17, 1967. Total running time: 40:10; Recorded at Columbia 30th Street Studio, New York, NY. USA, May 2, 1967 (tracks 1-3); May 1st, 1958 (tracks 4-6) and May 4, 1967 (tracks 7-9); produced by Andrew Kazdin (tracks 1-3 and 7-9) and Howard H. Scott (tracks 4-6); Vladimir Golschmann conductor; Glenn Gould piano; Columbia Symphony Orchestra.

Ludwig van Beethoven
Symphony No. 5 in C Minor, Op. 67
(Transcribed for Piano by Franz Liszt)

Joke, satire, irony, deeper significance: the back cover of Gould's gripping recording contained four imaginary reviews by an English critic (Sir Humphrey Price-Davies), a Munich musicologist (Dr. Karlheinz Heinkel), an American psychiatrist (Prof. S. F. Lemming), and the American correspondent to the Journal of the All-Union Musical Workers of Budapest. All were written by Gould himself…

LP release date: April 3, 1968. Total running time: 38:58; Recorded at Columbia 30th Street Studio, New York, NY. USA, November 22 and December 5, 7, 28-29, 1967; and January 8, 1968; produced by Andrew Kazdin.

Ludwig van Beethoven
Beethoven Sonatas Nos. 8, 14 & 23

Yet another scandal: Gould played the F-minor Piano Sonata, op. 57, at such a tortuously slow tempo that it seemed to fall into unrelated bits. "There is about the Appassionata – an egoistic pomposity, a defiant 'let's just see if I can't get away with using that once more' attitude—that on my own private Beethoven poll places this sonata somewhere between the King Stephen Overture and the Wellington's Victory Symphony."

LP release date: February 24, 1970. Total running time: 64:37; Recorded at Columbia 30th Street Studio, New York, NY, USA, April 18-19, 1966 (tracks 1-3); May 15, 1967 (tracks 4-6); and October 18, 1967 (tracks 7-9); produced by Andrew Kazdin.

William Byrd (1543-1623)
Orlando Gibbons (1583-1625)
A Consort of Musicke Bye William Byrde and Orlando Gibbons

"Orlando Gibbons is my favorite composer—always has been. I can't think of anybody who represents the end of an era better than Orlando Gibbons does." This profession of faith in the great English virginalist is more than an act of defiance: it harks back to Gould's early childhood puritanical experience.

LP release date: September 29, 1971. Total running time: 42:44; Recorded at Columbia 30th Street Studio, New York, NY, USA, June 14-15, 1967 (track 1); July 30 - August 1st, 1968 (tracks 2, 3, and 6); May 25-26, 1967 (tracks 5 and 7); and at Eaton's Auditorium, Toronto, Canada, April 18, 1971 (tracks 4 and 8); produced by Andrew Kazdin.

Wolfgang Amadeus Mozart 1756-1791
Piano Sonatas, Vol. 3

«The Sonata [No. 12] K. 332 was the first I began to study, I think, and I simply couldn't understand how my teachers, and other presumably sane adults of my acquaintance, could count this piece among the great musical treasures of Western man.»

LP release date: January 19, 1972. Total running time: 49:18; Recorded at Columbia 30th Street Studio, New York, NY, USA, January 30-31 and February 13, 1969 (tracks 1-3); August 11, 1970 (track 4-6); September 28-29 and December 16, 1965; May 16-17, 1966 (tracks 7-9); and August 12, 1965; May 16-17, 1966; January 22-23 and August 10, 1970 (tracks 10-12); produced by Andrew Kazdin.

Johann Sebastian Bach
The French Suites, Vol. II
and Overture in the French Style

Back to Bach, the composer of Gould's two new releases of 1974. The same year was notable for other projects: Gould recorded a Schoenberg set and the first episode of a television series Music in Our Time, both for the CBC, and he joined the French director Bruno Monsaingeon to create the four-part Chemins de la Musique (Music Paths) for French radio-TV. The same year witnessed Gould's only Grammy award—for his sleeve notes to the three Hindemith sonatas.

LP release date: May 4, 1974. Total running time: 46:35; Recorded at Eaton's Auditorium, Toronto, February 27 and May 23, 1971 (tracks 1-7); March 13 and May 23, 1971 (tracks 8-15); January, 10, 11, 24 and 31, 1971; February 27, 1971; and November 5, 1973 (tracks 16-26); produced by Andrew Kazdin.

Jean Sibelius (1865-1957)
Three Sonatinas for Piano, Op. 67
«Kyllikki» - Three Lyric Pieces for Piano, Op. 41

An experimental recording in which Gould looped several microphones at various distances from the piano. It is also a declaration of his love for the great Finnish composer, whom he had met in Berlin in the late 1950s at a performance of Sibelius's Fifth under Herbert von Karajan— "one of the truly indelible musical-dramatic experiences of my life."

LP release date: November 4, 1977. Total running time: 37:53; Recorded at Eaton's Auditorium, Canada, December 18-19, 1976 (tracks 1-3 and 7-8); and March 28-29, 1977 (tracks 4-6 and 9-11); produced by Andrew Kazdin.

Johann Sebastian Bach
Preludes, Fughettas and Fugues

In December 1979 Gould's longstanding producer Andrew Kazdin left Columbia. Gould produced his final recordings himself, beginning with this Bach album in January and February 1980. The cover shows Gould in the corner of a bare dilapidated room – more like the snapshot of a vagrant than the portrait of a pianistic genius. A doomsday scenario…

LP release date: September 1st, 1980. Total running time: 40:46; Recorded at Eaton's Auditorium, Toronto, Canada, October 10-11, 1979 (tracks 1-11); January 10-11 and February 2, 1980 (tracks 12-17); and January 20 and February 2, 1980 (tracks 18-24); produced by Glenn Gould and Andrew Kazdin..

The Glenn Gould Silver Jubilee Album

This LP is the first "grab bag" of unreleased recordings lying in Columbia's boxes, partly for lack of suitable companions, partly as fragments of unfinished projects. The second LP staged Gould's alleged "hysteric return" to the concert hall as part of a radio fantasy—aboard an oil rig in the Beaufort Sea, far away in the Canadian north!

LP release date: November 3, 1980.
Album 1- Total running time: 45:31; Recorded at Columbia 30th Street Studio, New York, NY, USA, January 30, 1968 (tracks 1 and 3-6); February 6, 1968 (track 2); December 14, 1963 (track 7); January 14-15, 1966 (tracks 10-12); July 30-31 and August 1st, 1968 (track 13); and at Eaton's Auditorium, Toronto, Canada, December 13, 1972 (tracks 8-9); produced by Andrew Kazdin (tracks 1-6, 8-9, and 13); Paul Myers (tracks 7 and 10-12); Glenn Gould, piano (tracks 1-6 and 8-13); Elizabeth Benson-Gray Soprano; Anita Darian, mezzo-soprano; Charles Bressler, tenor; Donald Gramm, baritone; Vladimir Golschmann, conductor; Julliard String Quartet (track 7); Elizabeth Schwarzkopf, soprano (tracks 10-12).
Album 2 - Total running time: 54.44. Recorded at Eaton's Auditorium, Toronto, Canada, July 1st and 7-8, 1980; produced by Glenn Gould.

Johann Sebastian Bach
The Goldberg Variations, BWV 988
1981 Digital Recording

The last recording to appear in Gould's lifetime, completing the discographical circle that had begun so spectacularly with the same work in 1955. "I would like to think that there is a kind of autumnal repose in what I'm doing, so that much of the music becomes a tranquilizing experience. It would be nice if what we do in the recorded state could involve the possibility of some degree of perfection, not purely of a technical order, but also of a spiritual order."

LP release date: September 2, 1982. Total running time: 50:58; Recorded at Columbia 30th Street Studio, New York, NY, USA, April 22-25 and May 15, 19, and 29, 1981; produced by Glenn Gould and Samuel H. Carter.

Johannes Brahms (1833–1897)
Ballades, Op. 10, Rhapsodies, Op. 79

The first of three piano recordings to appear after Gould's death. As in his early recording of the Intermezzi (see no. 11), Gould's playing of Brahms exudes an introverted tranquility and transfiguration that seems to emerge from another, distant world.

LP release date: March 1st, 1983. Total running time: 42:25; Recorded at RCA Studio A, New York, NY, USA, February 8-10, 1982 (tracks 1-4); and June 30 and July 1st, 1982 (tracks 5-6); produced by Glenn Gould and Samuel H. Carter.

all text reprinted with permission of Sony and taken from glenngould.com

FURTHER READING:

Wondrous Strange: The Life and Art of Glenn Gould
Kevin Bazzana, Oxford University Press

A Romance on Three Legs: Glenn Gould's Obsessive Quest for the Perfect Piano
Katie Hafner, Bloomsbury USA

Glenn Gould Reader
Tim Page, Vintage

Glenn Gould: The Ecstasy and Tragedy of Genius
Peter Ostwald, W.W. Norton

The Secret Life of Glenn Gould: A Genius in Love
Michael Clarkson, ECW Press

Leonard Bernstein on Glenn Gould:
www.leonardbernstein.com/cond_gould.htm

FURTHER VIEWING:

Glenn Gould on Television,
The complete CBC broadcasts 1957-1977.
Sony Classical

Glenn Gould- On & Off the Record
Image Entertainment

Glenn Gould- The Alchemist
by Bruno Monsaingeon
EMI-Warner Classics

Glenn Gould, Hereafter
By Bruno Monsaingeon
Ideale Audience

Glenn Gould, Extasis
Kultur Video

Glenn Gould, Genius Within, the Inner Life of Glenn Gould
Documentary by Michel Hozer and Peter Raymont
Lorber Films

Acknowledgements:

It was my great pleasure to cross paths with you over the course of these past three years while I researched, wrote and illustrated this graphic novel. You have all helped me in one way or another, and for that I am truly grateful. I'm thinking in particular of Brian M. Levine, Victoria Buchy of the Glenn Gould Foundation, Ron Davis, Jean-Jacques Lemêtre, Bernard Cazaux, who kicked off the project without knowing it, Thomas, Philippe, and many more.
Also for their precious help: Bogdan Roscic of Sony Music Entertainment and Robert Russ of Sony Classical International.
My eternal gratitude goes out to my family for their support and encouragement.
My thanks goes out to Miriam for her off-tempo life.
The anecdotes found in this book were inspired by the biographies and documentaries on the life of Glenn Gould. My imagination did the rest.

http://glenngould.ca

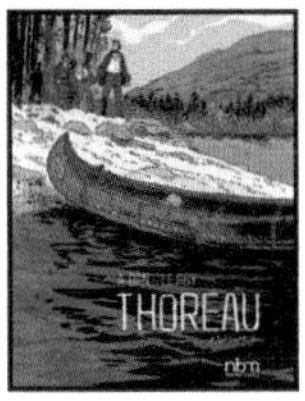
THOREAU
nbm

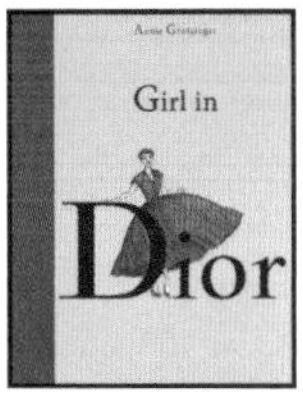
Girl in
Dior

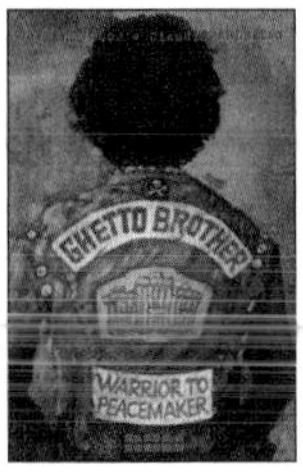
GHETTO BROTHER
WARRIOR TO PEACEMAKER

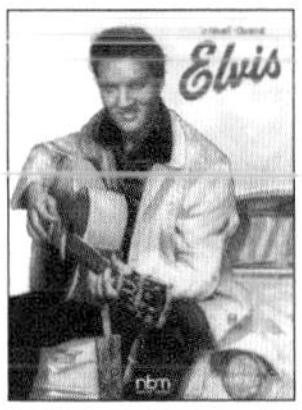
Elvis
nbm

NBM Graphic Novels
160 Broadway, Suite 700, East Wing,
New York, NY 10038
Catalog available upon request